T.D JAKES ENTERPRISES PRESENTS

CHURCH STRATEGIES
for the 21st century

T.D JAKES ENTERPRISES PRESENTS

CHURCH STRATEGIES
for the 21st century

Unless otherwise indicated, all Scripture quotations are taken from
the *New King James Version* of the Bible. Copyright © 1979, 1980, 1982,
Thomas Nelson, Inc.

Church Strategies for the 21st Century
ISBN 1-57855-997-9
Copyright © 2000 by T. D. Jakes Enterprises, Inc.
5787 S. Hampton Road, Suite 445, LB 125
Dallas TX 75232-2200

Published by T.D. Jakes Enterprises
5787 S. Hampton Road, Suite 445, LB 125
Dallas TX 75232-2200

DEDICATION

This handbook is dedicated to my wonderful wife Anna and my daughter Melissa for their encouragement and help over the last year. I am also grateful to my mother Euodias, a true woman of God who taught me never to give up.

INSTRUCTIONS FOR CD ROM:

We have provided for you a CD with various types of helpful forms. Review the forms from each section which are intended as samples and should be adapted to your organizations needs. Go through all the forms and laser print those applicable.

As you select a performance appraisal form keep the following in mind:

1. Is the form easy to read and understand?

2. Can one easily determine achievement based on the measurements used?

3. Is there space to provide suggestions for improvement and /or career development recommendations?

4. Is there space for the employee to make comments?

TYPES OF FORMS ON THE CD

- **Standard Performance appraisals**
  These performance appraisals are more general in application and will fit numerous occupations but may be limited in scope for some occupations.

- **Participative performance appraisals**
  This performance appraisal method allows the employee and the immediate supervisor the ability to collaborate and write comments concerning each area being evaluated. It helps the employer and the employee discuss areas of concern on both sides. It also helps the employee feel that they are really participating in their evaluation.

- **Job applications**
  The following are standard job applications. Every employee must have a job application on file as well as a background check. There are a variety of employment applications with different information formats.

INSTALLATION INSTRUCTIONS FOR WINDOWS

Double-click the ".exe" to access the Acrobat Reader contents. You may copy this software to your hard drive. Double click on any of the pdf documents to view the file. Acrobat Reader will then allow you to print the file.

TABLE OF CONTENTS

INTRODUCTION

The purpose of this handbook is to assist pastors, church administrators, lay leaders and faith-based organizations, in understanding how to better manage their organization. Today, churches are more vulnerable to law suits and unnecessary legal exposure. In addition, a paradigm shift is occurring. Society in many respects has become more secular, but also the secular agenda has moved many families, singles, teens, and the elderly toward the church and the social sector for answers and help. The federal government is also realizing that faith-based organizations can do social services more efficiently and effectively than government programs can. With this influx, the faith-based organizations especially must be prepared and careful how they handle their affairs and operations. Are the faith-based and social sector organizations ready?

Unfortunately, today there is a notion among churches that is very prevalent. It is that - *the principles of management apply only to business related organizations.* Pastors and laymen alike tend to feel that using business strategies shows a lack of trust in divine intervention and leadership. That belief is far from the truth. There is a need to train social sector organizations *(organizations that work in and with the grass-root communities)* as well as faith-based organizations, so they can become part of the exploding faith-based movement. The nonprofit social-sector is where management leadership is most needed today. If trained properly, social sector organizations can generate results far faster with better sustainable results than the typical secular corporate organization that has the money but may not have the commitment.

Churches and social-sector organizations are open for anyone who needs spiritual or social help. Not everyone, however, who comes to the door of the church comes with good intentions, or a real need. On many occasions, those who appear to be looking for help are really looking at how they can use the organization for their own personal gain through lawsuits, management malpractice accusations and felonious liability claims. Therefore, the church must be wise and on guard at all times. If a church is well organized with the knowledge to do the job, those skills are reflected in a well-managed staff and facility. A well-trained church can meet the many and varied needs it will encounter on a day-to-day basis. This handbook was developed to help in that training process.

As you go through the handbook, you will find worksheets labeled **TASKS.** These tasks will assist you in the learning experience so it is important that you complete each task. In addition, there are case studies, with illustrations drawn from actual situations, that are meant to help you in the learning process. This manual was prepared to provide maximum information. Keep in mind that not everything in this manual may be useable at this moment because of the size of your organization, but you will find it helpful as you plan and grow for the future.

In II Thessalonians 1:11-12 (nkjv) we read "Therefore we also pray always for you that our God would count you worthy of this calling, and fulfill all the good pleasure of His goodness and the work of faith with power, that the name of our Lord Jesus Christ may be glorified in you, and you in Him, according to the grace of our God and the Lord Jesus Christ." We have been called to a new level of excellence. It is hoped that this manual will help you toward reaching that goal.

▲

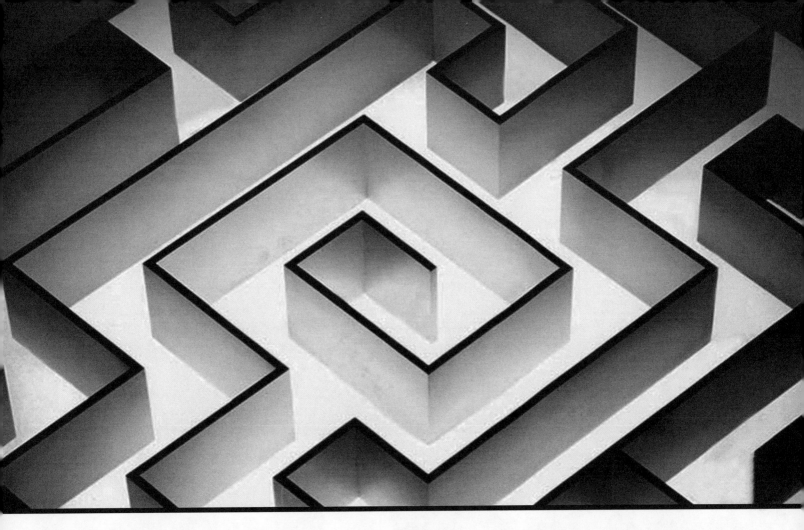

CHURCH STRATEGIES
for the 21st century

An Effective
Results Oriented
Church Administrator

AN EFFECTIVE - RESULTS ORIENTED CHURCH ADMINISTRATOR

Learning to manage "by the Book," the Word of God, is the first step in becoming an effective administrator. A chapter dealing with that topic comes later. An individual is not born to be a manager; one learns the skills to become an effective and results oriented manager. You are not a leader just because you manage the work of others. If being in a position of manager or supervisor does not automatically make you a leader, what does? How is a leader recognized or defined? What is the answer? A leader, whether a church administrator or business executive, will be recognized by his effectiveness and the *results* of his efforts. Results, results, results. These results will be evident in the success of the organization and the growth of its leaders and workers.

As part of the learning process we are taking classical management approaches and applying them to the nonprofit environment. The terms executive and administrator are used interchangeably throughout the manual.

An administrator manages people that work on their own to reach the articulated goals of the organization. Peter Drucker calls them, "knowledge workers." Knowledge workers are the pastors, Sunday school teachers, youth leaders, counselors, security personnel, computer information personnel, administrative assistants, and others.

As an administrator, you must focus on not only what the organization is doing but also what is going on outside the organization walls in the business, technical and social environment. The focus of many executives is the immediacy of what is happening within the organization. The organizational relationships, contacts, problems, challenges, and gossip - all of these elements reach to the administrator/executive. Often, the higher up one goes in the organization, the more his attention is drawn to problems and challenges inside the organization rather than to events going on outside.

A good illustration of this is the railroad industry in the United States. Its primary goal was to lay tracks across America, from the east coast to the west coast. That goal was ambitious and correct, but the railroad never really saw itself as a transportation industry. As technology increased, the barons in the rail industry did not keep up with what was going on outside of the world of trains and tracks. Modern transportation was getting faster and providing quality customer service and comfort at a totally new level. The train systems in America were not keeping up with change. Headlines flashed about trains derailing, arriving late, and customer satisfaction decreasing. Patrons were looking for new alternative ways to travel. Today in America, the passenger rail system is but a pale image of its illustrious past. It lags behind in the new transportation technologies and is now subsidized by the government in order to survive.

In Japan, however, a technologically advanced rail system that floats on an electrical magnetic field was developed. This rail system, called the "bullet train," is virtually accident free, provides on-time scheduling, quality service, and is widely used by the populace. Why the difference in Japan? The Japanese rail industry was looking inside at what was being provided, from the steam engines to diesel power. They also looked at what new services were being provided outside and how external changes could effect the passenger rail transportation. Jets were faster, providing more flights to more locations meeting customer demands for more services. The new Japanese rail service travels at 180 miles per hour with passenger seats similar to those provided on airplanes. The rail service usage has increased and their customers are happy and arriving on time.

An organization is a vital organ of society and fulfills itself by the contribution it makes to the outside environment. And yet the bigger and apparently more successful an organization gets to be, the more will inside events tend to engage the interests, the energies, and the abilities of the executive, diminishing his effectiveness on the outside. At some point, in the future he will wonder why he did not see the changes coming. An effective church administrator must keep an eye on what is going on around him, politically, economically, spiritually, and socially. The growth and success of his organization depends on that.

UNDERSTANDING ORGANIZATIONAL CULTURE

The organizational culture is a pattern of shared values and beliefs, which provides cohesiveness for members of an organization and provides rules of behavior.

Organizational culture (also called corporate culture), is the way you do business, how you run your organization or church, how you relate to the employees, how the employees perceive the organization, how everyone is expected to present themselves, and how you relate to the customers - your church members and community. In addition to describing your culture, you should also be able to define the management style of the leadership. Management styles can be participative, autocratic or team oriented. You should be able to describe organizational culture and leadership style in a few sentences.

TASK #1
Take a few moments and write out a description of your organization's culture and leadership style. After you have written it out discuss it with a few people in your discussion group.

_____

_____

_____

_____

_____

_____

_____

MAKING A CONTRIBUTION TO YOUR ORGANIZATION

One of the keys to being an effective church administrator is focusing on what is contributed to the organization, in work, in substance, in intensity, in maintaining standards, in overall impact, relationships with other superiors and associates and in spiritual leadership. In addition, the proper use of tools such as meetings and reports to monitor progress and articulate direction is important.

In order to be an effective church administrator one must be able to ask the question, "What can I contribute that will significantly affect the performance of the organization?" Many executives/administrators focus downward being occupied with the efforts rather than the results. They end up getting involved in activities in the church that consume a tremendous amount of time that should have been delegated to someone else. The administrator who focuses on efforts and stresses his downward authority is a subordinate. The administrator who focuses on contributions and takes responsibility for results is more, in the literal sense of the word, top management. He holds himself accountable for the performance of the whole organization and does not play blame games.

The focus on contribution turns the administrator's attention away from his own interests, his own skills, his own department, and toward the performance of the whole organization. The focus on contribution turns his attention to the outside, which includes all levels of the staff from whom you expect to get results. There is nothing more debilitating then to inwardly focus on your personal agenda and lose sight of the external factors, the total picture. The effective administrator will always come to think in terms of the church member, the customer, or the client, the total reason why the organization exists.

To address the question "What can I contribute?" is to identify unused potential. Those hidden areas that no one else has addressed should be looked at, by asking important questions that bring new and fresh ideas to the surface and can stimulate growth and new potential. What we expect in a good job usually is far less than what the individual is doing. The administrator is challenged to motivate and stretch that individual to new levels of performance. An administrator who accepts the ordinary, the mediocre, and does not ask the question "What can I contribute?" will aim low at the wrong goals for himself, and his subordinates. Aiming low creates a negative climate that creeps into all areas of the organization; everything becomes too difficult to do, new ideas are rare. "We don't do it that way" or "it can't be done" is on everyone's lips. This stagnates an organization and without intervention will cause it to die. An effective administrator will stimulate staff, offering ideas as well as soliciting ideas from the staff. Positive- momentum comments such as "We can do this" or "Let's make a difference" will begin to emanate from the staff. **An effective church administrator cultivates growth.**

Contribution can mean many different things, but there are major areas that can be earmarked by all organizations no matter what size they are:

1. Getting sustainable results
2. Building of values and their declaration
3. Building people for now and tomorrow

▲

Contributions must be made in all of these areas in order for an organization to maximize its people and its services. An effective administrator must learn to draw from the organization's "human resource pool" including full time and volunteer staff. It is especially true that in the church there is usually a tremendous amount of potential that is never tapped. Finding those talented people and challenging them or building them up will impact the success and growth of the organization.

> **KEY POINT:** *As administrators, focusing on contribution is a powerful way to develop people. People adjust to the challenges given to them. The executive who concentrates on contribution raises the sights and standards of everyone with whom he works.*

An administrator must also understand and define the core values of the organization. What does your organization stand for? Is it technical leadership? Discipleship? Best quality? Community involvement?

TASK #2

Use this page to write a detailed explanation of the core values of your organization. What does your organization stand for?

_____

_____

_____

_____

_____

_____

_____

_____

_____

_____

_____

_____

_____

_____

_____

_____

▲

_____

_____

_____

_____

_____

_____

_____

_____

_____

_____

MANAGEMENT FUNCTIONS

In whatever type of organization you oversee, there are fundamental management principles that you must understand in order to be successful. Every manager performs the following functions that are essential to the success of his job and the organization.

Function One – **Planning**
Planning what objectives to pursue during a future time period and what to do in order to achieve those objectives.

Proverbs 16:3
Commit your works to the Lord, and your thoughts (plans) will be established.

Proverbs 16:9
A man's heart plans his way, but the Lord directs his steps.

Luke 14:28-30
For which of you, intending to build a tower, does not sit down first and count the cost, whether he has enough to finish it-lest, after he has laid the foundation, and is not able to finish, all who see it begin to mock him, saying, "This man began to build and was not able to finish."

Function Two – **Controlling**
Controlling is measuring performance of a group or individual against the stated objectives, and determining the cause of direction change and what action to take.

Proverbs 4:25-27
Let your eyes look straight ahead, and your eyelids look right before you. Ponder the path of your feet, and let your ways be established. Do not turn to the right or the left;

▲

remove your foot from evil.

Function Three – **Organizing**

Organizing includes group activities, assigned activities, and providing the knowledge workers the authority to do the job.

> *Exodus 18:21b*
> And place such over them to be rulers of thousands, rulers of hundreds, rulers of fifties, and rulers of tens.

> *1 Chronicles 13:1*
> Then David consulted with the captains of thousands and hundreds, and with every leader.

> *2 Chronicles 2:2*
> Solomon selected seventy thousand men to bear burdens, eighty thousand to quarry stone in the mountains, and three thousand six hundred to oversee them.

Function Four – **Staffing**

Staffing is determining what types of people are needed (human capital), how they will be recruited and how they will be trained.

> *John 15:16a,b*
> You did not choose Me, but I chose you and appointed you that you should go and bear fruit, and that your fruit should remain.

Function five – **Leading**

Leading means directing your staff and their group-behavior toward the stated goal.

> *Proverbs 28:2,3*
> Because of the transgression of a land, many are the princes; but by a man of understanding and knowledge right will be prolonged (maintains order).

There are very definite steps in performing each function. They are:

Planning
- Determine the present status of the organization
- Set the objectives for your organization
- Forecast the future as much as possible
- State actions and resource needs
- Evaluate proposed actions
- Revise plans, if needed
- Communicate throughout the process

Controlling
- Establish standards
- Review the results and compare

▲

- Correct any problems
- Make adjustments in order to stay on course

Organizing

- Identify work to be performed
- Assign duties
- Group duties into job functions
- Group duties into small chunks
- Assign work to be performed establishing accountability and extent of authority

Staffing

- Determine human resource needs
- Recruit potential employees
- Select employees
- Train employees
- Control the number of staff and quality
- Communicate throughout the staffing process

Leading

- Communicate and explain the objectives
- Develop performance standards
- Coach and mentor
- Reward subordinates
- Praise
- Provide a healthy environment
- Communicate on a regular basis

MANAGEMENT SKILLS

There are some very important skills required for management. You cannot make the assumption that an individual who likes people will make a good manager. That is not always the case. That person may be gifted in certain areas but not have the personality or the skills to be a manager. It is paramount that those people who work directly under the executive or administrator and have been placed in leadership/management roles have the necessary skills. These include:

Decision-making skills – Involves targeting situations or conditions in the organization that require change, reviewing possible courses of action, and executing those decisions.

Planning skills – Involves deciding what objectives to pursue during a future time period and what to do in order to achieve those objectives.

Administrative skills – Involves understanding and performing the organizing, staffing, and controlling functions of management.

Human relations skills - Involves being able to understand human behavior and work well with people.

Technical skills - Involves having specialized knowledge and analytical ability; in addition, having the ability to use the technological tools and techniques that are available for a specific discipline.

TASK #3

For each skill listed below, give an example of how that skill is utilized in your organization.

Decision-making skills

_____

_____

_____

_____

_____

_____

Planning skills

_____

_____

_____

_____

_____

_____

Administrative skills

_____

_____

_____

_____

_____

_____

Human relations skills

_____

_____

_____

_____

_____

Technical skills

_____

_____

_____

_____

_____

_____

STRATEGIC PLANNING

Habakkuk 2:2a
Write the vision, and make it plain on tablets, that he may run who reads it.

In order for a group of people (a church) to know where they are going, there should be a map or a plan. The plan can change, it can grow or downsize, it can move fast or slowly, but there should be some type of plan. Churches *need* to develop strategic plans. In most cases, the vision comes from the Pastor. That vision is then formulated into a plan. It must be noted that having a plan will help the organization save money, stay focused, and reach its planned goals.

Strategic planning is a tool; that is all it is, a tool, period. As a tool, it is used to help an organization do a better job - to focus its energy and to ensure that members of the organization are working toward a common goal. In short, strategic planning is a disciplined effort resulting in fundamental decisions being made and actions taken that will shape and define what an organization is, what it does, and why it does it, with a focus on the future. *(Adapted from Strategic Planning in Public and Non-profit Organizations)*.

Strategic planning is about setting goals and developing an approach to achieve those goals. Remember that strategic planning is ultimately no more and no less than a set of decisions about what to do, why to do it and how to do it. Strategic planning implies that some organizational decisions and actions are more important than others. We know this to be true. For example, it is impossible for a ministry to do everything that needs to be done in the community but the tough decision has to be made as to what is most important for the community. The same decision-making process applies to the organization as a whole.

STRATEGIC PLANNING VERSUS LONG-RANGE PLANNING

Although used interchangeably, strategic planning and long-range planning are different. *Long-range planning* is generally considered to mean the development of a plan for accomplishing a goal or set of goals over a period of several years. It is assumed in the process of long-range planning that future conditions will be relatively stable. In today's volatile environment, most long-range planning is limited to from 18 months to two years. *Strategic planning* on the other hand stresses the importance of making decisions that will ensure the organization's ability to successfully respond to future changes in the environment as well as wisely taking advantage of the current economic/social climate.

Strategic planning and management is only successful if strategic thinking supports it by others in the organization. Thinking strategically means asking, "Are we doing the right thing?" With a definite purpose in mind, an understanding of what is going on in the social/stakeholder environment, (the community) in essence, looking at the "big picture," you can develop a strong strategic plan.

STRATEGIC PLAN DISCUSSION POINTS

As a team, begin to discuss each one of these discussion points. In order to develop a solid strategic plan there needs to be a consensus. This is a good place to start.

- Do we want to develop a strategic plan for our ministry?

- Describe what the vision of the ministry is (see next page).

- What are we called to do?

- What are our priorities?

- What are our values; what do we believe?

- Is there synergy between our values and the vision?

- Is our vision reaching out?

- Do we have the manpower to accomplish the vision?

- Do we have the knowledge to accomplish the vision?

- Do we have the finances to accomplish the vision?

• How far ahead should we plan? Why?

• What types of teams need to be developed in order to accomplish the vision?

• What are the organization's internal strengths?

• What are the organization's internal weaknesses?

• What external opportunities will help move the ministry forward?

• What external threat will hold the organization back?

• How do we get everyone to "buy in to" the vision?

• Will this vision and plan serve our constituents?

TASK #4

With the Senior Pastor and leadership, develop what the vision of the house (the church) is presently. Using the bricks below as the foundation write one part of the vision in each brick. For example: *To develop strong families in the church.* It should be understood that the vision is the foundation from which the strategic plan is developed.

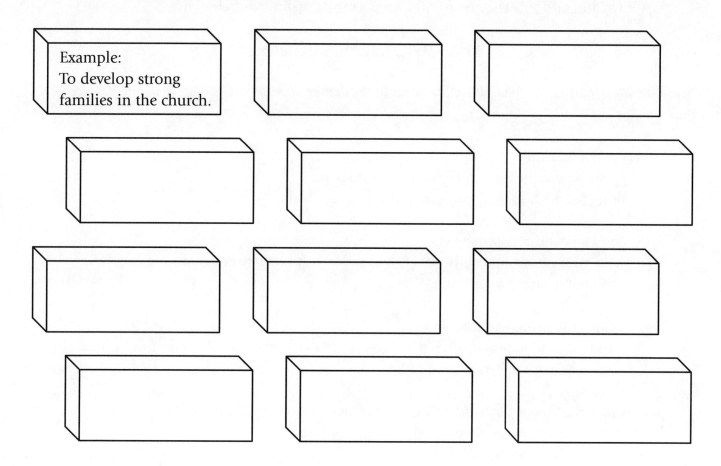

TASK #5

> Example:
> To develop strong
> families in the church.

For example, if one of the bricks is to *develop strong families in the church,* the next step is to ask how can we accomplish this task? The following are the types of questions that should be asked:

- Define families: Households with two parents? Single parent? Teenagers? Children under 13 years of age?

- How will we know that we are accomplishing the task of making families strong?

- What do we have to do to accomplish this task?

- How much will it cost?

- What is the impact on the environment (facilities)?

- How many more staff members will need to be hired?

- If we don't do this task, how will it impact the organization/church?

EFFECTIVE TIME MANAGEMENT

Becoming an effective church administrator requires the development of habits that should be practiced over time.

1. *Control your time.*
   Know where the time goes and how it is spent.
   Bring as much time as you can under your control.

2. *Focus on outward contributions.*
   Gear your efforts to results rather than work. Ask, "What results are expected of me?"

3. *Build on strengths, not weaknesses.*
   Capitalize on your own strengths and the strengths of others. You cannot build on weakness; your efforts will be futile.

4. *Concentrate on a few major areas; you cannot do everything.*
   Superior performance will produce superior results.

5. *Make effective decisions.*

The right step at the right time, the right move at the right time is essential. Knowing   that the decision will be made based on "dissenting opinions" rather than "consensus on the facts," it is dangerous to make fast decisions. Fast decision making is seldom the answer.

What is more important than fast decision making is making a few fundamental decisions, with the right strategy. In order for an executive or church administrator to make the right decisions, he must have time to make quality decisions. As an effective decision-maker, you must first determine how much time is available and how it will be allotted. The question is frequently asked, "Where did the time go?" An executive needs to find out where time has been going and how it is has been spent before he can plan what he will allocate time to. There are three steps that an effective executive takes in controlling where his time goes.

- Record time
- Manage time
- Consolidate time

Listed below are principles that, if applied, will help you, the executive, control more of your time and get better results.

Principle #1
Use time in large quantities.
Working on a report ten to twenty minutes here and there is a waste of time. It takes that much time or longer to really get into the report. Moving on to something else, even if you feel it is important is counterproductive. If you are meeting with an individual, don't be in a hurry. A rushed meeting leaves both you and the individual feeling that you did not cover all that was important. If the meeting is about something that is truly important, at least an hour is recommended. Depending on the circumstances, you may need to allow even more time.

Knowledge workers require a lot more time because they are dealing with *intrinsic* duties and not extrinsic duties. For example, if you are building a new building you know how much lumber needs to be used, what the measurements are for each room, and how much cement is needed. These requirements are hard-and-fast and easily measurable and controlled. However, the knowledge-worker may be involved in activities that are not hard-and-fast and he or she must deal with intangibles. Although a knowledge-worker, department head, executive director or subordinate primarily directs themselves, they must understand what is expected of them and why. They are focusing on the performance goals and results of the organization and will need instructions, information, and updates. This takes time.

Principle #2
Meet with the staff on a regular basis so that important questions can be asked and answered.
The art of asking questions is essential. Questions are the keys that open doors that reveal what a person is thinking, needing, and understanding. By asking the right questions, the executive saves time and learns faster.

Principle #3

Keep employees focused on the task.

Often the more that people have to work together, the more time will be spent interacting rather than working and accomplishing the tasks. This is especially true in nonprofit organizations that deal with social issues on a day-to- day basis. There are meetings and more meetings and very little gets accomplished. *See principle #6*

Principle #4

When making a decision regarding people, set aside a large amount of time to think it over.

Many executives take weeks to make a crucial decision. Thinking through the issue thoroughly will result in a better outcome.

Principle #5

Identify time wasters that have developed as a result of the lack of a system or the lack of foresight.

Do crises continue to reoccur time after time, year after year? If the same crisis occurs a second time, it shows lack of foresight and it results in time wasted. If the executive has the foresight, he will develop a system or a routine to deal with such crises. A routine is a repeated systematic approach to deal with situations. This enables less-skilled people to handle potential problems.

Principle #6

Time wasters often result when too many people are involved in a project.

It is commonly thought if you have more work you should hire more people. This is not always the case and you have to evaluate the situation. Haphazardly hiring more people may lead to a larger but ineffective work force. More time is spent on interacting, communicating, and meeting than on working. If the executives of an organization spend a great amount of time on problems of human relations, feuds, friction, territorial disputes and questions of cooperation, then the work force is too large. If an organization has too many people doing the same thing they tend to get in each other's way.

Principle #7

Excessive meetings are a sign of a deficient organization.

When a group is meeting, they are not working. Excessive meetings, which are repetitive and non-productive, create sub meetings ,both formal and informal and may cause a communication logjam. There are exceptions to the rule at the executive level because some meetings are essential. However, they should not be the main demand on an executive's time.

Principle #8

Poor information distribution contributes to wasted time.

Misinformation, no information, duplicate information, changing information, withheld information and too much information all contribute to wasted time in the organization.

Principle #9

The higher up you move, the more demands there are on your time.

The effective administrator knows that he has to consolidate his discretionary time. Some ways to do this include working at home one day or one morning per week and scheduling problem sessions and reviews only on two days out of the week, for example.

Principle #10
An organization that is not capable of perpetuating itself has failed.
An organization has to develop the leaders for tomorrow. Human capital has to be renewed. An organization should steadily upgrade its human resources.

An organization which just perpetuates today's level of vision, excellence, and accomplishment has lost the capacity to adapt. The old adage is "If it ain't broke, don't fix it." Since the one and only thing certain in life is change, an organization with that philosophy will not be capable of survival in a constantly changing world.

Principle #11
The most common cause of executive failure is inability or unwillingness to change with the demands of the position
The executive who is moved to a new position or given additional responsibilities and continues to do everything exactly as he has in the past may experience some difficulty and even failure. One must focus on what new contributions can be made to this new position or new organization.

Principle #12
Understand the importance of human relations.
Human relations is an extremely important factor in time control that cannot be overlooked. The key to maximizing your staff is the human relations factor. Areas to address are:

1. Communications

2. Teamwork

3. Self-development

4. Development of others

KEY POINT: *People will meet the challenges they place on themselves as well as challenges presented to them. Their growth is based on the level of achievement they have set. If they demand little of themselves, they remain stunted. If they demand a great deal from themselves, they grow to giant stature.*

TASK #6

For the next month keep a record on these pages of everything you do during the work day and your off time as well. You will be very surprised how you spend your time.

Date _____ Time _____ Task Performed _____

_____

Date _____ Time _____ Task Performed _____

_____

TASK #6 Cont'd

Date _____ Time _____ Task Performed _____

_____

Date _____ Time _____ Task Performed _____

_____

Date _____ Time _____ Task Performed _____

_____

Date _____ Time _____ Task Performed _____

_____

Date _____ Time _____ Task Performed _____

_____

Date _____ Time _____ Task Performed _____

_____

Date _____ Time _____ Task Performed _____

_____

Date _____ Time _____ Task Performed _____

_____

Date _____ Time _____ Task Performed _____

_____

Date _____ Time _____ Task Performed _____

_____

Date _____ Time _____ Task Performed _____

_____

Date _____ Time _____ Task Performed _____

_____

Date _____ Time _____ Task Performed _____

_____

Date _____ Time _____ Task Performed _____

_____

Date _____ Time _____ Task Performed _____

_____

TASK #6 Cont'd

Date _____ Time _____ Task Performed _____
_____

Date _____ Time _____ Task Performed _____
_____

Date _____ Time _____ Task Performed _____
_____

Date _____ Time _____ Task Performed _____
_____

Date _____ Time _____ Task Performed _____
_____

Date _____ Time _____ Task Performed _____
_____

Date _____ Time _____ Task Performed _____
_____

Date _____ Time _____ Task Performed _____
_____

Date _____ Time _____ Task Performed _____
_____

Date _____ Time _____ Task Performed _____
_____

Date _____ Time _____ Task Performed _____
_____

Date _____ Time _____ Task Performed _____
_____

Date _____ Time _____ Task Performed _____
_____

Date _____ Time _____ Task Performed _____
_____

Date _____ Time _____ Task Performed _____
_____

Date _____ Time _____ Task Performed _____
_____

▲

TASK #6 Cont'd

Date _____ Time _____ Task Performed _____

_____

Date _____ Time _____ Task Performed _____

_____

Date _____ Time _____ Task Performed _____

_____

Date _____ Time _____ Task Performed _____

_____

Date _____ Time _____ Task Performed _____

_____

Date _____ Time _____ Task Performed _____

_____

Date _____ Time _____ Task Performed _____

_____

Date _____ Time _____ Task Performed _____

_____

Date _____ Time _____ Task Performed _____

_____

Date _____ Time _____ Task Performed _____

_____

Date _____ Time _____ Task Performed _____

_____

Date _____ Time _____ Task Performed _____

_____

Date _____ Time _____ Task Performed _____

_____

Date _____ Time _____ Task Performed _____

_____

▲

TASK #6 Cont'd

Date _____ Time _____ Task Performed _____

_____

Date _____ Time _____ Task Performed _____

_____

Date _____ Time _____ Task Performed _____

_____

Date _____ Time _____ Task Performed _____

_____

Date _____ Time _____ Task Performed _____

_____

Date _____ Time _____ Task Performed _____

_____

Date _____ Time _____ Task Performed _____

_____

Date _____ Time _____ Task Performed _____

_____

Date _____ Time _____ Task Performed _____

_____

Date _____ Time _____ Task Performed _____

_____

Date _____ Time _____ Task Performed _____

_____

Date _____ Time _____ Task Performed _____

_____

Date _____ Time _____ Task Performed _____

_____

Date _____ Time _____ Task Performed _____

_____

MANAGEMENT ETHICS

The question that has been asked by many managers is, "What is ethics?" Simply put, ethics involves learning what is right and wrong, and then doing the right thing. However, "the right thing" is not as straightforward as one would think. Most ethical management dilemmas in the organization are not clearly back-and-white issues such as, "Should I lie to my pastor or counselor?" "Should I steal money from the tithe box at church?" The obvious answer is no in these situation but there are many gray areas. Many assert that there is always the right thing to do and it is based on moral principles. Others assert that deciding right or wrong is based on the situation and it is ultimately up to the individual.

Within the context of work, business ethics means knowing what is right and wrong in the workplace and doing what is right. This includes relationships between employer/ employee and the churches stakeholders, the congregation. Management ethics is crucial in times of organizational change; values that are taken for granted are brought into question during stressful times. For example, during times of financial difficulties and layoffs if the employees feel they cannot trust management or question their ethics they may say, "Management could care less about us." "It isn't fair we're being sold down the river." or "The leadership knows more than they are saying and is keeping us in the dark." When there is a crisis in an organization, it is imperative that management retains strong moral leadership. There are certain situations that can send messages to the employees that you, as a leader, are not ethical. Some of these situations are:

Tainted leaders or managerial mischief
Unfortunately, managerial leadership is not exempt from the temptations and problems that plague others. There are many issues that are either illegal or unethical that people in leadership have become involved in. Misuse of funds, moral misconduct, and lying top the list.

Moral conundrum
As a leader in your organization, a moral maze or conundrum lies before you. Issues such as misuse of funds, wrongful use of resources, and mismanagement of contracts are dealt with on a daily basis. The right ethical business decision must be made. Listed below are some misconceptions about business ethics that will help in understanding the impact on your organization.

1. *Business ethics is not based on a religious experience.*
   One can be religious and unethical. There are groups that adhere to a code of honor to tell the truth at all costs, but they are not religious in nature. A true relationship with God and adhering to Biblical principles will affect your ethical beliefs and morals, encouraging you to "do the right thing." *(See Management by the Book)*

2. *The organization's employees are ethical so they don't need training in business ethics.*
   All organizations should address the issue of business ethics. An organization is composed of people from all lifestyles with their own perception of what is ethical. In business there needs to be a standard of business ethics that all adhere to.

3. *Theologians or educators should teach business ethics.*

Pastors, administrators, deacons, managers, supervisors and organization leaders should all be students of business ethics and teach and mentor others in ethics as well.

4. *Business ethics is unnecessary — it is obvious that everyone will "do good."*

It is expected that all people will be honest and not steal. But if dishonesty has been a recurring problem in the organization then a policy of honesty should become part of the "code of ethics." A code of ethics helps the members of an organization with their priorities and focus regarding certain ethical values in the workplace.

5. *Ethics cannot be legislated.*

Ethics cannot be legislated; however, they can be managed indirectly by example. The behavior of the pastor, administrator or lay leader will strongly influence the behavior of employees in the organization/workplace.

BENEFITS OF ETHICS IN YOUR ORGANIZATION

1. *Ethics programs help maintain a direction in tough times.*

Business ethics is fundamental in times of change. Leaders find themselves dealing with situations that bring into question the issue of right and wrong. Applying ethical principles consistently can have a calming effect on the staff.

2. *Ethics programs support growth and health among executives.*

In an article titled "Unethical Behavior, Stress Appear Linked (Wall Street Journal, April 11, 1991, p. B1), it was stated that a consulting firm tested a range of executives and managers. Their most important finding was that emotionally healthy executives who measured high on a battery of tests were more likely to score high on ethics tests. It is important that the leaders in your organization stay mentally healthy. This can be accomplished by the HR department creating programs and regulations for the leadership and employees, such as: adequate vacation time taken regularly and consistently, personal days off, management teams that deal with employee problems, adequate health insurance, etc.

3. *Ethics programs help avoid acts of omission..*

Focusing on ethics tends to help the organization detect issues and violations early so they can be addressed. If a violation is not properly reported, it can be considered a criminal act. For example, a 501c3 nonprofit engaged in profit-making enterprise is in violation of IRS regulations.

4. *Ethics programs create a strong public image.*

The fact that an organization regularly gives attention to its ethics can portray a strong positive image to the public. People see those types of organizations valuing people over money. These organizations are considered to be of high integrity.

THE TEMPLATE OF A HIGHLY ETHICAL ORGANIZATION

The following are principles that have been tracked in highly ethical organizations. When you perform an ethics audit, make sure that you consider these principles. They should be reflective of the leadership in the organization.

1. **The organization is at ease in working with diverse people.** People feel welcomed. There is legitimate concern about the community around the organization.

2. **The organization is fair** with both its employees and constituents. The organization's leaders are genuinely interested in the members of the organization.

3. **The leadership believes responsibility falls on the individual** rather than collectively. The organization becomes more than just a job to the individual, it becomes part of him or her.

4. **There is a purpose.** This purpose articulates the way the organization operates. This is highly valued by the employees and management. The employees know why they are there and how their work has effected the community or the world.

5. **There exists a clear vision** which is reflected in integrity throughout the organization.

6. **The vision is accepted** and owned by the leadership.

7. **Contribution and integrity are rewarded.**

8. **Policies and practices of an organization are fair and ethical.** Everyone is treated the same. There are no mixed messages and no bent rules that can jeopardize the integrity of the organization.

9. **Every significant management decision has an ethical values aspect.**

10. **Everyone is expected to work through conflict** whether with employees or with the people the organization serves.

TASK #7

DISCUSSION GROUP - ETHICAL DILEMMAS

These dilemmas below do not necessarily deal with religious organizations, but each scenario can be applied to numerous contexts. Discuss each scenario in your group.

- A client asked for a product from us today. I gave him the price on the product and he said he could not afford it. I knew the competition sold the same product for a much lower price. Should I tell him about the competition, or let him go without getting what he needs? What should I do?

- I am the bookkeeper for the church and have been in the position for over 12 years. The church accounting records have always been perfect. I had been praying for some time for divine help to pay off my credit cards. After service, in the church parking lot, I found a roll of $100 bills, which totaled $3000, which was exactly what I needed. Has God supplied my need? What should I do?

- Our organization is predominately white and we are interviewing for a new Information Technology person. The most qualified person interviewed is an Asian female, but she does not speak English well. We also have many Vietnam veterans that attend our meetings. What should I do?

- Because of a drop in donations, a nonprofit organization is planning to lay off several people. As a manager, you are briefed of the layoff, but you are told to say nothing. One of your employees gleefully tells you that he is getting ready to buy a new car and remodel his house next month. He is one of those to be laid off. What do you do?

- You are a computer repairman in your organization. While repairing a computer, you find downloaded files of hard-core pornography. The user of the computer is a leader in your organization. What do you do?

- You find out that the only counselor you have on staff in your organization is married and is having an affair. He is a tremendous counselor and has helped literately hundreds of people in your organization. He has brought back numerous people from the edge of total destruction. What do you do?

- You are fund-raising for a particular project in your organization and have collected a large number of donations. A fire occurs and money is needed to make repairs. What should you do?

TASK #8

DISCUSSION GROUP — ETHICAL DILEMMAS

Use this page to list ethical dilemmas that you have dealt with and discuss them with members of your group.

Dilemma #1 _____

_____

_____

_____

_____

_____

_____

_____

_____

_____

_____

Dilemma #2 _____

_____

_____

_____

_____

_____

_____

_____

_____

_____

Dilemma #3 _____

_____

_____

_____

_____

_____

_____

_____

_____

_____

_____

A SEASON OF CHANGE

Change is an organizational reality. If it were not for change, planning would be pain-free because tomorrow would be no different from today. There would be no uncertainty.

Every organization whether faith-based or secular, goes through times of change, no matter what the organizational culture. There may be changes in the mission of the organization, changes in staff, downsizing, mergers and even closings, or the total reshaping of the organization. As an executive – a leader, you must adapt and help the organization go through the changes as it grows and develops; if you fight against it – you will lose. Organizations that change too slowly will have even bigger problems in later years.

As you push your faith-based or social-sector organization to another result-oriented level, you will face resistance. Some people cling desperately to the past saying, "This is the way we have always done it for years." They hold on to what's familiar and hide in the comfortable routines to avoid the possibility of having to change. Change always means giving up something and the more that people perceive they are giving up, the more they drag their feet.

Another reason why people defend the old way of doing things is to maintain personal stability. They feel more in control. They fight against change out of fear of how it may affect their future.

Some people resist change as a way to get even with the leadership. So they "beat up and bad mouth" the organization in retaliation for changes implemented that they do not like. The more a person dislikes unpredictability, the more resistant he is.

Lastly, some resisters of change are well-intentioned people who may think their organization is making a mistake and try to stop it. They have the organization at heart and have enough nerve to take a stand.

When the winds of change hit your organization, resisting does more harm than good. Resisting change takes effort. Instead of trying to hold on to the past, encourage your people to grab on to the future.

Frequently people will develop a negative mind-set no matter what the organization's goals are. This mind-set or attitude will be based on faulty assumptions, wrong thinking, etc.

False notions are developed from false information. Below is a list of factual and fictional ideas that become prevalent during change.

Fiction	Fact
This will go away. "Things will go back to normal just wait and see."	**Change is here to stay.** Things may settle as time goes on, but they will never be the same.

Fiction	Fact
It will help if I get upset about what is happening. "I will fight this to the end!"	**Controlling your emotions increases your control over the situation.** It won't do the organization any good if you walk around upset; stay positive.
My career is ruined. "I'm going to have to start all over again"	**Progress often masquerades as trouble.** Give yourself time to get a better view of the situation. Look for the opportunity. If you can't find an opportunity, make your own.
I can just keep doing my job like I have been. Why fix something that isn't broken?"	**If the organization is changing you probably need to change too.** Examine your work routine; see if you are in step with the new tempo of the organization. If you see change happening take it as evidence that you need to change as well.
All these problems prove that changes are bad for the company. "Things used to run a lot smoother than this but these changes are creating all kinds of problems."	**Problems are the natural side effect of the change process.** Don't forget that frequently on the road to getting better, things will appear to get a little worse. But they do get better.
Top management knows more than they are saying. "The organization is keeping us in the dark."	**The odds are that management is being as open and straightforward as the situation permits.** The change process can create gaps in information. In many cases higher management doesn't have all the answers that are needed. The truth sometimes can be a moving target.
Management could care less about us. "It isn't fair; we're being sold down the river."	**Management has to make tough decisions, and it's impossible to keep everyone happy.** The natural tendency is to look for someone to blame. It's always easier to accuse upper management when you don't like what's happening.

Fiction	Fact
I'm not in a position to make a difference. "All these changes are not my idea, it's not my responsibility to make things work. There's nothing I can do."	**You are either part of the solution or part of the problem.** During times like this people often feel like victims. Don't act helpless. You may surprise yourself with how much you can accomplish and the contribution you can make toward helping the organization through the changes.
Top management is supposed to make those changes work. "Top management put this thing together; now let's see them pull."	**If you work here, this is your plan.** Top management is responsible for developing the overall game plan and calling the plays. You, the employee, are supposed to run the plays and make them work.

TASK #9

1. *Has your organization worked its way through change? If so, describe.*

2. *Is change good for your organization? Why? How should your organization change? Use the space below to answer these questions.*

_____

_____

_____

_____

_____

_____

_____

_____

_____

_____

_____

BECOMING A CHANGE LEADER

It's understandable that a person would be upset or disappointed about certain aspects of a change. But how long should you let these feelings go on?

W. Clement Stone, the president of Combined Insurance and the author of numerous books, said, "There is very little difference in people. But that little difference makes a big difference. That little difference is attitude. The big difference is whether it is positive or negative. As the administrator, be sure you give strong direction and information to the employees. Listed above were some of the common myths that run rampant during any organizational change. Below are important points to help the employees.

- Control your attitude

- Take some ownership of the change

- Choose your battles carefully

- Be tolerant of management mistakes

- Keep your sense of humor

- Don't let your strengths become weaknesses

- Practice good stress management

- Support management

- Invent the future instead of trying to redesign the past

As the administrator, remember the following items about your staff as your organization changes: People need to know where you stand.

- They need to communicate with the people that they work with.

- They need to know what they can expect from the changes.

- They need to continue to understand the value and the rules of the organization.

- People do not function well if they feel that there is no predictability.

ORGANIZATION GROWTH STYLES AND CHANGES

An organization develops through a process of stages. As it passes through these developmental stages, changes occur that can result in improving the organization and lengthening its life. A normal organization grows in roughly 5-year steps. Every 5 years or so the organization finds itself at a new threshold or behind in its development.

Organizations will differ in their growth process. Each stage may have a "crisis zone," An organization does not have to go through these "crisis zones" if they plan well. As a rule of thumb the stages of development are as follows:

Step one: Developmental

Step two: Restructuring

Step three: Empowering

Step four: Strategizing

Step five: Partnering

STEP ONE: DEVELOPMENTAL

This is the pioneer stage, when the world is your oyster. Nothing can go wrong; every idea is a good idea. The church is filling with new people who are excited about coming; the word is out. Everyone is doing whatever it takes to get the job done, putting in long hours with low pay or in some cases no pay at all or just volunteering. Everything is reactive with no real plans in place or any real structure but there is confidence in the future. In this euphoric phase, spending is done freely and there is usually no accounting system in place.

The leadership style is autocratic. The young pastor has the vision. Communication is frequent and informal as you may meet in the parking lot before or after services. Ideas are plentiful. Everyone feels a part of what is happening and enjoying the excitement.

DEVELOPMENTAL CRISIS

Suddenly, there is too much work to be done and more staff is needed. The pastor is now spreading himself too thin and the management is not focused on the primary goals of the church. More employees are brought on but they don't carry the vision like the founding group. New ministries are springing up with no real direction. The pastor is overwhelmed with more management duties that take him away from his primary duties of the ministry. The pastor tightens down on all activities not wanting things to get out of control. A more sophisticated accounting system is needed. New employees are hired at higher pay to get more quality workers.

STEP TWO: RESTRUCTURING

An administrator is hired to oversee the church duties and help the management become more efficient. The pastor pulls away from the day-to-day affairs and focuses more on the ministry aspect. Job roles become more specialized. Meetings are now restricted to department heads. Salaries increase.

RESTRUCTURING CRISIS

The leadership at the top finds itself less informed about what's going on "in the trenches" which includes the different auxiliaries and departments. The organization grows more complex. Conflict increases among the autonomous groups. Rigid rules are put in place causing the organization's members to feel restricted. More meetings are called with less productivity. Employees are torn between taking initiative and following procedures. Employees become attracted to the competition.

STEP THREE: EMPOWERING

"Let's build a new church; let's start a new ministry to the homeless; and let's start a missions program overseas." The leadership starts focusing on expanding, and the new visions are compatible with the present direction of the organization. Communication is via e-mail or in writing. The pastor/leadership learns to delegate more. Department managers take control of their areas by holding significant meetings to keep everyone apprised. More financial controls are put in place to measure income and waste. Human Resources takes on a bigger role. Hiring becomes more critical. More perks and titles are added.

EMPOWERING CRISIS

Leadership finds it difficult to give up authority and control. Expansion does not relate to the vision. Departments want to stay autonomous and do not share information. Top leadership is too far from the primary activities. Accounting systems are not standardized.

STEP FOUR: STRATEGIZING STAGE

Formal planning procedures are put in place. Decision-making is left to the department heads. Accounting and MIS is centralized. The congregation is being served. Finances are adequate for the congregation size.

STRATEGIZING CRISIS

The leadership is distracted from doing a quality job. The staff begins to nurture resentment and lack of confidence. Too many programs and activities overload everything and everyone. Problems take longer to solve; adherence to procedures takes precedence. The congregation senses discord. Income and attendance may decrease.

STEP FIVE: PARTNERING

Problems are solved quickly through team leadership and collaboration. Staff is sensitive to the needs of the congregation. Infrastructure supports ministry and growth.

TASK #10

1. *Describe in detail what stage(s) your organization is at in its development. Explain why you think this is so.*
2. *Join your discussion group and discuss the stages and their effect on your organization.*

_____

_____

_____

THE RIGHT PEOPLE

An important area to be addressed now is the hiring process. Poor hiring decisions can affect many areas in your church, such as other staff members' performance and the amount of dollars wasted on training. In some cases it can cost $6,000 plus to train and get a new employee functioning and up to speed. If the wrong hiring decision is made and the wrong person is put into a position, money will be definitely wasted.

A church on the East Coast hired a secretary for the pastor relying on a gut feeling without any real professional investigation into the person's background or experience. Her name was given by one of the members who stated, "I don't know her well but I think she can do the job." The person was hired. A few weeks later the pastor realized that he was not getting calls and noticed that church members were giving him negative looks in service. He finally approached one of the members and asked what the problem was. To his surprise and dismay, he was advised that his new secretary was very impatient on the telephone with people. She had said to one member when he had called for hospital visitation, "The pastor's real busy and he may not have time to get to the hospital. You'll most likely be out by the time he gets to see you." Further investigation convinced the pastor that the person representing him as his secretary was a poor fit; she did not belong in that particular position or organizational culture.

In another situation, an individual was hired by a very large church on the West Coast to be the director of the youth department. The pastor and the staff were very people oriented, as they should be. There were activities for the family, the elderly, the singles, but not much for the youth. The new youth director's job was to develop relationships and activities with the youth and lead them toward a closer relationship with the Lord. Weeks went by with no results; six months went by, no measurable results. Finally the pastor sat down with the youth leader and after candid discussions found out that the youth leader was really interested in evangelizing and traveling and holding youth crusades. His aspirations did not fit with the needs of the church. Very shortly after the conversation the youth leader was asked to resign. Although the person hired had good intentions, he did not fit. The church did not perform their due diligence in evaluating the candidate and thus the wrong person was hired. So much time and money was spent and wasted and the youth department was in disarray.

Here is another actual situation which really brings home the importance of finding the right people for the job. A Christian church school was totally brought to its knees because the custodian that the church hired was acutely dysfunctional and was sexually molesting children and stealing. After a bloody court battle and lawsuit, the church had to close its doors forever. Sadly, this all occurred because the church did not do their due diligence in checking his background and thoroughly interviewing the individual.

The church secretary's temperament did not fit the job. The youth leader did not fit the position in which he was placed. The custodian had not been thoroughly checked out to see if he fit the organization and the school environment he was being placed in. The important question in hiring is, Does the person fit? How do you find the right person? What can be done to be fairly confident that the right person has been hired? Will the new employee fit reasonably well into your organizational culture? In order to know if a person will fit, you first must understand your organizational culture.

STOP GUESSING - HIRE THE RIGHT PERSON

One of the main reasons why the wrong person is hired or the person doesn't fit with the organizational culture, (and it's realized after they are hired) is that in most cases there is no screening process when hiring a new employee. This seems especially true with nonprofit organizations. An individual shows interest, volunteers regularly, and is eager to help and it is assumed that that person will make a good employee. This is not always the case. Let's say such a person is hired and offered a professional position in the organization which pays between $30,000 and $40,000 annually. Without warning, the new hire two months later walks into the administrator's office and says he or she is not happy, has found a better job and is leaving. The employee's leaving can cost the organization up to $6000 or more to recruit rehire and retrain a replacement. In-depth interviewing will help prevent these kinds of situations in many cases.

Also, many individuals pulled from socially economically, and educationally deprived backgrounds enter the work force lacking the basic skills and work ethic so prevalent in earlier generations. Organizations can no longer assume that applicants possess even the most basic competencies required to perform the job. Getting individuals to produce the level of work needed to keep the organization competitive is one of the crucial challenges of the new millennium. To start the process, the organization should review hiring procedures and philosophy.

HIRING SKILLS INVENTORY

To examine the hiring procedure in your organization, consider the following hiring skills inventory. These questions address the major considerations of a successful hiring effort.

1. **Have you defined the type of person that does well in your organization?**
   Refer to the organizational culture section and review the task.

2. **Are your procedures consistent and well-defined?**
   Is employee selection conducted without clear procedures or performed in a haphazard way? If so, this can result in high turnover, discrimination, lawsuits or loss of your best applicants.

3. **Is everyone well informed?**
   Often, too many people are involved in the hiring process which can cause a communications breakdown. A few people should be responsible for screening and making timely decisions

4. **Are you tracking recruiting costs?**
   For example, how much did it cost to replace the last receptionist who left the organization?

5. **Are you cultivating new contacts and sources for applicants?**

Sources such as colleges, churches, and business should be considered.

6. **Are you considering the versatility of candidates?**

Many people are hired for a single job but end up doing a variety of tasks. Small organizations should attempt to hire multitasking type people or be willing to retrain when needed. You must hire for the future.

7. **Do you, "the employer," have a good reputation?**

Have you developed a reputation as an organization that treats its employees well? Quality people are drawn to quality organizations.

On many occasions an organization will hire additional people because of a perceived need. The rational to hire new people may sound good, but they may not be needed. Use the following check-list to help you in deciding if you need to fill a new position.

1. What is the purpose of this new job?

2. Who is presently performing these tasks?

3. How long have the employees who presently perform this task been overloaded?

4. Is this added influx the result of a temporary increase in activity or is the pace more permanent?

5. What will be the initial goals of this position and how long will it take to accomplish them?

6. What is the best that can happen if we fill this position with a good person?

7. Is there enough work for a full-time position? Can it be performed by a part-time employee?

8. Can some of the overload duties be switched to another area within the same department or location?

9. Is this a true need or can the systems in this function be streamlined for better productivity?

10. How much will this new position cost?

11. Is there a sufficient labor market from which to choose?

12. Will this position exist 24 months from now?

13. Have we checked with all other parties involved to determine if everyone feels there is a need?

14. How will other departments view adding this position?

15. What impact will the creation of this new position have on the jobs from which the tasks are being removed?

16. What is the worst that can happen if we do not fill this position?

KEY POINT

Before you ever think about hiring a person, you must answer the above questions keeping in mind. 1. What do you want this person to do? 2. What are the competencies her or she must have (what kind of tasks do you expect the person to perform)?

TASK #11

As part of the learning process list the competencies that you want the next person you are hiring to have. Note: You must decide what the position is before you start.

_____

_____

_____

_____

_____

_____

_____

_____

_____

_____

_____

_____

_____

_____

_____

_____

JOB AUDIT

The purpose of the job audit is to evaluate the requirements needed to do the job so that you can write a job description. When completing a job audit be as thorough in describing the job tasks as possible. Questions to be asked during a job audit are as follows:

1. What duties will the person perform? (Be specific in the description.)

_____

_____

_____

_____

2. What tools, services, and/or accommodations does a person need to complete these duties?

_____

_____

_____

_____

3. Who supervises the person in this position?

_____

_____

_____

_____

4. With whom will this person interact, both in and out of the organization?

_____

_____

_____

_____

5. What formal training does the person need to perform the job, if any?

_____

_____

_____

6. What skills does this person need to complete this job? (Include technical, interpersonal, organizational and problem-solving skills.)

_____

_____

_____

_____

7. How is the person performing this job evaluated?

_____

_____

_____

_____

The more information gathered, the more thorough the job description will be.

RESUMES AND APPLICATIONS

In the recruiting and hiring process numerous resumes will come across your desk. How effectively you review resumes and applications to reach a clear decision is essential. Before you begin reviewing, decide on the type of person you are looking for and the skills that you want him or her to possess. When reviewing resumes, divide the review into five categories:

1. **Overall appearance**

   Are there errors in spelling? Is proper grammar used? Is the printing readable? Is it printed on good quality paper with envelope? Does it look like it was copied from a book, "too perfect?"

2. **Organization**

   Does the resume provide the information you need? Did the applicant do his or her homework and anticipate your needs? Does the resume provide a clear path to the information, or is there no rhyme or reason to its structure?

3. **Education/training**

   Keep in mind that only relevant education should be considered. Examine the motivation of someone with too much education. Is this person really interested in the position or looking for a place to rest his or her hat before moving on. Check all educational institutions by telephone.

4. **Experience**

   When you review the experience section of a resume, consider thefollowing: Does the applicant list duties versus responsibilities? (What was actually done?) Is there a list of accomplishments? How long did the applicant hold each position? Are the job titles authentic? Does the applicant demonstrate how acquired skills fit into the position sought?

5. Other relevant activities

   You may find a variety of information in this category. These might include college activities, community involvement, awards, church-related activities and functions, hobbies, and participation in sports. All of these provide insight into the type of person that the applicant is.

TASK #12

Resume #1 - Review and critique the following resume.

Clay B. Potter
555 Eastville Rd.
Old Ridge, New Jersey 44444
(555) 321-7890

EXPERIENCE:

1995 to present   **Civil Engineering Company**
Old Ridge, New Jersey
Facilities manager worked with 35 people

1990 to 1991   **Security Services Inc.**
Baltimore, Maryland
Security Guard supervisor

1989 to 1990   **Consolidated Construction**
Dallas, Texas
Construction worker

1981 to 1989   **Potter Construction Company**
Old Ridge, New Jersey
Family construction business foreman on large construction projects

EDUCATION: **Graduate of Old Ridge High School**
Old Ridge, New Jersey - Graduated 1988

Barley's Auto Mechanics School
Attended - specialized in exhaust systems

OTHER ACTIVTIES:

Enjoy parties, movies, and football

TASK #13

Resume #2- Review and critique the following resume.

ANNA W. LEE
6316 BRYNMAWR LANE
WILBUR, VA 76543
(555)-420-1234

CAREER OBJECTIVE:	To serve in a Christian organization where my skills can be used, but also a place where everyone loves God and reaches out to people in need.
EXPERIENCE 1979 to 1980	**COMMERCIAL CREDIT CLERK** Manover Trust, Linkhorn, New York Credit reports, Complied monthly reports for loan offiers and board of directors.
1980 to 1984	**COMMERCIAL LOAN CLERK** Third Virginia Bank, Brewer, Virginia Prepared loans for 27 banks for computer entry. Responsible for input payment documantation for loans in excess of thirty million dollars.
1984 to 1988	Part-time student, Bookkeeping, Homemaker
1988 to 1994	**CO-OWNER OF "COMPU - TRAIN** Wilbur, Virginia Trained clients in use of computers for job prepiration
1994 to Present	**OWNER OF NEEDLE POINT SEWING SHOP** Wilbur, Virginia Sales and markating of sewing supplies
EDUCATION	**Barrington College - West Providence, RI** Diploma Major: English literature 1991 GPA 3.65 Joined Adjuct proffessor staff **Lake Taylor Community College - Wilbur Virginia** Accounting theroy and practice - 1986 to 1988
	Refernces upon request

EVALUATING COVER LETTERS

Tips for reviewing cover letters:

1. **Is it an original letter?**

   Job hunters can send out hundreds of letters. With today's laser copiers, an applicant can send a clean copy that looks like an original. If the letter looks poorly copied, most likely one letter has been written that will be sent to every prospect. If an applicant cannot take the time to write a letter specifically to your organization, that can send a negative message.

2. **Is the spelling and grammar correct?**

   With today's computer with spell check and grammar check there is no reason for poor grammar and spelling. If a cover letter crosses your desk and it shows poor spelling, possibly the individual is computer illiterate or has poor reading skills. There are numerous reasons for poor spelling and grammar.

3. **Has it been written in proper business format?**

   The letter should be written in a readable, organized manner. For example, it should not be written in memo form.

4. **Is the letter addressed to a specific person?**

   A letter that is addressed to "To Whom It May Concern" or "Dear Sir" shows that the individual has not done his or her homework; has not researched the organization to find out to whom the letter should be forwarded.

5. **Does the letter tell you who the person is?**

   Some applicants write well, so well, that you really cannot get a glimpse of who they are. In these situations if the resume looks promising and the telephone interview goes well, a face-to-face interview is the next step.

▲

TASK #14

Review and critique the following cover letter.

Brandon Taylor
3434 Longview Ave.
East Elmer, Texas 45678
(289)-345-7890

CNBC   August 5, 2000
Tom Wendell
CBNC Tower East
Albany, New York 29456-2349

Dear Mr. Wendell:

This letter and resume is in response to your ad in the Broadcasting & Cable maga-
zine dated August 1, 2000.

For 20 years, I have been involved in all aspects of television and audio production.
My experience encompasses music recording, digital audio editing, audio for television and television directing.

I have been in management level positions for 16 years of my career. As Director of
Engineering and Satellite communications for King Broadcasting Network in Daytona
Beach, Florida for seven years, I supervised 100 on-line staff. I developed a "work
team" environment that increased productivity, and allowed us to produce 8 hours of
programming per day, instead of 4 hours per day. I also supervised all international
productions in seven foreign countries

While at King Broadcasting I assisted in developing, the company's 5-year master
plan.

I look forward to meeting you. I will call to set an appointment on August 7, 2000

Cordially,

▲

TASK #15

Luke McCarthy
729 Walnut Trail
Redwood, California 23456
679-824-3456

August 12, 2000

Dr. Lawrence David
West Oak Church
78 flower street
Saratoga, California 23456

Dear Pastor:

This letter is in response to your ad in Christianity Today for a church Administrator. For several years, I have been involved in management. I am familier with all aspects of the church. My level of skills can keep people moving ahead and motivated.

My management skills took me after college to Cooper Lake church for a year, I have been working as a salesmen for a local printing company since leaving Cooper for six months.

You will also note that I have a Masters degree from LaSalle University in management. I am convinced that you will love my mangaement skills. I am a Christian, I have been attending church for a year and a half.

I am available to be interviewed at any time on Monday or Fridays between 9am and 3pm. I will provide references if you are serious about hiring me. Please do not contact Cooper Church, the Pastor has a very busy schedule and he does not accept calls from non-church members.

Sincerely

APPLICANT REVIEW SHEET

When reviewing applicants, you can break the evaluation into eight categories.
Rate the applicant in each category with *one* being the worst and *five* being the best.

Position: _____

Applicant name: _____

	RESUME	COVER LETTER	APPLICATION

Grade Level	1	2	3	4	5
• Clarity	☐	☐	☐	☐	☐
• Education	☐	☐	☐	☐	☐
• Experience	☐	☐	☐	☐	☐
• Legibility	☐	☐	☐	☐	☐
• Neatness	☐	☐	☐	☐	☐
• Related Hobbies	☐	☐	☐	☐	☐
• Career continuity	☐	☐	☐	☐	☐
• Related experience to the specific job	☐	☐	☐	☐	☐

BACKGROUND CHECKS

Reference checks are a valuable way for employers to communicate with one another about an applicant. However, in recent years, lawsuits resulting from negative reference checks have garnered a great deal of negative publicity. It is, therefore, important for employers to be knowledgeable of their rights as well as the rights of the applicant.

There are several types of background checks. These include credit checks, criminal record checks, driving records, and past employment checks.

CREDIT CHECKS

Utilizing credit checks for employment purposes is regulated by the Fair Credit Reporting Act (FCRA). Credits checks are often performed for positions that involve financial responsibilities, especially if the position involves handling large sums of money or exercising financial discretion. If the position does not entail this type of responsibility, the employee should not be subject to a credit check. This could be misconstrued as a violation of privacy. It is, therefore, a good practice to limit the use of credit checks to situations where the position demands good credit references.

There are two types of credit checks: investigative consumer credit reports and consumer credit reports. An investigative consumer credit report includes a written report along with interviews from business associates, neighbors, etc. Written notice must be given to an applicant before an investigative credit check is performed. In addition, the applicant should be briefed as to the types of questions that will be asked.

 The consumer credit report is a written report issued by a third party. If an applicant is denied employment because of the credit report, the applicant must be informed and furnished with the name of the credit agency that issued the report.

CRIMINAL RECORDS

Employers may want to consider doing a criminal background check for positions that involve a high level of unsupervised contact with the public. Examples of this type of position would be security guards, teachers, childcare, and eldercare personnel. Private employers are able to acquire criminal records at the state level, if there is proven need. In many states, the employer would have to demonstrate that the applicant would be in close contact with the public and that securing the conviction record would be in the best interest of the public.

Obtaining criminal conviction records does not mean that this information can be used in making the hiring decision. Some states have laws prohibiting discrimination against people with criminal records. Check your state's Department of Labor.

DRIVING RECORDS

Employers should check driving records of applicants who will be using church vehicles before the applicant is hired and periodically during their employment. The employer could be held liable for negligent hiring if he or she knows or should have known about anything contained in the record such as drunk driving and speeding violations. Employers also should check to see if the applicant has a valid driver's license.

Employers should be as thorough as they can be, within the limits of the law, when checking into an applicant's background. Reference checking reduces the risk to the employer when hiring a new person.

PAST EMPLOYMENT CHECKS

When verifying employment with a former employer, it is likely that the former employer will be willing to provide ONLY the dates of employment and the position of the employee. Legal action resulting from negative reference checks is on the rise. A defamation suit could result if a former

▲

employer gives out false and negative information about an applicant. Defamation is defined as the unprivileged publication of a false statement tending to harm the reputation of another person. Because of increased litigation, many employers have a "say nothing" policy.

Saying nothing appears to protect the company from liability but this is not always the case. Employers can be sued by other employers if they fail to disclose negative information about an applicant that could negatively impact the inquiring organization. For example, an individual applies for a job at a private church school and the school calls the previous employer for a reference. The former employer does not tell them that the individual was fired because he exposed himself to children at the daycare center. The church could be facing lawsuits failing to disclose this pertinent piece of information.

This basic concept of negligent hiring can be extended to situations where the employer failed to investigate the background of the applicant and therefore placed the applicant in a position that could be dangerous to others. A church hires a bookkeeper and does not bother checking references and the employee is later caught embezzling money. If it turns out that he has a previous similar offense, the employer faces lawsuits based on negligent hiring. If the employer had looked into the background of the person, this information would have been discovered.

Reference checking is a double-edged sword. There are potential consequences for not checking references (negligent hiring lawsuits) and there are potential consequences if you do check references (defamation lawsuits). The important thing is to know what is the right course of action in each situation.

When you are asked to provide a reference on a former employee, be sure the former employee knows the company's reference checking policy and obtains his or her written permission before providing references. Document the positive and negative performance evaluations and refer to these documents when giving a reference. It is important to provide truthful information; truth is an "absolute defense" to a defamation charge. Never volunteer information. Do provide job-related information. Make sure that you identify to whom you are giving the information to and be sure to take down their name, title, address, and telephone number. Advise them that you will return the call. This allows the former employer to verify the identity of the potential employer.

▲

THE INTERVIEW PROCESS – GETTING TO KNOW YOU

In most small and medium sized organizations the person who does the interviewing is usually the supervisor, pastor or the administrator, and in many cases none of them have the necessary interviewing skills to make a sound decision. Usually what occurs is the halo effect, the person being interviewed might say something that the interviewer likes, or the interviewer may like the way he or she speaks and ends up overlooking what the person really is about and hires them anyway. I remember a supervisor that decided whom to hire by finding out what part of the country they came from, another decided by finding out the interviewee's church affiliation, and another would decide by how well the resume was prepared.

An interview can take about an hour or more and during that time the interviewer hopes to glean enough information to make the right decision to hire or not to hire. In most situations, an hour is not enough time. Since most interviewers are the supervisor or someone elected to hire for the open position, they have only a certain amount of time to spend on interviewing, and normally there is no preplanning.

The problem that occurs over and over again is that very rarely are the right questions asked. Who is this person? Will he or she fit in the organizational culture? When interviewing an individual, one must get to know the person and understand what his or her real capabilities are. One of the best interview techniques that gets positive result is Behavior Based Interviewing (BBI). This process can help reveal who the person is and what you can expect. The following are questions that can help to reveal the interviewee's integrity, honesty and trustworthiness.

BEHAVIOR BASED INTERVIEW QUESTIONS

1. Discuss a time when your integrity was challenged. How did you handle it?

2. What would you do if someone asked you to do something unethical?

3. Have you ever asked for forgiveness for doing something wrong?

4. If you ever saw a coworker doing something dishonest, would you tell your boss? What would you do about it?

The following are questions that can reveal personality, temperament and ability to work with others.

1. What motivates you the most?

2. If I call your references, what would they say about you?

3. How would you describe your personality?

4. What brings you joy?

5. If you took out a full-page ad in the town newspaper and had to describe yourself in three words, what would those words be?

6. Do you consider yourself a risk taker? Describe a situation in which you had to take a risk?

7. Tell me about a work situation that bothered you.

8. What kinds of people would you rather not work with?

9. What previous job was the most satisfying and why?

10. What do you think you owe to your employer?

11. Have you ever had to resolve a conflict with a coworker or client? How did you resolve it?

ISSUES THAT THE INTERVIEWER SHOULD BE CONCERNED ABOUT

1. The interviewee does not take the time to find out about the organization.

2. The interviewee accepts your salary or hourly terms and then tries to up the offer.

3. The interviewee is rude to those he or she comes in contact with in the office.

4. The interviewee dresses inappropriately.

5. The interviewee did not set goals at his or her former job.

6. The interviewee arrives late for the interview.

7. The interviewee provides references that cannot be reached.

8. The interviewee is over-qualified.

9. The interviewee reveals confidential information about his or her former employer.

10. The interviewee lacks enthusiasm.

11. The interviewee appears angry during the interview.

12. The interviewee quit his/her job without giving notice.

13. The interviewee appears to lie about certain matters.

14. The interviewee talks inappropriately about other people.

100 THOUGHT PROVOKING INTERVIEW QUESTIONS AND STATEMENTS

1. What do you think sets you apart from the other applicants?
   (The interviewer is asking why should he hire you instead of the other candidates..)

2. Describe the best boss you ever had?
   (This description can also help you understand what the interviewee expects in a boss.)

3. What spreadsheet programs are you familiar with?
   (If a person says that they have computer experience, they should be familiar with at least 2 or 3 spreadsheet programs.)

4. Did you bring your resume?
   (If the interviewee did not bring a resume, that means he or she is not prepared for the interview.)

5. What are some of the reasons that you are interested in this position?
   (A good interviewee has researched the job beforehand; the response to this question will tell whether or not he or she has done the homework.)

6. Why do you want to leave your current job?
   (Sometimes from the response you can tell if he or she is hiding something.)

7. Are you willing to stretch the truth if needed?
   (What you are really asking is, Will you lie? If he or she says yes, beware.)

8. Is money a strong incentive for you?
   (What you really want to know is: Did the applicant leave his or her last job because of money or lack of job satisfaction.)

9. Are you involved in extracurricular activities?
   (If the interviewee is not involved in activities outside the job, will he or she have difficulty being a part of a team at work?)

10. You must have interviewed for a number of jobs, why haven't you been successful?
    (If the interviewee starts a "pity party", he or she may not be a premium candidate. It may also show a lack of motivation.)

11. What are your personal objectives for the year?
    (This question can possibly show if the person plans and is interested in self-improvement.)

12. In the last four years you have had three jobs, why?
    (Moving to too many jobs could be a signal of a problem.)

13. Why can't you look me in the eye?
    (Good eye contact can connote sincerity and truthfulness. Lack of eye contact may be construed as a sign of weakness, poor self-esteem or evidence of lying.)

14. Would you recommend your last place of employment to others?
    (If he or she says no, find out why. It may tell why the interviewee wants to leave.)

15. "I absorb what concerns me directly." How do you feel about that statement?
    (This question will help you understand if the interviewee is concerned about others or just about his or her own needs.)

16. What interests you the most about the available position?
    (This will let you know if the interviewee has really thought about the job.)

17. What on-line service do you use?
    (This will help you understand if the interviewer is computer literate.)

18. Are you smart?
    (The response will help you understand if the interviewee has good self-esteem and a positive image.)

19. What accomplishments do you feel most proud of?
    (This will help you understand what the person has accomplished, if he or she is an achiever.)

20. I don't really like how you answered the questions at all.
    (This statement will rattle the interviewee and possibly reveal another side of the individual's personality.)

21. I just don't know if you are the right person for this position. You have not convinced me.
    (Hopefully this statement will bring something out that the interviewee has not told you.)

22. How do you save time when working on tasks?
    (This will help you understand if the interviewee has basic organization skills.)

23. What risks did you take in your last job? What were the results?
    (The real difficult decisions can only be made if one is willing to take risks.)

24. Name three books you have read in the last six months.
    (Being well-read is a plus.)

25. Do you exercise regularly?
    (This question will help you find out if the interviewee is fairly healthy. If the person is extremely overweight and says that he or she exercises, beware.)

26. Describe a typical day in your present job.
    (This will help you understand what the person really does.)

27. What are your weekends like?
    (This will help you understand if the person has a wholesome lifestyle.)

28. Tell me about yourself.
    (This is an open statement and can get the person to start talking. The person may end up revealing more than he or she had planned to.)

29. Did you have difficulty finding our office?
    (If the person had difficulty, or was late, perhaps he or she didn't plan ahead.)

30. Did you really accomplish all those tasks or were you just in the room when they happened?
    (Resumes are embellished so the person can look better than he or she really is. This question will help get to the truth.)

31. In your previous job how much work was done on your own and how much as part of a team?
    (This question will help you clarify what responsibility the interviewee really had.)

32. How do you let a person know that you hear and understand what he or she is saying?
    (What you want to hear from the interviewee is that he or she gives feedback, communicates understanding, or mirrors)

33. Did you enjoy working at your last job?
    (If the interviewee portrays the last job in a negative light, beware and ask more questions.)

34. Were you ever dismissed from a job for a reason that seemed unjustified?
    (If the person starts complaining about a situation, beware.)

35. Do you take work home, daily, weekends?
    (This will help you find out if the person is a "company man" and will go the extra mile but keep it in perspective.)

36. Is your wife able to keep up with you intellectually, or is she mainly concerned with the home?
    (You are asking, Will the pressures of this job affect your marriage; does your wife understand what you do?)

37. Are you innovative? Give me an example.
    (This question will help you see if the person is creative.)

38. What kind of career development activities have you participated in during the past years?
    (This question will help you understand if the interviewee has been involved in self-improvement.)

39. Did you supervise any committees or special team projects at your last job?
    (This question will help the interviewee express his or her possible leadership ability.)

40. Do you really think that you can do this job? Explain why.
    (What you are really saying is, Help me justify giving you this job.)

41. Have you taken on new job responsibilities at your present job?
    (This question will help you find out if the company thinks enough of the person to have given him or her additional responsibilities.)

42. The interviewee walks in late to the interview. Did you allow yourself enough time to get here?
    (There is usually no excuse for being late for a job interview.)

43. How would you describe your present boss?
    (This question can reveal the type of management style the interviewee had been exposed to. If he or she is extremely negative about his or her former boss, it could indicate a problem.)

44. Does stress bring on physical illness?
    (Stress can cause low productivity and high absenteeism if not handled correctly.)

45. Why do you want to switch careers at this stage of your professional life?
    (If the person was a success in his or her former career, why does he or she want to change?)

46. What was one of your greatest challenges on your present job?
    (The interviewer should describe how he or she faced difficult situations. Ask for   examples.)

47. Can you give some examples of your leadership ability?
    (If the interviewee cannot give solid examples, her or she may not have been a leader.)

48. Where would you like to be in three years if we hire you?
    (If the person wants to be president in three years, he or she is unrealistic. If the person wants to grow with the company, that's more realistic.)

49. What type of people do you have little patience with?
    (This question will help you understand how the person wants to be treated, and what type of impression he or she would like to project.)

50. In your resume, there is a large time gap. Why is that?
    (A time gap may reveal a problem like prison, prolonged illness or some other reason.)

51. Are you overqualified for this job?
    (This question may rattle the interviewee, giving you a better idea of who he or she is.)

52. What do you expect from a supervisor?
    (What you are trying to find out is the type of supervisor the interviewee works well with.)

53. What do you consider your major weakness?
    (If an individual says that he or she has no weaknesses, the question is then raised whether or not the person is truthful. Everyone has weaknesses.)

54. How did you prepare for this interview?
    (This question helps you understand if the person is a planner.)

55. When do you plan to retire?
    (If the person is an older interviewee, this question will help you understand how long he or she plans to be around.)

56. Please take this sheet of paper and write two paragraphs telling why you would like this job.
    (This process will show two things: 1. Writing skills and 2. Organized thinking.)

57. To what professional associations do you belong ?
    (Belonging to professional associations is a plus.)

58. If you could turn back the clock, what would you do differently in your present or past job?
    (This question will help you understand if the person has regrets about his or her past.)

59. Name ten of your favorite TV shows.
    (If the person can name ten TV shows, he or she may be a couch potato and lack motivation.)

60. Tell me some inside information about your last job.
    (If the interviewee starts telling you confidential information, what will he or she say about you.)

61. Will your previous employer be a good reference?
    (What you are really are asking is, Are you on good terms with your previous employer?)

62. In your performance appraisals what strengths and weaknesses were discussed?
    (This will help you understand the person better, if he or she is truthful.)

63. What causes you to perform poorly?
    (What you are really asking is, What are your weaknesses?)

64. Have you ever been fired?
    (If the interviewee is truthful and says yes, that could show integrity on his or her part.)

65. How do you know a listener is comprehending what you are saying?
    (What you want the interviewee to say is that he or she wants feedback from the person.)

66. Silence— Just look at the interviewee with skepticism for 30 seconds or more. Instead of actually asking a question, use silence to see how the interviewee handles himself or herself. Will he or she use this time to ask a question, offer any information or remain quiet and calm until the interview resumes.

67. Describe projects you have started and completed at work.
    (Have the interviewee explain those projects that he or she started, not the ones they were involved in.)

68. What are some of the things that your supervisor did that you disliked?
    (This question will provide room to discuss and find out more about the person and his or her work environment.)

69. Did you ever consider leaving your present position before?
    (What you want to find out is if this is the interviewee's first bailout attempt from his or her job or has the person tried to leave before.)

70. If you are in a group of friends who talks the most?
    (What you want to know is if the interviewee is a loner, if he or she feels comfortable interacting in a group setting.)

71. How much do you know about us?
    (This question lets you know if the interviewee has done his or her homework.)

72. Do you volunteer for projects on the job?
    (Volunteering does show initiative on the person's part.)

73. What makes this job different from your current or last job?
    (What you are really asking is, What skills would you bring to this job if we hire you?)

74. When should or shouldn't you take a risk?
    (The interviewee's response will help you understand if he or she is balanced or a loose cannon.)

75. Was succession planning implemented at your company? Why weren't you considered?
    (Succession planing is usually found at the executive level. This question would be appropriate for a leadership position.)

76. When is it not appropriate to tell the truth?
    (This interviewee's response to this question will give you insight into his or her character.)

77. How do you spend your free time?
    (You want to see if the person is proactive and industrious even in his or her spare time.)

78. What are your greatest achievements?

(This gives the interviewee an opportunity to blow his or her horn. It will reveal how industrious and aggressive the person really is.)

79. Are there any conditions of personal business, health, or family that would limit your flexibility in taking on a new task or assignment?
(What you are really asking is, Do you have any hidden problems?)

80. Have you ever received awards or commendations?
(This will help you understand what the interviewee has accomplished.)

81. We all miss opportunities. What opportunities have you missed?
(This question will help you find out if the interviewee is satisfied with himself or herself, and looks forward to new opportunities.)

82. What do you think about office romance?
(Office romance should be kept out of the office, romantic situations cause a tremendous amount of wasted time.)

83. Would you be in a position to work overtime if required?
(If the person says no that could be a problem if you require overtime.)

84. Describe your decision-making responsibilities in your last job.
(If a person claims to have managed at his or her last job, he or she should be able to explain the responsibilities.)

85. "The only way to get something done is to do it yourself." Comment on that statement.
(What you want to find out is whether the interviewee is a team player.)

86. What motivates you?
(Some good responses: meeting goals, positive feedback, team effort. Many will say money. If that is the case, he or she may not stay with you long.)

87. Would you like to own your own business?
(The response to this question may let you know if the interviewee is just passing through to collect a check to start a business. You might be the competition.)

88. Do you bend the rules?
(Bending the rules and being flexible are two different things. Beware.)

89. Why do you want to work here?
(What you are really asking is, Why do you want to leave your other job?)

90. How has your training and education prepared you for the job you are applying for?
(The response will help you understand how much job experience the person really has.)

▲

91. Have you experienced times when you felt you were capable of making decisions but did not have the authority?
    (If the answer is yes, ask why they didn't have the authority.)

92. Give me quantitative proof of your management skills and performance.
    (A good response would be: increased attendance by... lowered overhead by.... Increased productivity by...)

93. Have you always been an exempt or nonexempt employee?
    (Exempt are those who are salaried. Nonexempt are those who are paid hourly. Usually management types are salaried.)

94. For what things did your boss compliment you?
    (This will tell you a lot about how the person performed his or her job.)

95. Using examples, convince me that you can adapt to a wide variety of people, situations and environments
    (This will give you insight into their experience.)

96. What are your strengths in relation to the job you are applying for?
    (A good response would be some of the following: knowledge of job, organized, team player, a person of integrity, good communication skills.)

97. Are there any other offers that you are considering?
    (What you are really asking is, Is your organization the only one interested in this person.)

98. Were you treated fairly in regard to advancement options?
    (What you are really asking is if the interviewee was passed over for a promotion. This question may also get the person talking about situations on his or her job.)

99. Are you experienced at public speaking?
    (Public speakers are self-assured and confident in themselves. This can be a real asset as a group leader.)

100. Do you own a computer?
    (It would be a concern if the interviewee was not computer literate.)

Can you think of other interview questions? Add them below.

_____

_____

_____

_____

▲

Session Topic: _____

Presenter: _____

Date: _____ / _____ / _____

NOTES

_____

_____

_____

_____

_____

_____

_____

_____

_____

_____

_____

_____

_____

_____

IDEAS TO TAKE WITH YOU

_____

_____

_____

_____

_____

_____

_____

_____

_____

_____

_____

_____

_____

_____

_____

_____

_____

_____

_____

BOOKS AND OTHER MATERIALS

_____

_____

_____

_____

_____

_____

_____

_____

_____

_____

_____

_____

Session Topic: _____

Presenter: _____

Date: _____ / _____ / _____

NOTES

_____

_____

_____

_____

_____

_____

_____

_____

_____

_____

_____

_____

_____

_____

IDEAS TO TAKE WITH YOU

_____

_____

_____

_____

_____

_____

BOOKS AND OTHER MATERIALS

CHURCH STRATEGIES
for the 21st century

Help! The Press Is Coming

The media is always looking for news. Their job is to get as many people as possible to buy their newspapers or watch their television news show. Television, radio, and newspapers are always looking for news no matter what the topic is. The church pastor or administrator must be prepared for any type of situation that might arise. A national event occurs and the press wants you to comment. A tragedy happens at your church and you find a TV news truck planted in front of your church; the press wants to know what happened and why. Remember, when dealing with the media, always be open and positive as much as possible under the circumstances. While they, the media, may understand that you do not have the full story, reporters will become irate if they think that information is being withheld from them. Always give as much information as possible without jeopardizing the organization by releasing confidential information. A positive dialogue with the press is necessary.

When being interviewed by the press, never say "no comment" as a response to a reporter's inquiry, even if there is no information to be given. As the spokesperson, make sure that the reporters feel that they are getting information as quickly as possible. If you don't know the answer to the question, you should respond with a reply such as, "We are still examining that particular issue" or "I don't want to give out misinformation. We are gathering the facts as we speak" or "As quickly as I get the information, I will be giving it to you." As long as a pledge is offered to get the information to the reporters as soon as possible, you will be fine but do not say it if you cannot deliver. The spokesperson should be able to tell the media when they will have access to the information through news briefings, prepared statements, or interviews.

CRISIS INTERVIEWING

In order for an organization to be prepared for a crisis, planning is the key. Reporters can be intrusive and obnoxious during a crisis, seeking information so they can give their version of what happened to the audience. Be prepared to answer the following:

- What happened?

- Was anyone hurt?

- Why did it happen?

- How is the community affected?

- What are you doing to fix it?

▲

TASK #16

List below three or four catastrophes that have happened in your town that could happen to you.

_____

_____

_____

_____

_____

_____

_____

_____

_____

_____

_____

_____

_____

_____

_____

_____

_____

_____

_____

_____

_____

_____

_____

_____

▲

Assemble the key leadership in your organization to list the "what ifs" they might have to deal with if there were flooding, a fire, an earthquake, or a shooting. Planning ahead gives the organization's key people the luxury of considering several possible solutions. There are several steps to be taken during a crisis and dealing with the media. They are as follows:

- Interview those members of the staff that were involved in the crisis as soon as possible while details are still fresh in their minds. It allows the leadership to understand what happened and why. A decision should be made as to what specific person involved in the crisis should be interviewed. This also allows the leadership to "media train" that person in what to say so that the organization can be portrayed in the least damaging light.

- An official spokesperson must be chosen and an additional person should be picked as the backup spokesperson just in case the other person is not available for some reason.

- The spokesperson must have credibility with the media; he or she should be a fitting representative of the organization. The spokesperson should be composed, well spoken, and able to handle the stress of an interview by the media. Their face will be seen by possibly millions and will be representing your organization. Choose wisely.

- Organization executives should also be prepared to have a news conference soon after the incident occurs. Depending on the severity of the crisis this could occur up to 48 hours after the event.

- Someone in the organization should be in charge of the logistics for the news conference, such as:

  Location for news conference
  Lighting
  Sound system
  Ample telephones for e-mail
  Breakout press box

If your organization does not have space for a news conference, look into using a hotel or conference center.

- Standby statements should be prepared to address a potential crisis. They should be written with input from and agreed upon by the leadership. These standby statements should be written in simple, easy to understand terms. The statement explains (if applicable) that the leadership plans to resolve the problem as quickly as possible.

For example: If there is a fire in the school, immediately release a statement saying that plans are being made to relocate classes to another location.

If there has been a shooting, immediately release a statement that all parents have been notified, counselors have been called in, and the authorities have taken charge.

If there is a child molestation, immediately release a statement that the parents have been contacted and the authorities are on-site and in communication with the parents.

- Prepare a list of names and numbers of reporters from television, radio stations and newspapers as well as publications covering your organization's industry. You should develop a good relationship with key people in each of the media outlets. To do that let them know what you are doing during the good times.

- Each media must be dealt with differently. For example, when being interviewed by television reporters, use short "sound bites" of 15 to 20 seconds rather than a long drawn out statement that is going to be edited anyway. Use as much time as you need before you respond, but avoid pauses that make you look suspicious. Newspaper reporters on the other hand have more time and room for lengthy statements.

PREPARING FOR THE MEDIA INTERVIEW

What do you do during an interview? What do you wear, and what do you say? If you are not prepared, the media will be in total control and use the opportunity to their advantage. Whether the interview occurs on the street, in your church, or in the studio, the interview principles are primarily the same.

A key point to remember is to never accept a cold call from anyone. You should always prepare for an interview. Make sure you know what you are being interviewed for. On numerous occasions, a pastor has been told to come in for an interview on television or on radio and the pastor's perception is that he is being interviewed from a positive point of view. However, when he gets there, the tables are turned and the interview takes on a negative slant. Always maintain a positive approach and if something is said in a negative manner, turn it around to a positive one. For example: "Why are you fleecing your flock?" You respond, "Our church is audited every year by a certified public accountant and our financial records are available to all congregation members to see. As a matter of fact the church has just finished the angel tree project and we raised more money than any other church in the community." If you keep the interview on the high road and reflect negative questions with positive responses you cannot go wrong.

Do not get into discussing your political position. This can be a volatile issue that can put you in a very sensitive position.

If you are a pastor or religious leader, speak from a biblically based foundation. Most reporters are liberal and have no idea what the Bible says, and don't understand it. Use scripture from time to time to get your point across. In addition, avoid getting into doctrinal discussions during interviews on radio or television. This is not the time to prove your doctrinal position.

Try to stay away from using "ah" when you are lost for words. Take a second or two to think about the question and then say the reporter's name if you need more time. Then repeat the question. What I understand you to say is that…" or "That is a good question."

Avoid using "Christian" words like "spirit filled" "getting saved," "healing the broken hearted," "holy ghost." These words certainly are not bad, but when used with people who don't understand them and in volatile situations the words have no impact or may give opportunity for unfair and unlearned remarks.

Wash your face. Most of the time nervous people will sweat under the hot lights. Before going on TV wash your face with very cold water which will help to close the pores on your face.
When on television always look at the interviewer not the camera. When on radio look at the inter-viewer and not at the microphone.

Keep the following points in mind when preparing for an interview.

1. Watch or listen to the interview show on which you are planning to appear. Notice what slant the moderator takes. Does he or she give the interviewee time to speak? Does he or she cut off the interviewee?

2. Make sure that you call the station and find out what the topic will be and who will be on the program with you. The topic may be fine but the other guests on the program could make the program more negative than positive. You may be included with some-one of a questionable background. Questions to ask:

   "Who are the other guests?"

   "How long will the interview be?"

   "Will you be accepting telephone calls?"

   "In order to be prepared can you give me a list of the questions
   or if a list is not available, some idea of what you will be asking.?"

3. Prepare notes that you can use during the interview. Use light blue 9x12 cards or folded 8 1/2x11 paper. Make sure that the information is typed in a large font size so you can see it easily.

4. Line up someone to record your interview so that you can have a record of what was said.

5. Listen to the types of questions that are asked just before commercials. In order to hold the audience's attention the moderator may ask a stinger question or make an inflamma-tory statement. For example: "We understand Rev._____ that your flock pays you a very handsome salary. It must a good amount. I see you arrived at the station in a 1999 Mercedes today. We'll be right back after these messages."

6. Do not take anything personal. If you do, you will lose control and end up getting your-self into a negative conversation.

7. Do not talk over the interviewer. Although what you are saying may be true, talking incessantly makes you come off looking like a "know it all."

8. Tell the truth. If you do not know something, say so. For example, "That's a very good question but I really don't know."

9. Don't use negative phrases like "Don't go there." "Why did you ask me that?" "I don't care about..." "I don't listen to this show." "The audience has no idea..."

10. When on television limit the use of your hands, leave them folded in your lap only gesturing once in a while to emphasizes a point.

11. No matter how friendly the interviewer appears to be, stay on your toes for what ever you say is on the record. Remember you are always being interviewed even when the interview is over. Even if you say, "This comment is off the record" you are leaving it up to the reporter to decide. They do lie.

12. Keep to the high road. Never get involved with off-color discussions, gossip, or rumors. Present yourself with dignity and integrity. Never comment on another ministry or organization in a negative way. It has been done in the past and proven to be an albatross around the person's neck that made the comment.

13. There are no bad questions, only the potential for bad answers. Make sure that you listen to the question, and understand what is being asked. Always end on a positive note.

HOW TO DRESS FOR TELEVISION - WOMEN

1. Women should avoid provocative clothing, extremely short dresses and low necklines. Your appearance can detract from the message. Make sure that your attire has an appropriate place for a lavaliere microphone to be clipped on, for example a jacket lapel or vest.

2. Avoid large earrings, necklaces and bracelets. Noise from large jewelry can be picked up by the microphone.

3. Wear a light application of makeup.

4. Avoid white dresses or herringbone patterns. Dark blues, grays, or browns are preferable.

5. Take someone with you who you can see from the TV set and can tell you if your hair is out of place or if your jacket needs adjusting.

HOW TO DRESS FOR TELEVISION - MEN

1. Although it may look nice, avoid flashy jewelry. It reflects light that can be a problem for the camera..

2. Avoid white shirts and narrow stripe shirts.

3. When sitting down make sure your jacket is unbuttoned which will give you a more comfortable and relaxed look.

4. Use the television makeup that the makeup person provides.

5. It is always standard procedure to bring someone with you to see how you look on the set.

CASE STUDY #1

The pastor, to his dismay, is advised while on vacation that one of the church employees has been picked up for bank robbery. The pastor flies back home from vacation and immediately goes to the church. Since this person was part of the administrative staff, the press is waiting for him for comment. The pastor jumps from the car into a sea of cameras and microphones.

Pastor A "I have no comment, stay away from me....no comment....you're just itching to put me on the six o'clock news....no comment," the pastor says as he rushes through the crowd and into the church.

Press A "Why are you afraid to comment? Did you know that this man was a felon? What are you hiding? Why won't you talk to us?"

Pastor B The pastor gets out of the car and stops, not trying to push through the press. "I have just arrived back in town. I don't have any information for you at this time and I don't want to give you misinformation. At the appropriate time, we will have an official statement, but we must remember the gentleman in question is a private citizen. No comments will be made until we get all the facts. Thank you."

Press B "Are you surprised that Mr. _____ was picked up by the police and arrested for robbery?"

Pastor B "As I stated before, I do not want to give you any misinformation, but at the appropriate time, we will have a comment. Thank you." The pastor walks calmly into the church.

CASE STUDY #2

A famous pastor is recognized with another woman in a red-light district. A reporter is notified, pictures are taken, and he ends up on the front page of the local and national newspaper. The press contacts the church. The administrator is put on the spot. He receives a telephone call from the press, which he accepts.

Reporter C "Rev._____ was caught downtown in the red-light district with another woman and he's married with children and supposed to be a religious leader. Has he been taking care of her and paying for her apartment? How much church money was going to her? Are you going to ask him to leave or just forgive and forget? Where is he now? He is not answering his telephone at home."

Administrator C "Look, your guess is as good as mine. I saw the story in the paper and everybody is mad and upset. If you want my opinion, I think that the board should remove him as soon as possible. We are trying to find out who the woman is. We are a good church with a lot of good leaders and parishioners. The pastor must be using money from the church for this other woman."

Reporter C "So you're saying he did take money and the leaders in the church knew about it, but looked the other way?"

Administrator C "No, that's not what I said."

Reporter C "That's what I heard you say, sir."

Key Point: *Do not take cold calls from the press. However, if you have to, keep the interview on the positive side.*

Administrator D "The only comment we have is that the church has been a part of this community for the last 20 years and we have been involved in all types of projects that have benefited the city. This situation is a real concern but we really do not want to comment until the church leadership has addressed the issue which they are doing now. We will get through this, together. Thank you for calling."

CASE STUDY # 3

The maintenance man is seen with one of the children from the Christian school, which is housed at the church. The child tells her parents that she was touched inappropriately (the accusation is untrue) and the irate parent goes to the press and threatens to sue. The press contacts the principal of the school.

Principal #1 A local reporter calls and the principal responds, "No comment!!!" and tries to hang up the phone.

Reporter #1 –"Is it true one of the children was raped at the school? We demand to know!"

Principal #1 – (yelling into the telephone) "We are not saying anything until we talk to our lawyer!" He slams the telephone down.

Principal #2   A local reporter calls and the school principal answers the phone

Reporter #2 "We just heard from a parent that a child was raped at your school by the maintenance man!"

Principal #2 "Everyone at our school goes through a thorough background check before they are hired. We are just as disturbed by these allegations as you are. At this point I cannot comment any more until we get all the facts, but I can assure you we will have a full investigation into this matter. Thank you for calling."

Reporter #2 "How old is this guy? Where does he live? Does he have a prison record?"

Principal #2 "I assure you we will provide all necessary information to the authorities who are looking into the allegations. It would not be prudent to say any more until after the investigation. After all, we are dealing with a person's reputation here. Thank you for calling." He hangs up.

TASK #17

Prepare for your on-camera interview. Rehearse with a member of your discussion group

Note:
If you have the textbook but have not attended our seminars, our "Help The Press Is Coming" video is available for purchase. Use it as a training tool for your staff. Order today!!!!

Session Topic: _____

Presenter: _____

Date: _____ /_____ /_____

NOTES

_____

_____

_____

_____

_____

_____

_____

_____

_____

_____

_____

_____

_____

_____

IDEAS TO TAKE WITH YOU

_____

_____

_____

_____

_____

_____

_____

_____

_____

_____

_____

BOOKS AND OTHER MATERIALS

_____

_____

_____

_____

_____

_____

_____

_____

_____

_____

_____

_____

Session Topic: _____

Presenter: _____

Date: _____ / _____ / _____

NOTES

_____

_____

_____

_____

_____

_____

_____

_____

_____

_____

_____

_____

_____

_____

_____

IDEAS TO TAKE WITH YOU

_____

_____

_____

_____

_____

BOOKS AND OTHER MATERIALS

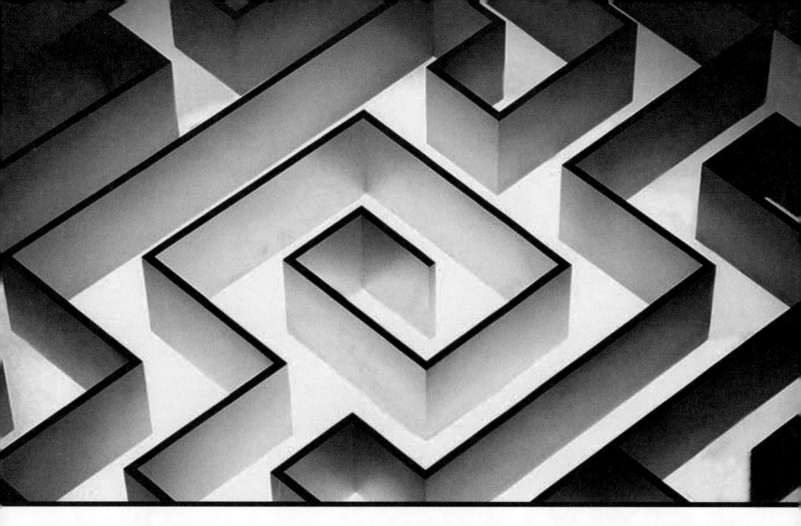

CHURCH STRATEGIES
for the 21st century

Outside The Walls

A young pastor called me at my office and asked if he could come in to see me and talk to me concerning information for grants, foundations and funding for the church. He understood that there were all types of state, federal and foundation money available for faith-based entities to help them in social endeavors for the community. There are funds available for faith-based entities, but it is important that the church first develop a strategy to avail themselves of those funds.

How does a church develop a strategy for securing grants and external funding? The key is building a framework that causes external funding sources to want to help you do what you do best, help people. The following process, if followed, will help you in developing a total strategy that may help you become eligible for funding.

1. Survey your congregation

It is so important to know who is sitting in the pews in your church. Are they business people, managers of stores, social service professionals, policemen, carpenters, plumbers? Understanding who sits in the congregation is the first step. In order to find out who they are a survey should be taken and everyone in the congregation should be invited to fill out the survey sheet.

In order to help the congregation understand why the survey is being done, it must be conveyed that the church is preparing to embark on a new approach to ministry. In order to do that it is necessary to know who the congregation members are so those who are interested can be fit into the master plan. The survey will also open the door to the network in the church. One would be surprised to know that a church congregation is a network into the community that can be used quite effectively. Once the survey has been completed and all forms have been turned in, the work begins.

2. What is the church's niche?
Where is God leading your church? What should the church be involved in? This question must be addressed. While seeking the Lord, you can also pick some of your congregation members to give their input. If one of those surveyed is a social worker, sit with him or her and discuss what the community's needs are and how the church can help. Drive around the community and look for yourself. Are there a large number of youth? Elderly? Is your church near a prison or detention home? Are factories closed? There may be a need for training of some type to get people back to work. or to help those that are economically disadvantaged.

CASE STUDY #1

A young Pastor was brought into a newly formed church with a membership of about 75. The congregation was eager to take what they had learned from God's Word and the Pastor's preaching and make it come alive in the community. The church was not wealthy but they began realizing that there were many elderly who owned property around them that could not attend church, but had just as many needs.

The houses were rundown and needed refurbishing. The Pastor had already surveyed his congregation, finding that he had three professional carpenters, one electrician, and several housewives who had great sewing skills. The members were also made up of young couples eager to work; some were professionals, some not. The church offered one of the elderly homeowner's help to refurbish his house, which he gladly accepted. Money was raised by the congregation to cover the refurbishing which was approximately $6,000. The local paper got wind of the story and more donations came in to help. Adding to what they already had they were able to refurbish another home for another of the elderly citizens. The momentum continued, more donations came in, the city offered money and by the time it was all over a whole block of some 15 homes were refurbished. In addition, because of the social responsibility of the church more people came to visit thus adding to the congregation. Because of their success, the church was able to apply for a state grant to fund more home refurbishing.

CASE STUDY #2

A church in the Midwest had a fairly large congregation whose members were mostly blue collar working folks. The pastor was able to share his vision of reaching out into the community. The church had just purchased a strip mall made up of about 10 stores. They opened a beauty salon in one of the stores. The ministry skills survey had revealed that there were many women with cosmetology backgrounds. Two of the ladies felt that operating the salon could be their ministry, allowing them to teach young men and women a new skill. Another one of the stores was used as a computer center to train the unskilled in computer repair and operation. Another store was used as a classroom for a GED program to help young people and adults get their high school diploma. There were several people that had human resource backgrounds and they opened a part-time employment office which helped not only the community but members of the church as well.

CORE COMPETENCIES

Listed below are several areas that have been recognized as 'Best Practices." Best Practices are those programs that have been identified by both state and federal agencies to be most successful in meeting social needs. As your organization decides what direction to take in serving your community, consider what best practice fits your organization and community. Use the Needs Assessment form to find out what skills or areas of interest are in your organization. This will help you to decide what areas you should focus on.

- **Jobs**
  Training
  Mentoring

- **Entrepreneurial Development**
  Economic Development

- **Education**
  GED
  ESL
  Life skills

- **Housing**
  Refurbishing
  New construction

- **Health**
  Screening
  Training

- **Legal**
  Assistance

- **Substance Abuse**
  Prevention
  Outpatient

- **Therapeutic**
  Basic communication and interaction. There is a need for people who can really listen and interact with youth as well as adults. Just being able to listen can be a useful skill for ministry.

- **Financial Management**
  Personal financial skills

- **Spiritual Growth**
  Mentoring
  Training

- **Parenting/Fathering**

- **Mentoring**

- **Recreation**

- **Care Team Development**
  Elderly
  Disabled

- **Technology Development**

- **Food Services**

EXAMPLES OF EFFECTIVE PROGRAMS

There are churches all over the United States that are getting involved with the community by bringing the church to the community, taking the church outside the walls and reaching lives that otherwise may not be touched. A holistic approach, touching the soul and then teaching a skill is the key. The following is a list of some of the outreaches that many churches are participating in. They serve to encourage you to launch out and begin new outreaches in your church.

Please be careful to adhere to all local and state regulations.

Truck Driving School

Reaching men and women that lack strong employable skills has been answered by a church that has started a truck driving school. A member of the church who is a professional driver runs the school. Partial funding comes from the state while the remainder is funded by student tuition. Eighteen-wheeler rigs may be leased or purchased used. A large parking lot can be used for the beginners; classroom space can be provided by the church if available.

Hair Salon

Young women especially who lack their GED can get started in this field easily, while working on their GED. The salon is a school to train young ladies in the skill of hair styling and other related services like nail care. Space will be needed for styling chairs and a classroom. Members of the church can use the service as well as the general public.

Construction Company

Those churches that are in urban settings can use building refurbishing and construction as a means to reach the community. Numerous churches have started construction companies either run by a member of the church or an outside consultant. Teaching a young man or woman a trade like plumbing, carpentry, brick masonry, or electrical work can give them the economic push needed to be successful. The revenue from the refurbishing or new construction can serve as the funding for the next project, so that it will not be a continual financial burden on the church.

Cleaning Company

There are several churches that have developed cleaning companies. These businesses clean offices, restaurant kitchens, and public facilities. Numerous municipalities provide public bids for the state and local buildings. The majority of those who work for the cleaning company may be those who have recently accepted Christ and have no real marketable skills. A cleaning business can be very lucrative but the turnover is very high.

Limousine Service

A limo business can be a great asset to the local churches in your area, providing quality on-time service for weddings, funerals, and special guests. Young men and women can be trained to drive the limousines with the proper licensing.

Moving Company

There are several churches that have formed moving companies. This type of business is primarily for men. However, if you add the service of packing, women can certainly be included.

Computer Lab/ Sales / Service

High technology should be a major focus of all churches that are interested in providing opportunities to learn new skills. A computer lab should contain not only computers for program training but also audio and video nonlinear editing, computer graphics, animation, and web design. Computer repair and sales can be a part of the computer lab as well.

Apparel Store

Most churches have members that are skilled seamstresses. An apparel store that sells custom-made as well as commercially made clothing can be a tremendous training place for skilled and unskilled individuals. The apparel store can also provide clothing alterations services as well.

Call Center

A call center can be expensive to start but can be very lucrative. The initial cost is in the start-up equipment. Call centers usually provide service to any type of company that needs to provide customer service by telephone. A call center can also be used as a training school.

FAST ATTACK MINISTRY

The television news tells the story of a family that has just been burned out of their single family home. Everything was lost — clothes, food, money, and memories — nothing survived. The Pastor sits staring at the television; his heart is moved. Finally he says, "Isn't that awful. We'll pray for them." On another evening of relaxation the Pastor sits and looks at the news. This time a shooting occurred leaving a 15-year-old boy dead in the street. The single mom is seen kneeling by his lifeless body screaming and crying for her dead son. The Pastor sits staring at the television; his heart is moved. Finally he says, "Isn't that awful. I'm going to remember that woman in my prayers."

Another story follows showing how a tornado passed through a small neighboring town destroying everything in its path; families are left without homes and possessions, and everything is gone. The television news reporter makes an appeal to citizens to send in money to help these unfortunate people. The Pastor calls the church treasurer and tells her to send $50 to help those who were victims of the tornado. The Pastor sits staring at the television again saying, "Isn't that awful. I'm going to remember those people in my prayers…Well we've done our part."

The three scenarios above happen in some form everyday. Our hearts and prayers go out to the victims of the tragedies but that is as far as it goes. The question has been asked by numerous church leaders, "What can we do? We are a small congregation and there are other churches more equipped than we are," they think. In other words, the leader is saying, "We can't change anything, we can't change our community, and we can't make a difference." The response to those statements is YES YOU CAN! The church, in its role as the flashpoint, must by its example empower people to make a change in their community and raise their level of compassion.

Television can have a numbing effect or create awareness of what needs to be done in the community. A Fast Attack Ministry (FAM) is the answer to this problem. This type of ministry does what its name implies — responds with a fast attack to the problem or need. FAM can have an awesome effect on your community for years to come. With FAM you have the ability to touch people where they are, quickly. The church can put together a Fast Attack Ministry with very little cost. The first step is finding the right people to be a part of FAM. The participants can be those who will be available for immediate response to needs in their communities. Members of the church that are skilled can be a real asset as well as those that may not be skilled but can comfort those who are in need.

Let us go back to those earlier scenarios and understand how FAM can help. In the first scenario a mother, father and three children are burned out of their home; they have lost everything. The Pastor sees the news story and immediately picks up the telephone to call one of the five FAM captains. The captain calls one or more of the five people he oversees. The team includes three men and two women. Each person is a member of the church with various occupations - a postman, housewife, carpenter, retired civil service worker, and a secretary. The team immediately arrives at the scene of the fire in the official vehicle for this ministry and makes contact with the family, providing the much-needed help. If the family has left the scene, the police, because they are aware of the ministry, advise the team where the family was sent. The church has an account with a local efficiency and rooms are reserved for the family for three nights, compliments of the church. The church clothing closet is contacted with the sizes of each person and within an hour clothes are delivered by one of the team members to the family. The church also has an account with a local food store and three days worth of food is delivered to the family at the efficiency. The FAM captain leaves the family a number to call for assistance during the next five days. The FAM team completes the operation in a matter of hours and a family is helped and will not soon forget the church that the team represented.

In the second scenario, a shooting occurred leaving a 15-year-old boy dead in the street in a nearby community that the church has been evangelizing. Immediately a special FAM team is contacted. This team has members who have Biblical counseling and crisis intervention skills which is very important in this type of situation. The team arrives and identifies itself to the police and tells them "we are here to help the family." The police will usually identify those that need support and counseling. Hotel rooms can be reserved, if needed. Someone familiar with funeral arranging can also be available a day or so later to assist in arranging the funeral. Food delivery can be headed up by one of the team members for the next two to three days. After the tragedy has passed, one of the pastors of the church can visit periodically to show support.

In the third scenario, a tornado passes through a small neighboring town destroying everything in its path; families are left without homes and possessions, and everything is gone. In response to the appeal for help, all the church FAM teams are called into action. All FAM vehicles, which include two vans and one Suburban, are loaded with blankets, food, clothing and first aid materials. Three teams are ready to roll equipped with phones and walkie-talkies. The teams arrive at the police and fire department headquarters and identify themselves. They help serve food and water to the victims and assist the rescue teams in any way they can. Ministry is also an important part of what the team does. Offering prayer and spiritual support is crucial.

In order to have a ministry that is recognized and accepted it must be well organized. It is important also that the police, fire, and rescue agencies know of the ministry. To help identify team members, each member should wear a special uniform. They should carry identification cards and use vehicles with the FAM logo on it. Each team should be well supplied with at least the following:

- Cell phones and walkie-talkies
- First-aid kits
- Directory of social agencies, clinics, etc.
- Blankets
- Contact information to leave with the victims

NOTES

_____

_____

_____

_____

_____

_____

_____

_____

ECONOMIC DEVELOPMENT CORPORATION

- *What is an Economic Development Corporation?*
  An Economic Development Corporation can be involved in numerous activities in its community. Some EDCs are formed by local municipalities to entice businesses to set up in their community, especially in the economically depressed areas, thus creating more jobs, job training, housing, and business counseling. A prime purpose of an EDC is to eradicate poverty in designated areas. This falls under the category of a charitable service. The articles and bylaws of the EDC must clearly state that the organization's mission is charitable and nonsectarian.

- *How can a church or organization benefit from forming an EDC?*
  In most cases major corporations, business entities, and foundations do not like to donate money to religious organizations. They do not want to be perceived as being biased toward one religion. In addition, many CEOs tend to give to their favorite charities or organizations. Because of its charter, an EDC is more eligible to receive financial gifts. Remember, an EDC

▲

is a nonsectarian. Corporations and foundations that see you as a social organization with a social agenda, not a religious agenda, will consider giving to you if you meet their criteria. This gives you the opportunity to apply for funding from a myriad of organizations and businesses nationwide.

Organizations that have a community / social agenda can create a great public image. The activities of an EDC can create positive community interest resulting in local donations. If your organization has developed social programs within the church, those social programs may be eligible for outside funding from foundations or corporations. Note: It is essential that you maintain data on all of the social programs that your organization is involved with. When approaching corporations or foundations, they look for solid results from what you have done. For example, you have an outreach to pregnant teenage girls from 12 to 18 years of age. The program provides counseling, prenatal instruction, adoption arrangements, homes for those who are without homes, and daycare services after the baby is born so the mother can work. Moreover, the results over the last four years have been tremendous. You have reached 375 girls, 134 girls put their children up for adoption, and 90 girls have jobs and are taking care of their child. Maintain as many statistical facts as you can; without provable facts you will not be funded.

- *Are there any special requirements to form an EDC?*
  Yes, you are required to file a 1023-application (501c3) for exempt status recognition with the IRS. You are also required to file an annual return called a 990.

  Note: It is imperative that you engage an attorney and a certified CPA for this process.

- *Are there any pitfalls in forming an EDC?*
  If you incorporate religious purposes and activities in the EDC and if you blend what the church does with what the EDC does, you will create problems for yourself. Remember the EDC is nonsectarian and nonreligious. In addition, you cannot incorporate profit-making endeavors that may jeopardize your 501c3 standing.

▲

TASK: #18

List those areas in your organization that help the community. Explain how.

_____

_____

_____

_____

_____

_____

_____

_____

_____

Session Topic: _____

Presenter: _____

Date: _____ / _____ / _____

<u>NOTES</u>

_____

_____

_____

_____

_____

_____

_____

_____

_____

_____

_____

_____

_____

IDEAS TO TAKE WITH YOU

_____

_____

_____

_____

_____

_____

_____

_____

_____

_____

_____

_____

_____

BOOKS AND OTHER MATERIALS

_____

_____

_____

_____

_____

_____

_____

_____

_____

_____

_____

_____

Session Topic: _____

Presenter: _____

Date: _____ / _____ / _____

NOTES

_____

_____

_____

_____

_____

_____

_____

_____

_____

_____

_____

_____

_____

_____

_____

_____

IDEAS TO TAKE WITH YOU

_____

_____

_____

_____

_____

_____

_____

_____

_____

_____

_____

_____

_____

_____

_____

BOOKS AND OTHER MATERIALS

_____

_____

_____

_____

_____

_____

_____

_____

_____

_____

_____

_____

_____

_____

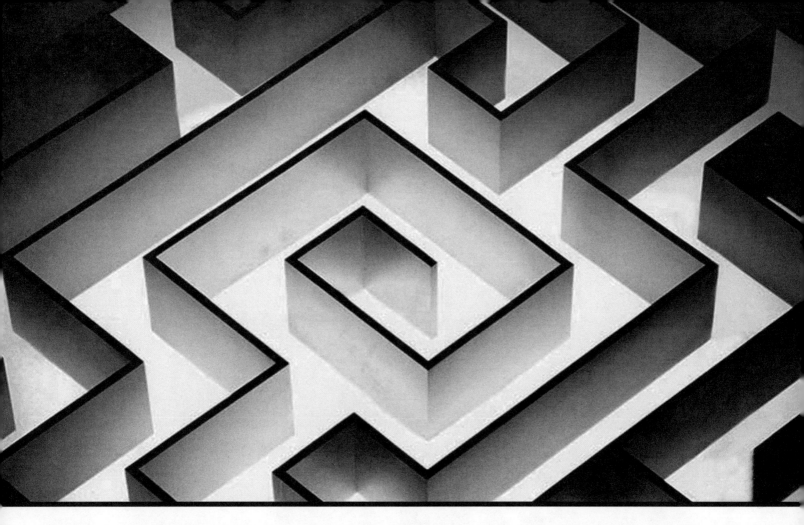

CHURCH STRATEGIES
for the 21st century

Management by the Book

There are all types of books and materials available that discuss numerous management skills and formulas. Books are available that can range from "first time manager" to "you're wrong they're right", "the best management style" "the new management" and the litany goes on.

Management by the Book is timeless and it works. Even if you have never attended college or had any advanced education, these are easy to understand Biblical principles that will work in every situation. The following is a combination of scenarios and scripture applications. It is hoped that you will see how management by the Book will be an asset to your decision making.

One of the primary principles in management is communication. We communicate with subordinates, church members, secretaries, bosses, mothers, fathers, children and through communication we make decisions. There are many leaders who have limited skills in communicating. I am not referring to just speaking, but understanding what the other person is saying. One of the first skills that must be learned is listening.

TASK #19

Select a scripture (one per week) and apply it to your everyday life. As a class function, pick a scripture and be prepared to elaborate on how that scripture applies to management principles.

COMMUNICATION SKILLS

Proverbs 18:13
He who answers a matter before he hears it, it is folly and shame to him.

Proverbs 18:2
A fool has no delight in understanding, but expresses his own heart.

Proverbs 10:19
In the multitude of words sin is not lacking, but he who restrains his lips is wise.

Proverbs 10:32
The lips of the righteous know what is acceptable, but the mouth of the wicked what is perverse.

Proverbs 11:9
The hypocrite with his mouth destroys his neighbor.

Proverbs 14:3
In the mouth of a fool is a rod of pride, but the lips of the wise will preserve them.

Psalm 34:1
I will bless the Lord at all times, His praise shall continually be in my mouth.

Proverbs 12:25
Anxiety in the heart of man causes depression, but a good word makes it glad.

Proverbs 21:23
Whoever guards his mouth and tongue keeps his soul from troubles.

Psalm 37:30
The mouth of the righteous speaks wisdom and his tongue talks of justice.

Proverbs 15:1a
A soft answer turns away wrath.

Proverbs 15:7
The lips of the wise disperse knowledge.

Proverbs 18:21
Death and life are in the power of the tongue.

SELF CONTROL

Proverbs 16:32
He who is slow to anger is better than the mighty and he who rules his spirit than he who takes a city.

Proverbs 13:3a
He who guards his mouth preserves his life.

Lamentations 3:25 a,b
The Lord is good to those who wait for him, to the soul who seeks Him. It is good that one should hope and wait quietly.

BUSINESS NEGOTIATIONS

Proverbs 16:7
When a man's ways please the Lord, He makes even his enemies to be at peace with him.

Proverbs 21:14
A gift in secret pacifies anger, and a bribe behind the back, strong wrath.

RELYING ON DIVINE INTERVENTION TO MAKE BUSINESS DECISIONS

Psalm 7:1
O Lord my God in you I put my trust.

Psalm 2:12
Blessed are all those who put their trust in Him.

Psalm 5:11
But let all those rejoice who put their trust in you.

Proverbs 3:25
For the Lord will be your confidence. and will keep your foot from being caught.

II Kings 4:7
Go sell the oil and pay your debt; and you and your sons live on the rest.

Nehemiah 9:31
For you are God, gracious and merciful.

Nehemiah 10:31
If the people of the land brought wares or any grain to sell on the Sabbath day, we would not buy it from them on the Sabbath or on any holy day; and we would forego the seventh year's produce and the exacting of every debt.

Job 4:5
But as for me, I would seek God and to God I would commit my cause.

Job 14:14
If a man dies, shall he live again? All the days of my hard service, I will wait, till my change comes.

Job 23:12
I have treasured the words of His mouth more than my necessary food.

Job 42:10
And the Lord restored Job's losses when he prayed for his friends. Indeed, the Lord gave Job twice as much as he had before.

Psalm 1:1,2
Blessed is the man who walks not in the counsel of the ungodly, nor stands in the path of sinners, nor sits in the seat of the scornful. But his delight is in the law of the Lord and in His law he meditates day and night.

Psalm 5:6
The Lord abhors the blood thirsty and deceitful men.

Psalm 7:8
The Lord shall judge the people; judge me O Lord according to my righteousness and according to my integrity within me

Psalm 25:4
Show me your words O Lord; teach me your paths.

INTEGRITY AND DISCRETION

Psalm 25:21
Let integrity and uprightness preserve me.

Psalm 26:11
But as for me I will walk in my integrity.

Psalm 41:12
As for me you uphold me in my integrity.

Proverbs 10:8
He who walks in integrity walks securely.

Proverbs 11:3a
The integrity of the upright will guide them.

Proverbs 2:11
Discretion will preserve you; understanding will keep you.

Proverbs 3:21
Keep sound wisdom and discretion.

Proverbs 19:9
And he who speaks lies shall perish.

Psalm 37:7
Rest in the Lord and wait patiently for him; do not fret because of him who prospers in his way.

Proverbs 19:1
Better is the poor who walks in his integrity than one who is perverse in his lips and is a fool.
Proverbs 20:7
The righteous man walks in his integrity; his children are blessed after him.

Proverbs 27:19
As in water face reflects face, so a man's heart reveals the man..

Ecclesiastes 7:1
A good name is better than precious ointment.

FINANCES

Psalm 37:21a
The wicked borrows and does not repay.

Proverbs 13:7
There is one who makes himself rich, yet has nothing; and one who makes himself poor yet has great riches.

Proverbs 13:22
A good man leaves an inheritance to his children's children, but the wealth of the sinner is stored up for the righteous.

Proverbs 13:11a
Wealth gained by dishonesty will be diminished.

Proverbs 15:27
He who is greedy for gain troubles his own house, but he who hates bribes will live.

Proverbs19:17
He who has pity on the poor lends to the Lord, and he will pay back what he has given.

Proverbs 20:14
It is good for nothing, cries the buyer; but when he has gone his way then he boasts.

Proverb 20:23
Diverse weights are an abomination to the Lord, and dishonest scales are not good.

Proverbs 22:7b
And the borrower is the servant to the lender.

Proverbs 22:26,27
Do not be one of those who shakes hands in a pledge, one of those who is surety for debts; if you have nothing with which to pay, why should he take away your bed from under you?

Ecclesiastes 5:19
As for every man to whom God has given riches and wealth, and given him power to eat of it, to receive his heritage and rejoice in his labor - this is the gift of God.

Ecclesiastes 7:12
For wisdom is a defense as money is a defense.

Ecclesiastes 10:19b
But money answers everything.

COMMUNITY INVOLVEMENT

Psalm 37:21b
But the righteous shows mercy and gives.

Psalm 41:1
Blessed is he who considers the poor, the Lord will deliver him in time of trouble

Psalm 56:11
In God I have put my trust; I will not be afraid. What can man do to me.

Psalm 66:10-12
For you O God have tested us, you have refined us as silver is refined. You brought us into the net; you laid affliction on our backs. You have caused men to ride over our heads; we went through fire and through water; but you bought us out to rich fulfillment.

Psalm 84:11c
No good thing will he withhold from those who walk uprightly.

Psalm 97:10
You who love the Lord, hate evil.

Psalm 101:5
Whoever secretly slanders his neighbor him will I destroy; the one who has a haughty look and a proud heart, him will I not endure.

Psalm 124:2a
If it had not been the Lord who was on our side when men rose up against us …..

Psalm140: 3
Set a guard O Lord, over my mouth; keep watch over the door of my lips

Psalm 140:4
Do not incline my heart to any evil thing; to practice wicked works with men who work iniquity;

DEVELOPING LISTENING SKILLS

Proverbs 1:5a
A wise man will hear and increase learning.

Proverbs 1:33
But whoever listens to me will dwell safely, and will be secure, without fear of evil.

Proverbs 10:19
In the multitude of words sin is not lacking, but he who restrains his lips is wise.

Proverbs 11:12
He who is devoid of wisdom despises his neighbor, but a man of understanding holds his peace.

Proverbs 18:15b
The ear of the wise seeks knowledge

Proverbs 19:27
Cease listening to instruction, my son, and you will stray from the words of knowledge.

CONFIDENTIALITY

Proverbs 11:13
A talebearer reveals secrets, but he who is of a faithful spirit conceals a matter

Proverbs 25:8
Do not go hastily to court; for what will you do in the end when your neighbor has put you to shame? Debate your case with your neighbor, and do not disclose the secret to another lest he who hears it exposes your shame and your reputation be ruined.

TEAM DEVELOPMENT / MENTORING

Proverbs 11:14
Where there is no counsel, the people fall; but in the multitude of counselors there is safety.

Psalm 133:1
Behold how good and how pleasant it is for brethren to dwell together in unity.
Proverbs 20:6
Most men will proclaim each his own goodness, but who can find a faithful man.

Proverbs 24:6b
And in a multitude of counselors there is safety.

Philippians 2:2b
By being like minded, having the same love, being of one accord, of one mind.

GAINING KNOWLEDGE

Proverbs 1:7
The fear of the Lord is the beginning of knowledge, But fools despise wisdom and instruction.

▲

Proverbs 8:34

Blessed is the man who listens to me. Watching daily at my gates, waiting at the posts of my doors. For whoever finds me finds life, and obtains favor from the Lord.

Proverbs 13:20a

He who walks with a wise man will be wise.

Proverbs 10:14

Wise people store up knowledge, but the mouth of the foolish is near destruction.

SHARING YOUR ORGANIZATION'S WEALTH

Proverbs 3:9

Honor the Lord with your possessions, and with the first fruits of your increase.

Proverbs 14:21

He who despises his neighbor sins, but he who has mercy on the poor happy is he.

MANAGING PEOPLE

Proverbs 3:27

Do not withhold good from those to whom it is due. when it is in the power of your hand to do so.

Proverbs 10:18

Whoever hides hatred has lying lips, and whoever spreads slander is a fool.

Psalm 75:5b,6

Do not speak with a stiff neck, for exaltation (promotion) comes neither from the east nor from the west nor from the south. But God is the judge He puts down one and exalts another.

Proverbs 3:30

Do not strive with a man without cause, if he has done you no harm.

Proverbs 11:25

The generous souls will be made rich, and he who waters will also be watered himself.

Proverbs 12:19

The truthful lip shall be established forever, But a lying tongue is for a moment .

Proverbs 14:17a

A quick-tempered man acts foolishly.

Proverbs 15:12

A scoffer does not love one who corrects him, nor will he go to the wise.

▲

Proverbs 16:27
An ungodly man digs up evil, and it is on his lips like a burning fire.

Proverbs 17:10
Rebuke is more effective for a wise man than a hundred blows on a fool.

Proverbs 18:1
A man who isolates himself seeks his own desires. He rages against all wise judgment.
Proverbs 20:5
Counsel in the heart of man is like deep water, but a man of understanding will
draw it out.

Proverbs 22:2
The rich and the poor have this in common, the Lord is the maker of them all.

Proverbs 24:23a
It is not good to show partiality in judgment.

Proverbs 26:20
Where there is no wood, the fire goes out; and where there is no talebearer, strife ceases.
No servant can serve two masters; for either he will hate the one and love the other, or else he will
be loyal to the one and despise the other.

Romans 12:9
Be kindly affectionate one to another with brotherly love, in honor giving preference to one another

AVOIDING VERBAL HARRASSMENT

Colossians 4:6
Let your speech always be with grace, seasoned with salt, that you may know how you ought to
answer each one.

WORKING WITH OLDER EMPLOYEES

Proverbs 16:31
The silver-haired head is a crown of glory, if it is found in the way of righteousness.

Proverbs 20:29
The glory of young men is their strength, and the splendor of old men is their gray head.

STRATEGIC PLANNING

Proverbs 13:19a
A desired accomplishment is sweet to the soul.

▲

Proverbs 19:21
There are many plans in a man's heart. nevertheless the Lord's counsel - that will stand.

Proverbs 15:22
Without counsel plans go awry, but in the multitude of counselors they are established.

Proverbs 16:9a
A man's heart plans his way, but the Lord directs his path.

Proverbs 20:18a
Plans are established by counsel.

Proverbs 21:5
The plans of the diligent lead surely to plenty, but those of everyone who is hasty, surely to poverty.

Proverbs 24:3,4a
Through wisdom a house is built and by understanding it is established; by knowledge the rooms are filled.

Habakkuk 2:2a
Write the vision, and make it plain on tablets, that he may run who reads it.

Luke 14:28,29,30
For which of you, intending to build a tower, does not sit down first and count the cost, whether he has enough to finish it- lest, after he has laid the foundation, and is not able to finish, all who see it begin to mock him, saying, This man began to build and was not able to finish.

CONFLICT RESOLUTION

Matthew 5:9
Blessed are the peacemakers for they shall be called the sons of God.

Matthew 12:25b
Every city or house divided against itself will not stand.

1 Corinthians 6:1-8
Paul admonishes Christians not to take their conflicts before the ungodly to seek resolution.

Romans 12:18
If it is possible, as much as depends on you, live peaceably with all men.

Matthew 5:23-26
First, be reconciled to your brother.

Ecclesiastes 10:4

▲

If the spirit of the ruler rises against you, do not leave your post; for conciliation pacifies great offenses. (If you are at odds with your superior, don't walk off the job in anger. Stay calm and schedule a meeting to reconcile the situation).

Philippians 2:4
Let each of you look out not only for his own interest, but also for the interest of others.

LEADERSHIP DEVELOPMENT

Proverbs 4:7
Wisdom is the principal thing; therefore, get wisdom. And, in all your getting get understanding. Exalt her and she will promote you.

Proverbs 4: 22
Keep your heart with all diligence, for out of it spring the issues of life.

Psalm 119:37
Turn away my eyes from looking at worthless things.

Psalm 25 :14
The secret of the Lord is with those who fear him.

Proverbs 6:6
Go to the ant you sluggard! Consider her ways and be wise.

Proverbs 6:16
(There are seven things that God hates)
1. A proud look
2. A lying tongue
3. Hands the shed innocent blood
4. A heart that devises wicked plans
5. Feet that are swift in running to evil
6. A false witness who speaks lies,
7. One who sows discord among the brethren.

Proverbs 20: 3
It is honorable for a man to stop striving since any fool can start a quarrel.

Proverbs 10:17
He who keeps instruction is in the way of life, but who refuses correction goes astray.

Proverbs 12:1
Whoever loves instruction loves knowledge, but he who hates correction is stupid.

▲

Proverbs 12: 23
A prudent man conceals knowledge, but the heart of fools proclaims foolishness.

Proverbs 13:16
Every prudent man acts with knowledge, but a foolish man lays open his folly.

Proverbs 14:15
The simple believes every word, but the prudent considers well his steps.

Proverbs 16:3
Commit your works to the Lord, and your thoughts will be established.

Proverbs 17:27a
He who has knowledge spares his words , and a man of understanding is of a calm spirit.

Proverbs 18:13
He who answers a matter before he hears it, it is folly and shame to him.

Proverbs 21:4
A haughty look, a proud heart, and the plowing of the wicked are sin.

Proverbs 21:29
A wicked man hardens his face, but as for the upright, he establishes his way.

Proverbs 22:24,25
Make no friendship with an angry man, and with a furious man do not go,
lest you learn his ways and set a snare for your soul.

Proverbs 22:29
Do you see a man who excels in his work? He will stand before kings; he will stand before unknown men.

Proverbs 23:12
Apply your ears to instruction, and your ears to the words of knowledge.

Proverbs 24:10
If you faint in the day of adversity, your strength is small.

Proverbs 27:2
Let another man praise you, and not your own mouth; a stranger and not your own lips.

Proverbs 28:20a
A faithful man will abound with blessings.

▲

Proverbs 29:11
A fool vents all his feelings, but a wise man holds them back.

Ecclesiastes 7:21a
Also do not take to heart everything people say.

Micah 6:8
He has shown you, O man, what is good. And what does the Lord require of you, but to do justly, to love mercy, and walk humbly with your God?

Zechariah 4:10
For who has despised the day of small things?

Matthew 20:16
So the last will be first and the first last. For many are called but few are chosen.

1 Corinthians 15:33
Do not be deceived: Evil company corrupts good habits.

ENCOURAGEMENT FOR THE LEADER

Isaiah 40:31
But those who wait on the Lord shall renew their strength; they shall mount up with wings as eagles, they shall run and not be weary, they shall walk and not faint.

Isaiah 41:9c
You are my servant, I have chosen you and have not cast you away: Fear not, for I am your God. I will strengthen you, yes, I will help you. I will uphold you with My righteous right hand.

Isaiah 43:1b,2
I have called you by your name; you are mine. When you pass through the waters, I will be with you; and through the rivers, they shall not overflow you. When you walk through the fire, you shall not be burned, nor shall the flame scorch you.

Isaiah 55:11
So shall My word be that goes forth from My mouth; it shall not return to Me void, but it shall accomplish that which I please. And, it shall proper in the thing for which I sent it.

Isaiah 58:12b
And you shall be called the Repairer of the Breach, The Restorer of streets to dwell in.

Isaiah 59:19 a,b
When the enemy comes in like a flood, the spirit of the Lord will lift up a standard against him.

Jeremiah 33:3
Call to Me, and I will answer you, and show you great and mighty things, which you do not know.

Joel 2:25
So I will restore to you the years that the swarming locust has eaten.

Joel 2:28
And it shall come to pass afterward, that I will pour out My spirit on all flesh; your sons and your daughters shall prophesy, your old men shall dream dreams, your young men shall see visions.

Zechariah 6b
Not by might nor by power, but by My Spirit, says the Lord of hosts.

Malachi 3:10b
And try me now in this, says the Lord of hosts, If I will not open for you the windows of Heaven and pour out for you such a blessing, that there will not be room enough to receive it.

Mark 10:27
With men it is impossible, but not with God; for with God all things are possible.

2 Corinthians 12:9
My grace is sufficient for you, for my strength is made perfect in weakness.

Philippians 1:6
Being confident of this very thing, that He who has begun a good work in you will complete it until the day of Jesus Christ.

TASK #20
Add more scriptures to this list:

_____

_____

_____

_____

_____

_____

_____

_____

▲

Session Topic: _____

Presenter: _____

Date: _____ /_____ /_____

NOTES

_____
_____
_____
_____
_____
_____
_____
_____
_____
_____
_____
_____
_____
_____
_____
_____
_____

IDEAS TO TAKE WITH YOU

_____
_____
_____
_____

▲

_____

_____

_____

_____

_____

_____

_____

BOOKS AND OTHER MATERIALS

_____

_____

_____

_____

_____

_____

_____

_____

_____

_____

_____

_____

_____

_____

_____

Session Topic: _____

Presenter: _____

Date: _____ / _____ / _____

NOTES

_____

_____

_____

_____

_____

_____

_____

_____

_____

_____

_____

_____

_____

_____

_____

_____

_____

_____

_____

_____

_____

_____

IDEAS TO TAKE WITH YOU

_____

_____ ▲

_____

_____

_____

_____

_____

_____

_____

_____

_____

_____

_____

_____

_____

_____

_____

BOOKS AND OTHER MATERIALS

_____

_____

_____

_____

_____

_____

_____

_____

▲

Session Topic: _____

Presenter: _____

Date: _____ /_____ /_____

NOTES

_____

_____

_____

_____

_____

_____

_____

_____

_____

_____

_____

_____

_____

_____

_____

_____

_____

_____

_____

_____

_____

_____

▲

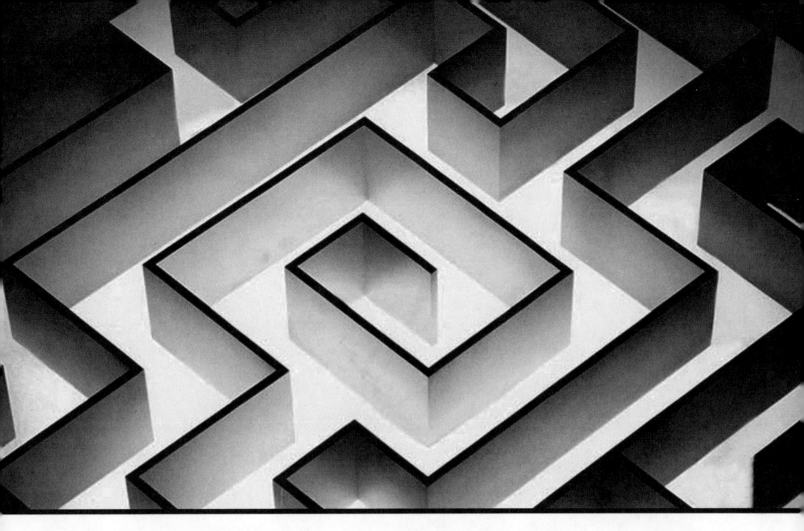

CHURCH STRATEGIES
for the 21st century

Smart Meetings

Because meetings can be a tremendous time waster, the first question to ask should be why a meeting is being held. Is it to inform? To make a decision? To give direction? The purpose of the meeting must be spelled out before it is called. When a visionary leads a meeting broad plans and images are voiced, leaving the listeners with many unanswered questions.

An effective administrator always states at the outset of a meeting the specific purpose of the meeting and what he hopes to achieve. The meeting should challenge and stimulate everyone in the room. When planning and scheduling a meeting, keep the following in mind:

1. A meeting defines the team, the group, or the unit.

2. A group of people meeting together can often produce better ideas, plans, and decisions than can a single individual, or a number of individuals who are working alone.

3. A meeting helps every individual understand both the collective aim of the group and the way in which his own and everyone else's work can contribute to the success of the group.

4. A meeting encourages participants to commit to carrying out the decisions made and do their part in meeting the objectives set.

5. For management, the meeting is the ideal place to show your leadership ability

6. A meeting is a status arena. Since a meeting is an opportune time for members to find out their relative standing, the "arena" atmosphere function is inevitable. Everyone is vying for a position in the pecking order. Keep in mind that a meeting can also be a negative experience ending with poor or no results. The challenge is to avoid this situation.

SIZES OF MEETINGS

There are typically three types of meetings:
The assembly – 100 or more people who are expected to do no more than listen to a speaker.
The council – 40 or 50 people who may be given an opportunity to comment, speak or ask questions.
The Team – Individuals who more or less speak on equal footing under the guidance of a chairperson.

BEFORE THE MEETING

The most important question that should be asked is, "What do you want to achieve in this meeting?" Alternatively, you could ask, "What would be the consequences if we did not hold this meeting?" You must define the objective.

Every item on the agenda can be placed in one of the following categories:

Clarification – In most cases one could fax or email a document that needed no comment. However, if there is a need for clarification or comments or it has great importance to the team, it would be proper to place it on the agenda although it may not require any discussion, conclusion, decision or action. Progress reports can also be considered "informative-digestive."

Collaboration – "What shall we do?" This category embraces all items that require something new to be devised, such as a new policy, a new strategy, or a new procedure. You are asking for ideas and input from the team so that you can arrive at the best conclusion.

Delegation – This is the "how shall we do it" function, after it has been decided what the members are going to do. Executive responsibilities are then handed out at the meeting.

AGENDA FORMAT

START TIME: 1:45 p.m.

END TIME: 3:15 p.m.

Item	Topic	Objective	Presenter	Time
(1)	Staffing	New hires	W. Smith	30 min.
(2)	Building program	Fundraising	L. Jones	20 min
(3)	Payroll	Increase benefits	A. Thomas	40 min

The agenda is a very important document. Review the following guidelines:

1. Do not be afraid of a long agenda if the chairperson can control the time. An hour and a half should give you plenty of time to cover the items on the agenda without stretching the meeting out too long. Extremely long meetings tend to exhaust the participants, thus less is accomplished.

2. Attach to the agenda a brief summary of each topic.

3. Do not circulate the agenda too early; two or three days ahead of time is adequate.

4. The early part of the meeting tends to be the best for the more difficult topics as attention spans wear down and fatigue sets in as time goes on.

5. Those topics that tend to unite should be in the beginning of the meeting and those discussion points that tend to divide the group should be in the later part of the agenda. However, always find a unifying item to end the meeting with.

6. A common mistake is to dwell on trivial topics that must be discussed. Keeping with the written time limit can solve this problem.

7. It is important to put the start time and the finish time on the agenda.

8. If meetings have a tendency to be long, the chairmen should arrange to start them one hour before lunch or one hour before the end of the workday. Generally, items that ought to be kept brief can be introduced ten minutes from a fixed end-point.

9. If reports are handed out during the meeting by a presenter, they should be brief and to the point. If they are too long, the participants will not read them.

10. Listing "Any Other Business" or "Open" is a classic time waster.

THE CHAIRPERSON - MASTER OR SERVANT

Having the right attitude as the chairperson is essential. There are three kinds of leader attitudes:

Pushy - The chairperson sees himself or herself as licensed to dominate.

Lackluster - Has no real motivation. Just satisfied to meet and talk.

Wobbler – This is the person who hopes to gain reassurance and support from the meeting to cover his own ineffectiveness and lack of decision-making skills

There is always a sense of power felt when chairing a meeting. It is often true that the chairperson's self indulgence is the greatest single barrier to the success of the meeting. The signal that the chairperson has lost focus is his continuous talking with hardly any discussion and little contribution from the other participants. The chairperson should limit himself to a few sentences to guide the participants. He actually is in a servant role in the meeting. The challenge of a meeting is to meet the objectives and get results.

There are two major roles played in a meeting.

1. *The team leader*
   It is usually the role of the chairperson to help the group join in the discussion without being overbearing which would certainly stifle participation.

1. *The task leader*
   The task leader is the person who drives a particular topic to closure. Tasks can then be either distributed among the group or designated to one person.

The team leader and the task leader can be the same person, if needed, or the task leader may also be the second in command.

THE STRUCTURE OF DISCUSSIONS

The structure of the discussion is similar to a mechanic talking to a customer:

"What seems to be the problem?"

There is usually something that needs attention, which is why most items are on the agenda to be discussed.

"How long has this been going on?"

An honest presentation of the facts and pertinent information is needed by all so that the situation can be addressed and a course of action decided on. For example, when did you notice there was a problem with the staff?

"Let's lift the hood and take a look"

A real close examination is made to see what is causing the problem, and to find out how things are going now. For example, "There was a breakdown in communication and that problem has been corrected."

"You seem to be over-heating."

When the facts are established, you can make a diagnosis and develop a solution.

"Fill the radiator with coolant and the problem should go away."

A single remedy may or may not be the answer. The committee should look at all of the options and then select the option that solves the overall problem.

CONDUCTING THE MEETING

Just as a driver of a car has two tasks, to follow his route and to manage his vehicle, so the chairperson's job can be divided into two corresponding tasks, to follow the agenda and manage the participants.

At the start of the discussion of any item, the chairperson should make it clear where they should be by the meeting's end. Are the participants to make a clear decision or just a recommendation? The chairperson should make sure that all the participants understand the issues and why they are discussing them. Give a brief overview if anyone is unclear about any of the issues covering the following:

1. The reason for the item being on the agenda

2. The story so far

3. The present position

4. What needs to be established, resolved or proposed

5. Courses of action that have been explored

6. Arguments on both sides of the issue

The chairperson then explains the meeting structure so that time will not be wasted. Sometimes the participants will have to review a draft document. If the document needs to be rewritten, that task should be delegated to a sub-committee to be brought back at the next meeting. At the end of the discussion, the chairperson should give a summary of what was discussed.

DEALING WITH PEOPLE

There is only one way to assure that a meeting starts on time, and that is to start on time. Latecomers who find that the meeting has begun without them learn the lesson.

Punctuality at future meetings can be effectively reinforced by the practice of listing late arrivals and early departures in the minutes. When the minutes are sent out you are telling everyone who was late and who left early. No one likes being put in a negative light.

Certain realities should be considered when dealing with people in a meeting. They include:

1. Psychologically, it has been proven that sitting at a square table face to face generates more opposition and conflict. (see illustration)

2. Sitting side by side at a round or oblong table diminishes the chances for confrontation. (see illustration)

3. Whom the chairperson sits opposite from can also be a factor. The chairperson can exploit the friendship-value of the seats next to him.

4. There is a "dead man's corner" which is the end seat on both the right and the left of the chairperson if sitting in a straight line.

5. Generally, proximity to the chairperson is a sign of honor and favor. Theoretically, the greater the distance the lower the rank.

CONTROLLING THE TALKER

There are participants that come to meetings that like to hear themselves talk. The easiest way to stop them is to latch on to a word or thought and jump in. "Develop a program - that is a good point Bob, how should we develop the program?"

GETTING THE SILENT TO SPEAK

1.   The silence of fear.

Some people become very nervous and have difficulty speaking. It is the chairperson's job to encourage them to speak and be courteous in his response although he may not agree.

2.   The silence of anger.

This is not hostility to the ideas but either toward the chairperson, the meeting, or the decision making process. Sometimes you will learn that this individual has something he needs to get off his chest. When it is relevant and appropriate, it is best to discuss it then.

3.   The helping hand.

Junior members of the group may unknowingly provoke disagreement from the seniors, which is normal. But if the discussion gets heated and the junior members feel their ideas and contributions are not appreciated or taken seriously, it is up to the chairperson to smooth things out. Let the junior members know their input is indeed appreciated. Discuss the juniors' ideas and contributions. Take notes (this is a plus) and refer to them later in the review (this is a double plus).

4.   Encourage healthy conflict.

A battle of ideas is healthy, however, it is important to discourage the clash of personalities. A good meeting is a cross flow of discussion and debate. The chairperson guides, mediates, summarizes and lets the participants work through the ideas. If two people get in a very heated discussion, bring in a neutral person that will deal with the issue in a factual manner.

5.   Watch out for suggestion-suppressers.

The elements of a meeting boil down to questions, answers, positive reaction, and negative reactions. Questions can only seek, and answers only supply information. There are three types of responses: information, opinion and suggestion. Suggestions contain the seeds of future success. If no one is allowed to make suggestions in meetings, you will find that a profitable meeting will soon become a sterile useless meeting. The chairperson needs to take special notice and respond courteously when anyone makes a suggestion and to discourage sharply the suggestion-suppressers. Requiring the suppresser to produce a better suggestion on the spot can do this.

6.   Come to the most senior leaders last.

If you work up the pecking order instead of down it, you are apt to get a wider spread of views and ideas. Often, once a senior person has spoken, others are apt to just follow along and not express their ideas, which in many cases are good ones.

7.   Close with a positive.

If an issue remains unsolved at the end of a meeting put it on the agenda for the next meeting. Set the time for the next meeting before you adjourn. Close the meeting and thank the group.

8. *Issue meeting minutes:*

   a) Date, time and place where the meeting was held.

   b) Names of all present and who chaired the meeting.

   c) Names of all absent that were schedule to attend.

   d) Names of late comers.

   e) Names of those who left early.

   f) All agenda items discussed and all decisions reached.

   g) If action items are listed, list name of person responsible.

   h) The time at which the meeting ended.

   i) Date and time of next meeting.

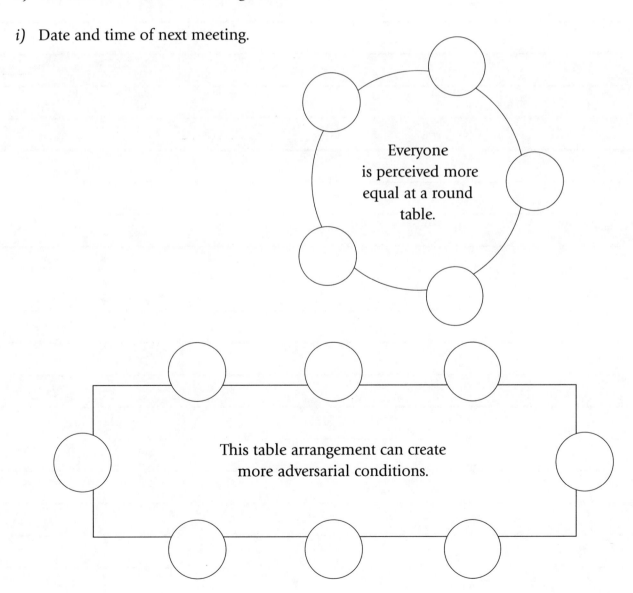

Everyone is perceived more equal at a round table.

This table arrangement can create more adversarial conditions.

Session Topic: _____

Presenter: _____

Date: _____ / _____ / _____

NOTES

_____

_____

_____

_____

_____

_____

_____

_____

_____

_____

_____

_____

_____

_____

_____

_____

_____

_____

_____

_____

_____

_____

_____

_____

THE PARLIAMENTARY PROCEDURE PROCESS

UNANIMOUS CONSENT

"If there is no objection....". These are the 5 most helpful word a chairperson will ever find.

In cases where there seems to be no opposition to routine business or no questions of great importance; and you have of a quorum; you can save time by obtaining Unanimous Consent (General Consent) from the assembly.

Parliamentary procedure is designed to protect the minority, and generally need not be strictly enforced when there is no minority (opposition) to protect. In these cases, a motion can be adopted without the Six Steps or even the formality of making a motion.

Any meeting can be ten times more productive if the chair will merely state, "If there is no objection." When no objection is heard, the chair states, "Since there is no objection, ... the motion is adopted." If someone objects, the chair proceeds with the traditional Six Steps.

Examples of situations which clearly call for Unanimous Consent are:

1. To correct or approve the minutes.

2. To withdraw one's own motion before the vote is taken. The maker may wish to withdraw his own motion; but the motion belongs to the assembly. Only the assembly may allow the withdrawal of a motion.

3. To suspend a rule on a matter clearly not controversial (as long as no Bylaw is violated).

4. To allow a speaker a few more minutes than the prescribed time.

5. To allow a guest speaker to speak in an order contrary to the approved agenda (or Rules of Order).

6. To divide a complex motion into logical parts for discussion, amendments, and voting purposes.

7. To close polls on a voting process after inquiring if there are any more votes. A motion to close the poll is necessary.

8. To elect a lone nominee by acclamation.

As long as you have a quorum and do not violate a Bylaw, these 5 words can allow a chair to quickly accomplish just about anything.

A MEETING VS. A SESSION

The words "Meeting" and " Session" are typically misused. Page 84 of Robert's rules of Order clearly indicates that a regular weekly, monthly, or quarterly meeting for an established order of business in a single afternoon or evening, constitutes a separate session. A meeting is actually a subset of a session, (for instance, the separate gatherings during an annual or biannual convention). The convention is a session, but its gatherings are meetings.

The significance of a session lies in the freedom of each session.
1. One session can not tie the hands of the majority at any later session, or place a question beyond the reach of a later session. The rights of the majority of one session can not adversely affect the rights of a majority of a later session. Powerful stuff!

2. One of Robert's rules of Order is that the same or substantially the same question can not be brought up a second time **during the same session.** So, if a session lasts longer than one gathering, a question may not be revisited for several gatherings.

3. Another Robert's rules of Order rule is that a question that is being postponed to a certain time must be postponed no further than the next session. But, if a session lasts longer than one gathering, the question would be postponed for a very long time.

The term "Meeting" does have its own special meaning:

1. **Regular (or stated) Meeting** – Refers to the periodic business meeting held weekly, monthly, or quarterly, as prescribed by the Bylaws. Each regular meeting normally completes a separate session.

    • If an issue was never reached on the agenda of one session, the issue could be carried forward as explained in Unfinished Business.

    • If an issue was reached in the agenda but not finally disposed of, it could be reached by the next session if the issue had been postponed (or made a special order), laid on the table, moved for reconsideration at the correct time, or referred to a committee.

2. **Special (or called) Meeting** – Is held at a time different from a regular meeting, and convened only to consider one or more items of business specified in the call of the meeting. Each special meeting normally completes a separate session.

3. **Adjourned Meeting** – Is a continuation of the immediately preceding regular or special meeting. An adjourned meeting takes up its work at the point where the preceding meeting was interrupted in the order of business. Each adjourned meeting normally completes the preceding session.

4. **Annual Meeting** – The only difference between a regular meeting and an annual meeting is that at an annual meeting annual reports from Officers and Standing Committees, and Election of

Officers are in order. Each annual meeting with its numerous separate meetings normally completes a separate session.

5. **Executive Session** – Any meeting in which the proceedings are secret constitutes an executive session. Boards, committees, and disciplinary sessions are normally held in executive session. Some organizations operate under the lodge system where every meeting is a secret meeting and held in executive session. Each executive session normally completes a separate session.

USING 3 STEPS TO GET CONTROL

If you wish to defeat, delay, or weaken a motion that you are against, you need to know when:

A.   You can interrupt the speaker with the precise modification or motion to prevent the assembly from adopting the motion;

B.   To amend the motion to an extent that not even the maker of the motion will vote for its approval;

C.   To prolong the debate to confuse the issue until someone moves to *Postpone Indefinitely or Calls for the Orders of the Day.*

The result is that you can **defeat a motion,** even when the majority is in favor of the motion. You can also do just the opposite – work towards the **adoption of the motion.** You can readily assure that a motion is adopted merely by anticipating and preventing your adversary's misuse of the 3 steps!

SIX STEPS TO EVERY MOTION!

Every motion requires 6 steps. The dos and don'ts are as follows:

Step 1   A member stands up, is recognized, and makes a motion.
Common Mistake: Members do not stand up, do not wait to be recognized, and typically start to discuss their motion before they make the motion!

Step 2   Another member seconds the motion.

Step 3   Without rewording, the presiding officer restates the motion to the assembly.
Common Mistake: Motion is restated differently from the wording of the maker!

Step 4   The members debate the motion.
Common Mistake: Debate gets out of control in temper, in duration, in relevance!

Step 5   Presiding officer asks for the affirmative votes & then the negative votes.
Common Mistake: The presiding officer states "All in favor" and fails to tell the

members what to do to vote (for example, "say aye", "stand up", "raise your hand", etc.), or the negative vote is never requested or counted!

Step 6   The presiding officer announces the result of the voting.
         Common Mistake: Presiding officer fails to pronounce the result of the voting!

SOME GENERAL EXCEPTIONS

For the sake of expediency, the chair can always say **"If there is no objection…"** and then declare what action the chair is going to take in the name of the assembly! If no one objects, the 6 steps are skipped and the motion has been adopted in 5 words. If someone objects, the chair follows the 6 steps, cheerfully.

On the other hand, not all motions require the 6 steps. Your power comes in knowing which motions do and which motions do not require the 6 steps.

Step 1. State the Motion:
Some motions are so important that the maker can interrupt the speaker and not even wait to be recognized by the chair! – *Question of Privilege, Orders of the Day, Point of Order, Appeal, Parliamentary Inquiry, Point of Information, Division.*

Step 2. Second the Motion:
Some motions do not require a second – Generally, if Robert's Rules of Order allow you to interrupt a speaker, you do not need to second (except *Appeal*).

Step 3. Chair Restates the Motion:
The presiding officer may help a person rephrase the motion.

Step 4. Discuss the Motion:
Some motions may not be debated because the debate would defeat the purpose of the motion – *Recess, Orders of the Day, Lay on the Table, Limit or Close Debate, Division of the Assembly, Division of the Question.*

Step 5. Vote on the Motion:
Some motions are made and passed without voting – *Question of Privilege, Orders of the Day, Point of Order, Division.*

Step 6. Announce Result of Vote:
The result of the voting must always be announced.

WHEN SIX STEPS DO NOT APPLY

We accept that the typical motion follow 6 steps.

1. Speaker stands, is recognized, and makes a motion.
2. Motion is seconded.
3. Presiding Officer restates the motion to the audience.
4. The assembly debates the motion.
5. The vote is taken.
6. The chair announces whether the motion was adopted or not.

Now let us review 2 privileged Motions and 4 Incidental Motions which do not require 6 steps. These motions can be used in public meetings.

Privileged Motions do not relate to the pending motion, but are of such immediate importance that they take precedence over any Main Motion.

1. Question of Privilege: As a member of the audience, you believe that you can not hear or see the proceedings, but you have a feasible solution. You have the right to stop the meeting, and have the problem corrected.

2. Call for the Orders of the Day: You notice that the agenda specifies the time for each portion of the agenda. You notice that the part you are interested in is scheduled for 9:25 am, and the time is now 9:16 am. The meeting is stuck with the 9:05 am item. You 'Call for the Orders of the Day'. This automatically forces everyone to abandon the 9:05 item and deal with next item.

   In both cases, you do not need to be recognized, or seconded. No one can amend or debate your motion! No vote is necessary. The 6 steps are not necessary.

Incidental Motions do not relate directly to the substance of the pending motion, but rather to the method of transacting the business of the motion. Incidental motions must be dealt with immediately.

3. Point of Order: During a meeting, you notice that someone (even the presiding officer) is disobeying Robert's Rule of Order. You state 'Point of Order' and explain your point. The Presiding Officer rules on your point and you help to keep everyone in line.

4. Point of Information: You have the right to understand the process and the potential consequences of the next voting. You have the right to stop business and have someone explain the process and consequences of the debate or the voting. The Presiding Officer can not ignore your request for information.

5. Division of Assembly: Whenever you doubt the Presiding Officer's hearing capabilities during a vote by loud ayes/nays, you can have the vote taken by having voters stand instead of yelling. You call for a 'Division of the Assembly' and the vote has to be retaken in a more accurate manner.

In the last 3 cases, you do not need to be recognized, or seconded. No one can amend or debate your motion! No vote is necessary.

6. Object to Consideration: Sometimes a sensitive or embarrassing motion is made. You can stop it before it is discussed by getting 2/3 of the assembly to agree with you to stop the motion **before it is discussed.** In this case, you do not need to be recognized, or seconded. No one can amend or debate your motion. A 2/3 vote is necessary.

If you know when the 6 steps do not apply, you can protect your rights as a member of an organization.

BYLAWS

Parliamentary Procedure is of no use, unless you are familiar with your organization's Bylaws. The best advice anyone can give you is to become familiar with the Bylaws and Constitution of your organization.

Typical Basic Bylaw Articles

I.   Name.
There must be no ambiguity as to the identity of the organization.

II.   **Object and Reason for the group's existence.**
This will help you keep the organization focused.

III.   Members.
This explains the members' rights, limitations, and qualifications. It clarifies issues such as fees, attendance, resignations, and membership.

IV.   Officers.
Explains methods for nominations, voting, elections, and filling vacancies, as well as term of office and duties.

V.   Meetings.
Details quorum, regular meetings, special meeting, and conventions.

VI.   **Executive Board or Board of Directors.**
(The board's composition, power, and quorum are clearly stated in this article.

VII.   Committees.
Standing committees must be described as to name, composition, manner of selection, attendance, and duties.

VIII.   Parliamentary Authority.
The rules of order must be clearly established. There are several, it could be Robert, Sturgis, Cannon,

Demeter, Riddick, etc. The important thing is to have a document that assures order. Regardless of the rule book, an organization is ruled first by local, state, and federal laws; and then by its parent organization; followed by any adopted special rules of order; and finally by its adopted parliamentary authority.

IX. Amendment of Bylaws.

Typically, a Bylaw can be amended with 2/3 of the collected votes, if a prior notice has been given during the prior meeting. Otherwise, it takes a majority of the entire registered membership to amend any Bylaw.

Some organizations have additional Articles for matters of Finances, Policies, or Discipline. You can adopt other articles to meet your particular needs.

THE AGENDA –RIGHTS AND ABUSES

The more serious an issue is, the more the reason to insist that the issue is included on the agenda, and that the agenda includes explicit starting time for each major section.

An agenda according to Robert's rules of Order.

I. Reading and approval of the minutes.
Motion to approve is not necessary. The minutes are either approved as read or as corrected, but without a vote.

II. Reports of Officers, Boards, Standing Committees.
This includes correspondence, treasurer's report, etc. Treasure's report is never adopted or voted upon unless it has been audited.

III. Reports of Special Committees.
Each report could conclude with a motion which the assembly must address.

IV. Special Orders.
Any motion which was adopted as a Special Order which guarantees that the motion will be dealt with before the meeting is adjourned.

V. Unfinished Business and General Orders.
Any issue which was not concluded, was postponed, or was tabled during the prior meeting. The secretary's minutes should inform the chair which items to add to this section.

VI. New Business.
This is when the chair and the parliamentarian can be surprised by the sequence of events. It is best to always anticipate issues the membership may present. It is at this time that announcements, educational programs, and speakers are introduced.

VII. Adjournment.

A motion to adjourn may be made at any time of the meeting. The assembly should never be forced to meet longer than it is willing to meet.

UNFINISHED BUSINESS, OLD BUSINESS.

"Old Business" means that you are reconsidering matters already disposed of. "Unfinished Business" means that you are continuing with matters which are currently not completed.

Before the current agenda is put together, the secretary advises the chair of the matters which were not disposed of from the previous meeting. Also, parliamentarian advises the chair which issues can be carried forward as "Unfinished Business". Therefore, the chair should never ask the members, "Is there any Unfinished Business." That questions can be answered only by the secretary and the parliamentarian.

There are really only a few reasons why a matter may be considered in the "Unfinished Business and General Orders" portion of the current meeting's agenda.

Questions left pending at the previous meeting:

1.   A question was being discussed and being dealt with when the previous meeting adjourned.

2.   A question was listed on the previous meeting's agenda as part of the unfinished business, but was not reached, when the meeting adjourned.

Questions NOT left pending at the previous meeting:

3.   A question was postponed (made current General Order) to the current meeting.

4.   Though not technically "Unfinished Business", any tabled matter may be taken from the table at this time as well.

Example:
Let us suppose that a group meets monthly.
In March, an issue is listed as "Unfinished Business" for the first time.
In March, the group adjourns without dealing with the issue.
In April, the issue can be taken up again as "Unfinished Business".
But, if in April the issue is not dealt with, the issue dies!
Of course, in May the issue may be introduced again, but only as "New Business".

ENTITLED TO BE HEARD

Who is entitled to be heard? When?

Any form of discussion on the merits of a motion is referred to as debate. You may not make a motion or speak in debate unless you obtain the floor, by being recognized by the chair. You may not stand (waiting to be recognized) until after the current speaker has yielded the floor.

When a motion is pending (during debate), the sequence of events is as follows:

1. The current speaker ceases his debate and yields the floor.

2. Other speakers promptly stand and state "Mr. Chair".

3. The chair recognizes the speaker who is entitled to speak next, based on the following general rules.

   a. The first person who stood up AFTER the speaker yielded on the floor.
   b. The maker of the motion, if he has not spoken yet.
   c. Whoever has not spoken on this motion.
   d. The person presenting an opposing opinion to the last speaker. The chair must allow the floor to alternate between opposing views.

If the chair fails to follow these rules, any member may raise a "Point of Order" or "Appeal from the Decision of the Chair."

When a motion is NOT pending, any of the following sequences apply:

1. Member "A" has been assigned to make a motion for which the Special meeting has been called. Member "A" is entitled to speak next.

2. Member "B" lays a motion on the table. Member "B" is entitled to speak next in order to Take the motion from the table.

3. Member "C" moved to Suspend the Orders of the Day in order to enable a certain motion be made. Member "C" is entitled to speak next and make that certain motion.

4. Member "D" urges the defeat of a motion so as to offer an alternate motion. Member "D" is entitled to speak next and make that alternate motion.

5. Member "E" states he wishes to Reconsider the vote on a motion. Member "E" is entitled to speak next.

PHRASES THAT SHOULD NOT BE USED

- "So moved"

This is a common statement which means nothing. One must state the actual motion so as to avoid confusion in the audience. Everyone has the right to know exactly what is being moved and discussed. "So moved!" is vague. State the actual motion, then say "So moved."

- **"I move to table"**

Actually, the correct motion is "Move to Lay on the Table". According to Robert's Rules of Order, this motion is in order only as a temporary interruption of the agenda, so as to allow something special and urgent out of turn. It is not intended to kill a motion. If a person wishes to kill a motion, let them use the correct motion – "Move to Postpone Indefinitely".

- **"Call for the question"**

This is not a motion. The chair should make sure that everyone has had an opportunity to speak. The chair should state that after one or two more speakers' comments, the vote shall be taken. It is critical that the chair not automatically stop the discussion when someone says, "Call for the question." The disorderly member who wishes to stop the discussion does not have more rights than the members who wish to discuss the issue. Actually a motion to stop the discussion ("I Call for or I Move the Main Question") would require a 2/3 vote to be adopted.

A MOTION CAN BE ADOPTED; YET STILL NOT BE FINAL

For every means of disposing of a motion, there is a means of returning the motion to the assembly, with certain slight limitations. You would think that once a motion is adopted (or is voted down), the question of the motion would be settled. To someone armed with Parliamentary Procedure knowledge, it does not mean any such thing. For example:

- **Move To Lay on the Table:** Anyone can Take for the Table, once the immediate urgency has been dealt with.

- **Move to Refer to a Committee:** Anyone can move to discharge the committee with previous notice. The motion could again return to the assembly.

- **Move to Rescind (annual or repeal):** Anyone, regardless of how he voted and without time limitations (but with previous notice), may move to annul a motion already adopted.

- **Move to Amend Something Previously Adopted:** Even after the assembly long debated and heatedly amended a controversial motion, anyone, with previous notice, can later move to amend it some more. This is the strange case of amending a motion that is not pending.

- **Move to Postpone Indefinitely:** Any motion which is killed may be reintroduced in a subsequent session of the assembly.

- **Move to Reconsider the Vote on…:** If a member votes on a prevailing side, he may Move to Reconsider the Vote at the same meeting. The result is that he will paralyze the majority's will by suspending all action which could be affected by the vote being reconsidered.

Robert's Rules of Order base Parliamentary Procedure on the potential of the majority to change its mind; the need to correct a hasty and ill-advised action; or the need to take into consideration a changed situation since a voting.

FOUR MOTIONS WHICH ARE ALWAYS OUT OF ORDER

A Main Motion reflects the will of the members of the organization. However, the following 4 motions are never in order, even if adopted by a unanimous vote:
Motions which conflict with laws (federal, state, or local), or with bylaws, constitutions, or rules of the organization;

1. Motions which present something already rejected during the same session, or conflict with a motion already adopted.

2. Motions which conflict with or present substantially the same question as one which has been temporarily disposed of .

3. Motions which propose actions beyond the scope of the organization's bylaws. (However, a 2/3 vote may allow this kind of motion).

But, what if the motion is in order, and you still do not agree with all or part of it? You can always protect your interests by amending the motion.

FIVE WAYS TO AMEND A MOTION

Motions are rarely perfect for everyone. Modifications are inevitable.

1. Between the time that a motion is made and before the chair states the motion, any member may informally offer modifying suggestions to the maker of the motion. The maker may accept or reject that member's recommendations.

2. After the chair has stated the motion, the maker of the motion may request unanimous consent from the members to modify the motion. Remember that at this time, the motion belongs to the assembly and not the original maker.

3. By means of the subsidiary motion to Amend, any member may propose changes to the motion, before the motion is voted upon. These proposed changes must be seconded and may be amended and/or debated.

4. If a motion requires further study, the members may vote to Refer the Main Motion to a Committee. When the committee returns the motion to the assembly, the committee normally proposes amendments for the assembly to vote upon.

5. Sometimes the motion is so complex that the only way to do it justice is for a member to urge its rejection and offer to propose a simpler version as a Substitute Motion. Upon defeat

▲

of the complex motion, anyone may propose the Substitute Motion.

Once a member learns which motions are out of order, how to make a motion, and how to amend a motion, the member becomes a productive member of the organization.

THREE WAYS TO AMEND A MOTION

As a matter of survival, the most common motion a church board member needs to know completely is the Motion to Amend a Pending Motion.

The difficult part is remembering that the more urgent <u>motions can not be amended</u> – Adjourn, Question of Privilege, Orders of the Day, Lay on/Take from the Table, Previous Question, Point of Order, Appeal, Parliamentary Inquiry, Suspend the Rules, and Reconsider.

During the Debate step of a Pending Motion, one may move to Amend the Pending Motion. All one needs to remember is that there are really only 3 basic processes of amendments:

Let's Amend this Sample Motion: I move that we buy new benches.

1.   You can Move to Amend by inserting words or paragraphs. I Move to Amend by inserting the phrase "not to exceed $5,000 dollars" at the end of the motion.

2.   You can Move to Amend by striking out (not deleting) words or the paragraphs. I Move to Amend by striking out the word "new".

3.   You can Move to Amend by striking out and inserting words or paragraphs. One can even Amend by Substituting (striking out and inserting) entire paragraphs or the complete motion. I move to Amend by striking out the word "new" and inserting the word "pre-owned."

You can also Amend the Amendment, before it is voted upon:

But you can only Amend the inserted or struck out words. You can not amend a separate part of the Main Motion not covered by the Amendment that is currently being discussed. After the current Amendment is voted upon, you can Amend the Motion again and Amend this new Amendment.

If you carefully review these 3 basic processes of amendments (insert, strikeout, and strike out/insert), you will agree that any other form is not an amendment. Only these 3 processes will reduce the chances of chaos and confusion that could occur during discussion of motions and amendments.

▲

UNAMENDABLE MOTIONS

The power to amend any motion leads to a quick compromise which pleases most of the board members. However, sometimes, amending a motion makes no sense.

In all of the motions listed in this section, the members either allow something to occur or they do not allow it. A member is either granted a request or is not. Normally, there is no half way position. Note that among the common motions listed below, if you can not debate them, then you probably can not amend them either.

1. Adjourn
2. Call for the Orders of the Day.
3. Call for the Division of the Assembly.
4. Lay on the Table/Take from the Table.
5. Dispense with Reading of the Minutes.
6. Objection to the Consideration of the Question.
7. Postpone Indefinitely.
8. Previous Question (Close Debate).
9. Parliamentary Inquiry.
10. Point of Information.
11. Point of Order.
12. Raise a Question of Privilege.
13. Suspend the Rules.
14. Appeal from the Decision of the Chair.
15. Reconsider a Motion.

Once you realize which motions you can make without the obstacle of an opposing debate or modification, you can then assure smooth sailing.

UNDEBATABLE MOTIONS

You can make some motions which no one can speak against, mostly because sometimes the right to debate does not make sense.

Some motions perform a time sensitive task where a discussion would be counter productive.
1. Call for the Orders of the Day.
2. Calls for the Division of the Assembly.
3. Lay on the Table/Take from the Table.
4. Division of a Question.
5. Suspend the rules.
6. Reconsider a Motion (most).
7. Dispense with Reading of the Minutes.

Some motions intend to prevent further debate. Discussing the motion defeats the purpose of the motion.

8. Adjourn.
9. Objection to the Consideration of the Question.
10. Previous Question (Close Debate).
11. Limit or Extend Limits of Debate.
12. Recess.

Some motions intend to perform simple tasks which require immediate attention.

13. Parliamentary Inquiry.
14. Point of Information.
15. Point of Order.
16. Raise a Question of Privilege.
17. Appeal from the Decision of the Chair (most).

If you know when others can debate your issues and when they can not, you will be better prepared to fairly make your point unopposed.

COUNTING VOTES AND VOTING RESULTS

Majority
…the Majority of the entire membership?
…the Majority of the members present?
…the Majority of the Votes Cast?

How should you count the blank votes, the illegal votes, the abstentions?

The basic requirements for adoption of a motion by any assembly with a quorum is a Majority Vote, except for certain motions as listed below. A Majority is 'more than half' of the votes cast by persons legally entitled to vote, excluding blank votes and abstentions. Majority does not mean 51%. In a situation with 1000 votes, Majority = 501 votes; but 51% = 510 votes.

> **Let's see an example:**
> - The chair instructs the members, at a meeting with a quorum, to vote by writing 'Yes' or 'No' on a piece of paper.
>
> - Of the members present, 100 are entitled to vote, but 15 abstain. Of the 85 votes cast, 10 are illegal (the members wrote 'Maybe'); and 5 were turned in blank.
>
> - The majority is any number larger than one half of the total of…
>   (legal votes cast) – (blank votes cast) + (illegal votes cast).
>
> - Of the 85 Votes Cast by members entitled to vote…
>   (75 are valid) – (5 are blank) + (10 are illegal) = 70 Votes Cast.
>
> - One half of 70 Votes Cast is 35. Majority is 36 votes.

2/3 VOTE

Robert rules specifies which motion will require at least a 2/3 vote for adoption. Notice it is not called a 2/3 majority. A 2/3 vote is generally not taken as a voice vote, but rather as a standing count, or some other easily countable fashion. Generally speaking, a 2/3 vote is required for adoption of any motion which...

1. Suspends or modifies a rule of order already adopted;

2. Prevents the introduction of a question to consideration;

3. Closes, limits, or extends the limit of debate;

4. Closes nominations or the polls;

5. Takes away membership or office.

There is a further requirement. As you can see from the following table, a **Previous Notice** is needed by some motions which require a 2/3 votes to adopt. A Previous Notice is an announcement of the intent to introduce the motion. A Previous Motion is typically given at least one meeting before the meeting when the proposal is to be introduced.

Votes Required to Adopt a Motion by a 2/3 Vote	
A Motion Not involving a ByLaw, the Constitution, or an issue listed as Special Order on the Agenda:	
With Previous Notice	Majority of votes cast
With NO Previous Notice	2/3 of votes cast; OR Majority of entire membership of the Organization
A Motion Involving a ByLaw, the Constitution, or an issue listed as Special Order on the Agenda:	
With Previous Notice	2/3 of votes cast
With NO Previous Notice	Majority of entire membership of the organization

Study this chart carefully and you will agree that it makes a great deal of sense.

2/3 VOTE VS. MAJORITY VOTE

The basic requirement for approval of an action is a majority vote. However, the following situations require a 2/3 STAND UP vote for approval. Notice that all of these motions rob the individual of his rights. As a compromise between the rights of the individual and the rights of the assembly, a 2/3 vote is necessary:

1. **Modify an Adopted Rule of Order or Agenda**
    a. Amend or rescind the Constitutions, Bylaws, or Agenda.
    b. Amend or rescind something already adopted.
    c. Suspend the Orders of the Day.
    d. Refuse to proceed to the Orders of the Day.
    e. Take up a Question out of its Order.

2. **Prevent the Introduction of a Question for Consideration**

3. **Modify the Extend of Debate**
    a. Limit or extend limits of Debate.
    b. Call for the previous Question.

4. **Close Nominations**

5. **Repeal an assignment**
    a. Take away membership or office.
    b. Discharge a committee.

6. **Make a Motion a Special Order**
    a. The chair should take a rising vote in those motions where a 2/3 vote is required.
    b. You can assure the victory of your ideas, once you are aware of the required amount of vote necessary for adoption of your motion.

RESCIND (REPEAL OR ANNUL)

You always have the right to annul or amend something already adopted.

Quite often it is obvious that a great deal of preparation and support has been quietly organized before a motion is presented to the members. The motion is adopted before you even understand the true purpose and potential consequences of the motion. Fortunately there are no time limitations to annul or amend any motion.

There are no arbitrary restrictions, just a couple of logical ones:

1. If on the day a motion was passed, someone moved to reconsider the vote on that motion.

2. If the motion you wish to rescind has been executed in an irreversible manner, you can not rescind it. However, any reversible portion can be amended. if no one outside the meeting is aware of the motion, the motion can probably be undone. If a part of the motion has not been executed, you can amend the unexecuted portion of the motion.

3. If a motion results in a contract and the other party has been informed of the vote, you can Rescind the motion.

4. If the motion acts upon a resignation, or results in an election/expulsion, and the person involved is officially notified of the voting, you can not Rescind the motion, Fortunately, Robert's rules allows for a reinstatement procedure and disciplinary removal of a person from office.

5. In order to Rescind a motion, it takes at least a 2/3 vote unless the membership has received a Previous Notice.

Simplified Rules of Order

Principles of Parliamentary Procedure

1. The purpose of parliamentary procedure is to make it easier for people to work together effectively and to help groups accomplish their purposes. Rules of procedure should assist a meeting, not inhibit it.

2. A meeting can deal with only one matter at a time. The various kinds of motions have therefore been assigned an order of precedence (see Table 1).

3. All members have equal rights, privileges and obligations. One of the chairperson's main responsibilities is to use the authority of the chair to ensure that all people attending a meeting are treated equally—for example, not to permit a vocal few to dominate the debates.

4. A majority vote decides an issue. In any group, each member agrees to be governed by the vote of the majority. Parliamentary rules enable a meeting to determine the will of the majority of those attending a meeting.

5. The rights of the minority must be protected at all times. Although the ultimate decision rests with a majority, all members have such basic rights as the right to be heard and the right to oppose. The rights of all members—majority and minority, should be the concern of every member, for a person may be in a majority on one question but in a minority on the next.

6. Every matter presented for decision should be discussed fully. The right of every member to speak on any issue is as important as each member's right to vote.

7. Every member has the right to understand the meaning of any question presented to a meeting, and to know what effect a decision will have. A member always has the right to request information on any motion he or she does not thoroughly understand. Moreover, all meetings must be characterized by fairness and by good faith. Parliamentary strategy is the art of using procedure legitimately to support or defeat a proposal.

Table 1.

ORDER OF PRECEDENCE OF MOTIONS

Rank	Motion	may interrupt speaker	Second Required	Debatable	Amendable	May be reconsidered
1.	Fix time to adjourn		X		X	X
2.	Adjourn		X			
3.	Recess		X		X	
4.	Question of privilege	X	X	X	X	X
5.	Orders of the day	X				
6.	Table		X			
7.	Previous Question		X			X
8.	Limit/extend limits of debate		X		X	X
9.	Postpone to a certain time		X	X		X
10.	Refer		X	X	X	X
11.	Amend		X	X	X	X
12.	Postpone indefinitely		X	X		X
13.	Main motion		X	X	X	X

Meeting Planner

MEETING PURPOSE_____

DATE: _____ START TIME: _____ END TIME: _____ LOCATION:_____

BY THE TIME WE LEAVE THIS MEETING, WE SHOULD HAVE ACHIEVED THESE RESULT:

Result No.	Priority A	B		Proceed Y	N

TO ACHIEVE THESE RESULTS, I WILL NEED

Result No. By Priority	These people:	This information/material	This much time:

THESE FACILITIES/EQUIPMENT/SPECIAL ARRANGEMENTS

	Costs Est.	Act.	Responsibility of:

PLAN AGENDA OVERLEAF

		Est.	Act.
Facilities & Equipment Costs	$		
Participant Costs	$		
Total Meeting Costs	$		

▲

Meeting Planner
Agenda/Outcomes

MEETING PURPOSE_____CHAIRPERSON _____

DATE: _____ START TIME: _____ END TIME: _____ LOCATION:_____

Item Time	AGENDA	Type*	DECISION/ACTION	Ref	Priority	Who	When

MEETING EVALUATION

WHAT WENT WELL	PROBLEMS TO OVERCOME	SOLUTIONS

ATTENDEES _____

ABSENT _____

NEXT MEETING DATE _____ START TIME_____ END TIME_____LOCATION_____

*TYPE INF (FOR INFORMATION), DIS (FOR DISCUSSION) ACT (FOR ACTION)

Meeting Agenda

DATE _____TIME _____PLACE_____

FUNCTION _____

ATTENDING _____

SCHEDULE

8:00 – 8:30_____

8:30 – 9:00_____

9:00 – 9:30_____

9:30 – 10:00_____

10:00 – 10:30_____

10:30 – 11:00_____

11:00 – 11:30_____

12:00 – 12:30_____

12:30 – 1:00_____

1:00 – 1:30_____

1:30 – 2:00_____

2:00 – 2:30_____

2:30 – 3:00_____

3:00 – 3:30_____

3:30 – 4:00_____

4:00 – 4:30_____

4:30 – 5:00_____

5:00 – 5:30_____

5:30 – 6:00_____

6:00 – 6:30_____

6:30 – 7:00_____

7:00 – 7:30_____

7:30 – 8:00_____

▲

Meeting Agenda

DATE _____ TIME _____ PLACE _____

FUNCTION _____

ATTENDING _____

SCHEDULE

8:00 – 8:30 _____

8:30 – 9:00 _____

9:00 – 9:30 _____

9:30 – 10:00 _____

10:00 – 10:30 _____

10:30 – 11:00 _____

11:00 – 11:30 _____

12:00 – 12:30 _____

12:30 – 1:00 _____

1:00 – 1:30 _____

1:30 – 2:00 _____

2:00 – 2:30 _____

2:30 – 3:00 _____

3:00 – 3:30 _____

3:30 – 4:00 _____

4:00 – 4:30 _____

4:30 – 5:00 _____

5:00 – 5:30 _____

5:30 – 6:00 _____

6:00 – 6:30 _____

6:30 – 7:00 _____

7:00 – 7:30 _____

7:30 – 8:00 _____

▲

PARLIMENTARY QUIZ #1

1.   Any meeting can be ten times more productive if the chair will merely make what statement?

_____

_____

2.   What is the difference between a meeting and a session?

_____

_____

3.   Name one of the six steps to every motion.

_____

_____

4.   When should incidental motions be dealt with?

_____

_____

5.   Parliamentary procedures are useless to you, unless you are familiar with your organization's bylaws.   ☐ True   ☐ False

6.   List the 5 typical bylaw articles.

_____

_____

_____

_____

_____

_____

PARLIMENTARY QUIZ #2

1. List the 7 elements of an agenda.

    _____

    _____

    _____

    _____

    _____

2. Who is entitled to be heard and when?

    _____

    _____

3. Name three phrases that mean nothing.

    _____

    _____

4. Name 2 of the 4 motions that are always out of order.

    _____

    _____

5. Name 1 way to modify a motion.

    _____

    _____

6. Name 4 unamendable motions.

    _____

    _____

PARLIMENTARY QUIZ #3

1.   Name 3 unbeatable motions.

_____

_____

_____

_____

2.   A 2/3 vote is generally not taken as a voice vote   ☐ True   ☐ False

3.   The basic requirement for approval of an action is a majority vote. However, there are situations that require a 2/3 STAND UP vote for approval. List 4 of the STAND UP vote situations.

_____

_____

_____

_____

4.   List 5 simplified rules of order.

_____

_____

_____

_____

_____

_____

_____

_____

_____

_____

_____

CHURCH STRATEGIES
for the 21st century

Risk Management

RISK MANAGEMENT / AVOIDING LIABILITY PROBLEMS

The purpose of risk management is to address those risk issues that the organization could be exposed to in its everyday functions including potential threats and the likelihood of their occurrence. The areas that should be considered are listed below. An organization can insure against liability if you rent or own the facility. Your organization should have **general liability insurance.** This covers you, for example, if someone walks in the church and falls down, a shelf or box falls on them or they trip over a camera cable. The organization should also carry **non-owned auto coverage,** which protects the organization when an employee is driving a family car for church activities. It is usually in the general policy, but make sure you check. If your organization puts on special events such as a church carnival for the youth you should purchase **temporary insurance** for that event. **Workers compensation insurance,** which can be very costly, is considered a necessity as it covers employee lawsuits. Churches that employ professional counselors should ensure that these professionals are covered under **professional liability insurance. Directors and Officers insurance,** or D&O is also essential. Organizations that handle large amounts of money should have fidelity coverage to cover possible criminal acts, which are specifically excluded from D&O. Areas under fidelity include theft, robbery, burglary, forgery, and crimes involving computers. D&O on the other hand, may protect the board from failure to implement proper controls that would have prevented the losses from the exposure covered under fidelity. (This concept can be very ambiguous; consult your insurance agent). The national center for non-profits advises that D&O insurance does not cover the following: fines and penalties imposed by law, libel and slander, personal profit, dishonesty, failure to procure or maintain insurance, bodily injury and property damage claims and suits by one board member to another.

Those organizations that have wealthy board members especially need to have D&O coverage. D&O as stated before is very expensive. Therefore, smaller organizations may consider limited coverage for what is realistically at risk. Some D&O policies are written for everything but what you may really need. Have a professional, other than the insurance salesperson, review the policy before you sign on the dotted line.

CONDUCTING RISK MANAGEMENT ASSESSMENT

Organizations should regularly undertake comprehensive assessments of potential risks to the organization. An assessment should occur at least twice per year by a team of staff members that represent the various components of the organization.

REVIEW OF PERSONNEL POLICY

Every organization must have up to date policies that outline and guide the relationships between staff and management. There has been an increase in lawsuits regarding wrongful termination, harassment, discrimination, and disagreements about promotions or salary issues. Parties to lawsuits include the organization, management and board members. Therefore, personnel policies must be reviewed at least once per year by an outside advisor who is an expert in employee law.

WELL DESIGNED INSURANCE COVERAGE

One must yearly study all insurance policies. If needed ask for clarification from your insurance agent in writing on their letterhead. (Refer to information above).

LEGAL PROTECTION

It is important to conduct a legal related audit of your organization. Ask yourself if there are any areas where you might unwittingly be violating the law.

RISK IN VOLUNTEER PROTECTION

Have the proper steps been taken to assure that volunteers are safe and are legally eligible to carry out the tasks?

FUND RAISING RISK

How are funds raised and allocated? Are there easy opportunities for misuse of funds?

RECORDS

Are all records centrally located and well labeled? Are critical documents including board minutes, leases, contracts, bylaws, and tax related information such as your exempt status letter all protected from fire and water damage? Personnel files should be under lock and key at all times and accessible only to the Director of HR or a designated executive. All files should be audited each year for proper labeling and content.

INTERNAL BUILDING SAFETY

It is very important that the facility is protected from possible liability issues. In many cases numerous items are overlooked and the organization can be open to liability and law suites.

SANCTUARY

The following are some important questions to ask regarding the safety of the sanctuary.

1. Are there cables on the floor from video cameras or other equipment?

2. Is there debris that may cause someone to trip?

3. Is there asbestos in the building?

4. Are the walking areas free from clutter?

5. Are the benches or chairs strong enough to hold overweight people?

6. Are there any low areas where one could hit their head?

7. Are the bathroom floors skid proof?

8. Is there a health safety person on staff?

9. Has a fire drill been practiced with the congregation?

10. Do you have fire exit maps?

11. Are all exit doors unlocked?

12. Are there electrical wires exposed?

13. Do you use "wet floor" signs?

14. Are there emergency lights in the building in case of power loss?

15. Are there battery-powered bullhorns located strategically?

16. Is the baptismal area skid proof?

17. Do you have security personnel?

18. Are electrical outlets covered with black soot, which indicates an electrical shortage?

19. Are office accommodations sufficient? Chairs that tip forward may cause an accident.

20. Are there first aid kits in multiple locations?

21. Are emergency numbers posted near telephones?

22. Is the staff trained in keeping a watchful eye for unsafe equipment or situations?

PERSONAL LIABILITY

1. Are all vehicle drivers registered?

2. Equipment coverage

ATHLETIC / PLAY GROUND AREAS

A church may or may not have a playground or athletic area that is owned by the church. The church must be aware of the problems that may occur. There are over 200,000 children each year that require emergency medical treatment for playground and athletic related injuries. It is the organization's responsibility to ensure that there are no hazardous areas. There are five areas that should be considered when evaluating the athletic and playground areas.

Play area

Make sure that the ground that the playground is on is safe. If the land was formerly used as a dump sight, it is important that the play area is examined for sharp objects and debris. seventy percent of playground injuries are due to falls. All of the play equipment should be installed on the safest part of the property avoiding concrete, asphalt, and stone chips. The safest surface for children to play on is sand as it absorbs the impact of a fall and can be cleaned easily. If the playground is indoors, rubber mats should be used.

Athletic and Playground Supervision

It is absolutely necessary to have proper supervision whenever use of the playground is authorized to avoid the possibility of liability. A typical ratio is 1 attendant and 1 aid for each 10 children. Fewer attendants are needed for older children. A whistle or bull horn should be available in case of emergencies.

Equipment

Make sure that all equipment that is purchased meets all state and local regulations. Information on a specific product can be obtained from the U.S. Consumer Product Safety Commission, Washington, D.C. 20207

Emergency Plan

An emergency plan should be in place if someone is injured in a supervised situation. A supervisor or assistant should have a cell phone at all times with emergency numbers available. All attendants and assistants should be trained in CPR.

Preventative Maintenance

All playground equipment should be checked periodically. A high rate of injury occurs from unstable equipment, jutting bolts, protruding nails and screws, and anchors that have worked loosed. A maintenance log should be kept of all repairs and related maintenance inspections..

FIRE PREVENTION

As you walk through the risk management process fire safety is an area of great concern. If a fire occurs it has the potential to take numerous lives. The following is a check that can be used when dealing with fire safety. Contact your local fire department for specific rules and regulations for your area.

One of the most common causes of fires is vandalism. Often external precautions were not taken making it easy for vandals to get into the building. The following should be checked:

1. Is there fencing to deter entry to the property?

2. Are there materials on the property that can be used to break in such as bricks, rocks, etc?

3. Are outside decorative windows covered with lexan or bars to prevent entry?

4. Are all external doors fire proof metal doors with non removable hinges?

5. Is there adequate lighting in the parking lots and around the building?

6. Are external doors re-keyed annually?

7. Are all external door key holders registered?

Internal precautions must be considered as well. If perpetrators get into the building other measures must be taken into consideration.

1. Is there adequate lighting left on in the building at night?

2. Does the building have a fire and burglar alarm system and is it checked periodically?

3. Is there a security person (s) on duty at night?

4. Are major corridor doors re-keyed annually?

5. Is there a sign-in sheet for night entry?

6. Are all paints, cleaning chemicals and other combustibles kept in a locked certified metal cabinet?

7. Does a security cruiser drive around the property on an irregular basis?

8. Are all external doors and windows checked more than once per night?

9. Are all key holders registered?

10. Video security cameras should be considered for large facilities that have several floors or multiple buildings.

It is also imperative that your church or organization have a fire drill at least once a year. The total congregation, Sunday school, and other departments should be involved in the fire drill.

TASK #20

In the space below, list those additional areas that you will review for any possible risks.

_____

_____

_____

_____

_____

_____

_____

_____

_____

_____

_____

_____

_____

_____

_____

_____

_____

_____

_____

_____

_____

_____

_____

_____

_____

TASK #21

DOCUMENTS AUDIT

This checklist is just a start to help your organization make sure that all important information and documents are accounted for. Check off each item as you complete each part of the audit.

CORPORATE CHARTER, BYLAWS AND CORPORATE SEAL

☐ *Is there a copy with an attorney?*

    Name

    Address

    City

    State/zip

    Phone number

    E-mail address

    Fax number

☐ *The 2nd copy of the documents are:*

    1. In a vault, where?

    2. Safety deposit box in what bank?

    3. Fireproof location

☐ *Other copies are located where:*

    1. _____

    2. _____

    3. _____

☐ *Who has the authority to have access to these copies?*

    1. _____

    2. _____

    3. _____

DOCUMENTS AUDIT

REAL ESTATE PAPERS/DEEDS

☐ *Is there a copy with the agent, bank or attorney?*

    Name

    Address

    City

    State/zip

    Phone number

    E-mail address

    Fax number

☐ *The 2nd copy of the documents are:*

    1. In a vault, where?

    2. Safety deposit box in what bank?

    3. Fireproof location?

☐ *Other copies are located where:*

    1. _____

    2. _____

    3. _____

☐ *Who has the authority to have access to these copies?*

    1. _____

    2. _____

    3. _____

INSURANCE POLICIES AND RELATED DOCUMENTS

☐ *Is there a copy with the agent, bank or attorney?*

    Name

    Address

    City

    State/zip

    Phone number

    E-mail address

    Fax number

DOCUMENTS AUDIT

☐ *The 2nd copy of the documents are:*
    In a vault, where?
    Safety deposit box in what bank?
    Fireproof location?

☐ *The 2nd copy of the documents are:*
    1. In a vault, where?
    2. Safety deposit box in what bank?
    3. Fireproof location?

☐ *Other copies are located where:*
    1. _____
    2. _____
    3. _____

☐ *Who has the authority to have access to these copies?*
    1. _____
    2. _____
    3. _____

CONTRACTS AND AGREEMENTS

☐ *Original copy with Attorney?*
    Name
    Address
    City
    State/zip
    Phone number
    E-mail address
    Fax number

☐ *The 2nd copy of the documents are:*
    1. In a vault, where?
    2. Safety deposit box in what bank?
    3. Fireproof location?

☐ *Other copies are located where:*
    1. Is the information on computer disk? Where?
    2. How many copies?

DOCUMENTS AUDIT

☐ *Who has the authority to have access to these copies?*

    1. _____

    2. _____

    3. _____

TAX RETURNS, RECORDS, IRS RELATED PAPERS

☐ *Is there a copy with the agent or bank?*

    Name

    Address

    City

    State/zip

    Phone number

    E-mail address

    Fax number

☐ *The 2nd copy of the documents are:*

    1. In a vault, where?

    2. Safety deposit box in what bank?

    3. Fireproof location?

☐ *Other copies are located where:*

    1. Is the information on computer disk? Where?

    2. How many copies?

    3. _____

    4. _____

    5. _____

☐ *Who has the authority to have access to these copies?*

    1. _____

    2. _____

DOCUMENTS AUDIT

ORGANIZATIONS MAILING LIST

☐ *Is there a copy with the agent or attorney?*

Name

Address

City

State/zip

Phone number

E-mail address

Fax number

☐ *The 2nd copy of the documents are:*

1. In a vault, where?

2. Safety deposit box in what bank?

3. Fireproof location?

4. Is the information on computer disk? Where?

5. How many copies?

☐ *Other copies are located where:*

1. _____

2. _____

3. _____

☐ *Who has the authority to have access to these copies?*

1. _____

2. _____

ALL OUT-DATED RECORDS

☐ *Where are they stored? With the agent or Records Storage Company?*

Name

Address

City

State/zip

Phone number

E-mail address

Fax number

DOCUMENTS AUDIT

☐ *Who has the authority to have access to these records?*

    1. _____

    2. _____

    3. _____

SAFE AND VAULT COMBINATIONS

Vault #1

Location of vault:

Combination:

Left #	Right #	Left #	Right #
Left #	Right #	Left #	Right #

☐ *Who has the authority to enter the vault*

    1. _____

    2. _____

    3. _____

Vault #2

Location of vault:

Combination:

Left #	Right #	Left #	Right #
Left #	Right #	Left #	Right #

☐ *Who has the authority to enter the vault?*

    1. _____

    2. _____

    3. _____

DOCUMENTS AUDIT

SAFE DEPOSIT BOX

☐ *Is the key with the agent or Attorney?*

    Name

    Address

    City

    State/zip

    Phone number

    E-mail address

    Fax number

☐ *Other key holders:*

    1. _____

    2. _____

    3. _____

☐ *Who has the authority to enter the safe deposit box?*

    1. _____

    2. _____

    3. _____

COMPUTER SECURITY

1. Can any user on a micro system enter the main system?
2. Do all computer users have passwords for both screen saver and on-line entry?
3. Is the computer system data "back-up" performed daily?
4. Is the main system wired to a UPS (un-interruptable power source)
5. Are passwords changed periodically?

DOCUMENTS AUDIT NOTES

_____

_____

_____

_____

_____

_____

DOCUMENTS AUDIT NOTES

TASK # 23 -

HELPFUL SOLUTIONS TO CHURCH ISSUES GROUP DISSICUSSION

Use the actual case studies listed below. Discuss what you would do in each situation as the Church Administrator and then refer to the following pages for the answers.

1. You hire teachers for your Christian school and after school has started you find out through the rumor mill that one of your male teachers has tested positive for aids. As the pastor you are concerned about the children, what do you do?

2. The church hires a female facilities manager. She injures her back loading heavy equipment. After she returns from sick leave with a doctor's certificate saying she could not lift heavy objects, the church administrator gives her a new assignment to load and unload heavy equipment and do all the outdoor landscaping by herself. Her absenteeism increased and she refused to do the work because of her back injury. The church administrator fired her.

3. A full-time staff member of the church is caught stealing but he says he was just inspecting the supplies. The room where the supplies are stored has only one key, that the church secretary has. The staff member was leaving the room carrying some of the supplies. The church administrator fires him on the spot. The former employee applies for a new job and lists your church as his last employer. The hiring company calls and asks for a reference.

4. A female employee of the church tells the church administrator that a male employee touched her inappropriately and said some very suggestive sexual things to her. The female employee said she wanted to file a grievance and have the situation investigated. The church administrator told her; "We don't have any particular process, just send me a memo." Nothing was done by the church administrator. The female employee got a lawyer.

5. A church policy states that applications will be kept on file for one year. An individual who interviewed for the position of principal of the new church school was turned down. He heard that someone was hired for the position three weeks after his interview. He went to the church and inquired about his application. He happened to know the person that was hired and knew that he had several years more experience than the person hired. He was advised by the secretary that she did not have his file. He was irate and accused the church of gross incompetence. He also said it was a racial issue because he was black. He got a lawyer and sued for discrimination.

6. During the summer season things are slow around the church. An employee of the church is asked to work in the church bookstore to cover for those going on vacation. The employee refuses. Insubordination is the refusal of an order from a supervisor or managerial personnel.

7. A young pastor is looking for a full-time Sunday school coordinator. A sixty year old former Sunday school director applies for the job. The pastor tells the interviewee that he was looking for someone younger. The interviewee list all of his credentials and successes as a Sunday school director. The pastor insisted that he wanted someone who had vitality, creativity and was younger. The interview ended and the interviewee contemplated filing an age discrimination suit.

8. The church administrator is interviewing a person for a secretarial position. He asks the applicant if she would have any child care problems if she got the job. The applicant responded that all of her children were in daycare and would not pose a problem. The administrator tells the applicant that her predecessor said the same thing and was out or on the telephone dealing with her kids frequently which interfered with her work. Kids get sick and that means that she would be out at least 3 or 4 times per month. He tells the applicant that he doesn't think she fits their needs and thanks her for coming in. The applicant leaves and says she's going to get a lawyer.

HELPFUL SOLUTIONS TO CHURCH ISSUES

There are all type of situations that can arise in your church that are not spiritual issues at all, but are policy issues that could create numerous problems for the church if not handled properly. Every church, regardless of their size, should have some type of policy manual. A policy manual will keep the church out of trouble and, hopefully, out of court. We will address policy manuals in another section of this handbook.

The most important thing that you should always remember when handling people is to ***treat everyone the same and fairly.*** Below are scenarios that will help you understand common managerial problems that may occur with your staff. *Use these illustrations as examples. Please note that we are not giving legal advice. If legal advice or other professional assistance is required, the services of a competent professional person should be engaged.*

Challenge #1 AIDS

You hire teachers for your Christian school and after school has started you find out through the rumor mill that one of your male teachers has tested positive for aids. As the pastor you are concerned about the children, what do you do?

Point #1
You must make sure that you understand that testing positive for HIV and having the disease itself are two different issues. A person can be tested positive for HIV and not be sick in any other way.

Point #2
Pastors, supervisors, and managers should understand their legal duty to protect the confidentiality of any employee's medical and personnel records.

Point #3

Employees with AIDS or who are HIV positive must be afforded the same rights, opportunities, and considerations as other employees with serious or life threatening illnesses.

Challenge #2 Constructive Discharge

The church hires a female facilities manager. She injures her back loading heavy equipment. After she returns from sick leave with a doctor's certificate saying she could not lift heavy objects, the church administrator gives her a new assignment to load and unload heavy equipment and do all the outdoor landscaping by herself. Her absenteeism increased and she refused to do the work because of her back injury. The church administrator fired her.

Point#1

Everyone must be treated fairly. Being a female is not the issue, the issue is that she was given work that would antagonize her injury. If the problem remains unresolved, the employee can bring it to the pastor or HR for a fair hearing. The goal is to resolve any honest differences of opinion about company policies, working conditions, and any other areas that may be creating problems.

Point#2

The church administrator knew that if he gave the woman the toughest jobs that required unusual physical effort she would most likely quit or he could fire her. This type of strategy will backfire and land your organization in court.

Challenge #3 Defamation

A full-time staff member of the church is caught stealing but he says he was just inspecting the supplies. The room where the supplies are stored has only one key that the church secretary has. The staff member was leaving the room carrying some of the supplies. The church administrator fires him on the spot. The former employee applies for a new job and lists your church as his last employer. The hiring company calls and asks for a reference.

Point #1

A lot of church HR departments and pastors are faced with this problem. You must be very careful. Defamation is the publication of false information that harms someone's reputation. You cannot be successfully sued for telling provable documented truth, but be careful. Even if you state that the employee was fired for dishonesty, you still could be in trouble if the employee could convince a court he was not actually guilty of the charge.

Point #2

Do not respond to requests for a reference unless you have been trained to do so. If you find yourself in that situation and there is no professional help use the following response: It is our church policy to give out the following information - the length of employment, date hired, date released, and position held. When the new employer calls take your cues from him. Don't volunteer anything. If the former employee had an acute problem and was fired for sexual harassment, as an example, refer the call to your attorney.

Challenge #4 Grievances

A female employee of the church tells the church administrator that a male employee touched her inappropriately and said some very suggestive sexual things to her. The female employee said she wanted to file a grievance and have the situation investigated. The church administrator told her; "We don't have any particular process, just send me a memo." Nothing was done by the church administrator. The female employee got a lawyer.

Point #1
You must have a grievance policy in your policy manual and it should not appear one sided. When an employee feels they will get a fair hearing through the grievance system, there is less chance that they will go to a government agency or the court.

Point #2
Treat every grievance seriously and explain that all information will be kept confidential. Only involve other employees and managers on a "need to know basis."

Point #3
Appoint an investigator from outside the department to interview witnesses and have them file a preliminary report.

Point #4
If after the investigation the employee is found guilty of violating the sexual harassment policy, take prompt and immediate action. Make sure all documentation is accurate and consists of the following: Notes of all the details of the complaint; what both parties said; what action the Church took in response to the allegations; how the employees reacted. Have the employee sign off on all the documents.

Point #5
Make sure that the church follows the grievance procedure in the same manner for all employees. Consistency is the key.

Challenge #5 Hiring

A church policy states that applications will be kept on file for one year. An individual who interviewed for the position of principal of the new church school was turned down. He heard that someone was hired for the position three weeks after his interview. He went to the church and inquired about his application. He happened to know the person that was hired and knew that he had several years more experience than the person hired. He was advised by the secretary that she did not have his file. He was irate and accused the church of gross incompetence. He also said it was a racial issue because he was black. He got a lawyer and sued for discrimination.

Point #1

If you do not have a policy for retention of applications, set one up. Applications should only be good for a stated period of time.

Point #2

If you have a policy of retaining applications, all applications must be reviewed during the period that relates to that position. All applications that have reached the "expiration date" must be destroyed.

Point #3

Using the policy of not retaining any applications is an option and a safe policy. However, it must be stated that applications are not retained and the applicant must reapply for each position.

Challenge #6 Insubordination

During the summer season things are slow around the church. An employee of the church is asked to work in the church bookstore to cover for those going on vacation. The employee refuses. Insubordination is the refusal of an order from a supervisor or managerial personnel.

Point #1

When an employee refuses to follow an order, it may be because they really don't understand your directive. Most employees are very cooperative. Make sure the employee understands what you want them to do and for how long.

Point #2

You can overcome employees' resistance by anticipating the fears that the employee has. The employee must also understand the consequences of refusing to follow the directive.

Challenge #7 Interviewing

A young pastor is looking for a full-time Sunday school coordinator. A sixty year old former Sunday school director applies for the job. The pastor tells the interviewee that he was looking for some-one younger. The interviewee list all of his credentials and successes as a Sunday school director. The pastor insisted that he wanted someone who had vitality, creativity and was younger. The inter-view ended and the interviewee contemplated filing an age discrimination suit.

Point #1

If an applicant is over the age of 18 and physically able to work, you must consider him or her for the position solely on the basis of qualifications for the job. Age should not be a deciding factor.

Point #2

To make sure you do not violate any EEO laws regarding hiring practices, especially in the area of age discrimination, always remain open to any applicant who feels that they are qualified for the position.

Point #3
Limit a job to workers of certain ages when, and only when, age is truly a job qualification. For example, police departments require that applicants be a certain age. Age can sometimes be a bona fide occupational qualification when public safety is a factor.

Challenge #8 Hiring

The church administrator is interviewing a person for a secretarial position. He asks the applicant if she would have any child care problems if she got the job. The applicant responded that all of her children were in daycare and would not pose a problem. The administrator tells the applicant that her predecessor said the same thing and was out or on the telephone dealing with her kids frequently which interfered with her work. Kids get sick and that means that she would be out at least 3 or 4 times per month. He tells the applicant that he doesn't think she fits their needs and thanks her for coming in. The applicant leaves and says she's going to get a lawyer.

Point #1
The administrator's fear could have been alleviated by stating "There are occasions when you would be asked to work later than 5pm, would you be able to meet that requirement?

Point #2
Number of children - This information can be used to eliminate mothers of school age or preschool children. Thus, it is highly suspect since it reveals nothing about an applicant's ability to perform the job.

QUICK NOTES CHECK LIST

There are items that do not fall under any particular topic but they are just as important. Remember this list may help in your effort to stay out of legal trouble. All of these examples and tips were taken from actual situations.

- **Put windows in all office doors so a person can look in if necessary.**
  One of the biggest problems with a male having a female in his office is the appearance of wrongdoing. Closed doors, with mixed company, in the office can be a problem, even if everything is innocent. To solve this problem cut a glass window in all doors where you hold counseling meetings, or interviews. Do not use blinds or shades on the windows as this makes it difficult for an individual to see what is going on in the room.

- **When meeting, with females especially, make sure the door is always left ajar.**
  If you don't have a window in the door, always leave the door ajar which serves the same purpose as having a window cut in the door.

- **Always have a witness when being interviewed by the media.**
  The press is known for misquoting people. Make sure that you record your interview or

have someone with you as a witness.

- **Do what you say you are going to do.**
One of the most serious violations in the church is making promises and not fulfilling them. Churches are being taken to court for making promises and not keeping them, for example, the promise to build a particular building or start a special program for which they are raising money but never follow through on. Whatever you promise to do, DO IT.

- **Carpet and cable**
Make sure that you have someone look at all the walk areas and stairs, making sure that there are no obstructions that might cause a person to fall.

- **Test emergency lighting**
Most emergency lights are rarely tested and you do not know if they work until the lights go out and then it too late. Someone might fall and create a liability problem. Check your emergency lights at least once per month.

- **Don't lock any doors during a service**
Emergency outlets must always be unlocked and ready for exiting; it is a violation of fire codes to have doors locked during a public meeting.

- **Be careful with full-body touching.**
In most churches today frontal hugging is normal. However, new people coming in may not feel comfortable with frontal hugging. Use discretion. Sexual harassment is a big issue today and anyone can be accused, if you are not careful. Use the handshake, side hug approach, or the two-hand approach. These are less likely to be interpreted as sexual harassment.

- **Don't slander from the pulpit.**
Defamation of character can create legal problems, even if the accusations are true. Stay away from slandering.

- **Do background checks on all those dealing with children.**
Your organization should get in the habit of doing criminal background checks on key people, especially those working with young children. This includes volunteers as well as staff members. If an individual refuses to allow you to do a criminal background check, he or she should be transitioned to another area. Be careful and use discretion.

- **Hire competent bus drivers i.e. city or private.**
One of the biggest issues with driver safety is getting drivers with clean records. Either have your insurance company do a driver background check or you order one yourself. Many organizations hire off duty professional drivers. Also, make sure that you have adequate insurance coverage.

- **Develop a policy manual.**
  Without some type of policy manual, you are driving your organization with blinders into a legal quagmire. A policy manual is a guidebook for the employer and the employee or the administration and the staff and should be used consistently regardless of your size.

- **Don't release a child to a stranger no matter what the claim.**
  Only release a child to his parent or individual who is authorized to pick him up. Use some type of identification code for each child and each parent. Ask the child who the person is that is picking them up if it is not the parent.

- **Remove offerings quickly.**
  Being cautious and wise is important. Count money in locked-down area. Don't make change from the basket.

- **Well-lit parking lot.**
  The parking lot, especially at night, can be a place where wrong doing might occur. Be sure that it is well lit. In addition, men should be posted outside as folks exit the building.

- **Pastors travel under an assumed name.**
  In most cases, this is not an issue, but for those pastors or executives that are concerned with being hounded by the press or individuals, traveling under an assumed is an option.

- **Control overly emotional people.**
  Some people that are taken with the moment and get overly excited can fall or get hurt. If they do hurt themselves, in most cases you will be paying the medical bills. Control the overly emotional.

- **Ask lots of questions to get insight about another person.**
  Questions can reveal a lot about a person's inner self and intentions. People who do a lot of talking learn less about the other person. Listen. Use silence to your advantage. When in a conversation with someone, leave long pauses, most people start talking when there are large silent gaps.

- **Stay detached when dealing with situations.**
  When you get emotionally involved you lose objectivity. At times, this may be difficult for some but it is important to keep your emotions in check.

- **Be observant.**
  For example, when you walk into someone s office, look at the office, the pictures, the desk, it will tell you a lot about the person.

- **Listen to the members of your church or organization.**
  You can pick up a lot of information by listening. The grapevine is a wonderful source of information and communication as well.

193

- **Work load**
  Realize that 20% of the people in your organization or church will do 80% of the work. This has always been an unfortunate reality in the church.

- **Always keep notes**
  For meeting, both formal and informal, it is important to keep notes. You can't remember everything.

- **Learn to use "but" or "however"**
  For example: "I couldn't agree with you more, but. Your point is well taken, however.

- **When some one is screaming, you speak softly.**
  If you speak softly the other person has to stop yelling to hear what you are saying.

- **Hire the best people to teach you what you don't know and need to learn.**
  Hire people smarter than you are.

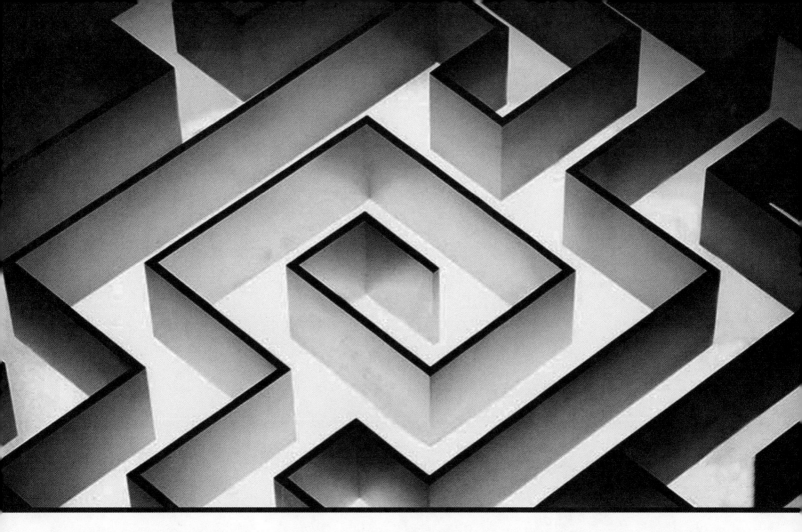

CHURCH STRATEGIES
for the 21st century

Building A Church

Building a church or any type of building project, if done correctly, can be a very rewarding experience. However, if proper planning does not occur, the building project can be a very negative experience. There was a pastor in the northeastern part of the states that built a 3 million dollar church facility. On opening day he stood in the pulpit before the doors were opened for the congregation to come in. As he looked out over the new sanctuary, he said, "This building is not what I wanted. For example, no one in the balcony can see me, unless they stand up." No matter what a church invests in a new building one million or one hundred million dollars, careful planning is the key to a successful building program. Below are listed the major steps that need to be addressed when building.

Building Committee

When the church congregation has decided that it wants to build a new church or add to the present facility, a building committee should be chosen and given full authority. It is advisable to choose qualified people:

1. Business owners

2. Business managers

3. Persons who have worked in construction or project management

4. Exemplary member(s) of the church

5. A person with accounting skills

6. An attorney (optional)

7. Pastor

8. Church board member(s)

9. Designated secretary

The church committee must be a cohesive team and should designate a team leader who has parliamentary law skills. Minutes should be recorded of all meetings. Once the committee is formed, the first step of the committee is to decide what type of facility they want. Should the sanctuary be built for future growth? How many Sunday school rooms do you need? How many offices are needed? Does additional land have to be purchased? How large of a mortgage can the church afford? Do you need a fellowship hall? These and many other questions need to be discussed thoroughly. In addition to a team leader, an *owner's representative* should be chosen. This person will represent the church at all prime contractor meetings and will sign change orders and other related documents as well. It is recommended that a retired businessperson or a church staff member be chosen for this job.

▲

A discussion log should be complied for each area of the building program.
A sample format for the log is as follows.

PROJECT DISCUSSION SHEET

Date:

Attendees:

DISCUSSION QUESTION: *EXAMPLE*

The church now seats 400 people. We have on average 375 people attending each Sunday. We are growing on average 10 new members per month. This will add 120 new members in one year. The question: Do we build a new church or add on?

DISCUSSION POINTS PRO:

1.

2.

3.

4.

5.

DISCUSSION POINTS CON:

1.

2.

3.

4.

5.

▲

PROJECT DISCUSSION SHEET

OTHER MATTERS RELATED TO THE SUBJECT:

COMMITTEE VOTE:

Name	☐ yes	☐ no	☐ abstain
Name	☐ yes	☐ no	☐ abstain
Name	☐ yes	☐ no	☐ abstain
Name	☐ yes	☐ no	☐ abstain
Name	☐ yes	☐ no	☐ abstain
Name	☐ yes	☐ no	☐ abstain
Name	☐ yes	☐ no	☐ abstain

FINAL DECISION - NARRATIVE FORM:

_____

_____

_____

_____

_____

_____

_____

_____

_____

_____

_____

▲

PROJECT DISCUSSION SHEET #

Date:

Attendees:

DISCUSSION QUESTION: *EXAMPLE*

The land that we wish to purchase cost $15,000 per acre. The seller is offering 30 acres
The question: Should we buy it?

DISCUSSION POINTS PRO:

1.

2.

3.

4.

5.

DISCUSSION POINTS CON:

1.

2.

3.

4.

5.

▲

PROJECT DISCUSSION SHEET

OTHER MATTERS RELATED TO THE SUBJECT:

COMMITTEE VOTE:

Name	☐ yes	☐ no	☐ abstain
Name	☐ yes	☐ no	☐ abstain
Name	☐ yes	☐ no	☐ abstain
Name	☐ yes	☐ no	☐ abstain
Name	☐ yes	☐ no	☐ abstain
Name	☐ yes	☐ no	☐ abstain
Name	☐ yes	☐ no	☐ abstain

FINAL DECISION - NARRATIVE FORM:

_____

_____

_____

_____

_____

_____

_____

LAND PURCHASE

If you are planning to purchase land, have the property inspected for toxic waste which may have been buried there. Often land developers and manufacturing companies use land to dump old paint cans, wood, bricks, and chemicals. They will then sell the land through a Realtor at a perceived low price; buyer beware. You, the new purchaser, are liable for the removal of all toxic materials and it could cost millions. After the property is inspected, you will be given a written report on the quality of the land. In addition, make sure you investigate who owns the property next to you. Will they be building a factory? Or light industry? When purchasing property, work through an attorney. Having a church representative negotiate the deal can be very awkward and may cost the church a lot more money than necessary. If a seller knows that a large organization is interested in the land it could stimulate the seller to raise the price. Zoning is very important. Some municipalities or counties have zoning regulations that must be considered. It is a mistake to purchase property without knowing if the zoning can be changed. Developing a relationship with the city counsel is very important when dealing with zoning issues.

At this juncture, it would be helpful to review the process involved in purchasing land. Purchasing property for a church facility can be very time consuming. A few of the questions to consider are:

1. *Is the plot of land large enough for what you want to build now and for future growth?* Often churches purchase property that fit their immediate needs. But what about a gym, fellowship hall, or expanding the sanctuary?

2. *Does the land have a clear title?*
   Without a proper title search by a qualified real estate lawyer or title company, the property should not be purchased. Included in the title search would be "mineral rights" search as well.

3. *Has the land been pre-inspected for toxic wastes?*
   Contractors have a tendency to dump construction waste on uninhabited property or properties that they own and then sell the property. BEWARE. A percolation test is also required to make sure that the property evacuates water properly.

4. *Who owns the property around you? What are they planning to do with their property?*
   Will there be a tavern built next to your church? A high activity entertainment center? A factory? If that is the case, it can have a negative impact on the value of your property if you plan to sell later.

5. *A church representative should not negotiate the deal.*
   In most cases, negotiating a deal is an art; it is better to leave the negotiating to a lawyer, or an experienced real estate agent. If a seller knows that a large organization wants to purchase the property, the price could move much higher.

6. *Proper zoning*
   Municipalities and counties have zoning regulations that should be considered.

Purchasing property that is improperly zoned or cannot have the zoning changed is a big mistake.

Once the land has been purchased and the decision has been made to build, the building committee has a framework to work from, it is now time to bring an architect in to design the building.

PROJECT MANAGER

If a church is planning to build a large complex it is recommended that a project manager be hired. A strong project manager is required to successfully lead the development team through the project. The project manager will handle all the day to day details of the job and he or she will be the single point of contact for the owner and will be an extension of the owners' staff. It is recommended that a qualified project manager be hired. The project manager can help you avoid numerous mistakes that could cost the church millions of dollars.

THE ARCHITECT

Choosing the right architect is essential to the total project. The architect must understand what you the client wants. If he or she cannot translate on to paper your vision for the building to be constructed then that company is the wrong company for your organization. The architect must be a member of the AIA (American Institute of Architects) and must hold a state license. If you are building a school use an architect that specializes in schools. When looking for a church architect find one that specializes in what you want to build. Note: Do not use a friend or member of the church as your architect. When it comes to tough negotiating or arbitration, it can destroy relationships. Business must be handled on a business level. When looking for an architect consider the following:

- **Visit some of the architects clients**
  Find out if the architect delivered on time. What was his design fee for the project. Did the owner provide easy to understand drawings? Did the architect give the client what they wanted?

- **Visit the architects office**
  Have them give you a full presentation. Ask them how much they grossed last year. Talk to the senior staff. Look at drawing of other projects.

- **Background check**
  Have your lawyer research for any litigation against the company. Have your lawyer check to be sure they are state certified.

- **Selection process**
  The committee should review and interview at least three architects. In many cases the architect may be willing to provide a basic rendering, you can use this to compare with other renderings and see if it meets the committees expectations.

- **Have the finalist give a presentations to the congregation**
  The congregation has to 'buy in" to everything. A presentation by the finalist would be appropriate.

INTRODUCTORY MEETINGS /CONCEPTUAL DESIGN

Once the architect has been hired and chosen a conceptual design begins with the owner and the architect working together to create what the client needs. That process starts with several phases:

Introductory meetings - In these meetings the owner (committee) and project manager clearly articulate what they want the final product (the church) to look like. Discussion points that should be covered in the initial meetings include:

- Type of worship

- Size of church (congregation)

- Ministry emphasis

- Future growth projections

- Television production

- Musical productions and stage performances

- Funerals

- Weddings

- Non-liturgical functions

- Communion

- Offering procedure

- Youth meetings

- Computer outputs (for those who use laptops)

- Average age of members

- Security issues

Each party should have minutes from each meeting to review and update. After the introductory meetings, which could be 3 or 4 meetings, the next phase of meetings is the conceptual design budget meetings.

DESIGN BUDGET

Based on the conceptual design meetings the next phase is the design budget. You have reviewed with the architect what type of building you want and what you want in it. The next decision is how much will it cost to build? Will you, the owner, get what you pay for? The architect can give you a general idea of cost based on his experience. In order to get the actual dollar cost of the building, the project will have to be, as they say in the industry, "put on the street."

PRIME CONTRACTOR

The same procedure that was used to find an architect can be used to find a general contractor. Visit churches in the areas that you find attractive, interview representatives of the church and find out the name of the prime contractor. After you have narrowed down the contractors to two or three, the committee should interview each company. Some of the questions that should be asked are:

- Are you a licensed contractor?

- What was the largest contract you have had in the last two years?

- Are you bonded? How much?

- Will you have a superintendent on site at all times?

- What do you require of your subs?

- Do you provide a project manager?

- How large is your crew?

- Will you be doing additional jobs while you are building our facility?

- Do you think that there will be any shortages e.g. of cement

- Have you worked before with the architectural firm that has been chosen?

- Are you in agreement with our payment procedure?

It should be noted that on larger more difficult projects, the more major subcontracts, such as mechanical and electrical may be negotiated and those subcontractors may be brought on board early in order to help facilitate the design process. For those subcontracts that are direct bids, the prime contractor will prepare bid tabulations, as outlined by the prime contractor. Bonding requirements will have to be outlined for both the prime contractor and the subs. The attorney or project manager representing the church can perform that for the organization. Subcontractor selection will continue into the construction phase, e.g. subcontractors for painting carpeting and fine finish work. These subs will be contracted after the earthwork and foundation subcontractors are underway.

A master schedule must be put together for all subcontractors, which is maintained by the prime contractor and reviewed with the owners weekly. The prime contractor will also coordinate the preparation and submittal of applications for all required certificates, permits and licenses. Those organizations involved including governmental agencies, boards, public works department, state and local traffic, transportation department, city council, environmental protection agency, public and private utilities and river authorities will need coordination as well. The prime contractor should submit applications to obtain utilities such as water, sewer, electrical, natural gas, telephone and any others that may be required for the project construction and for operation of the facility after it is occupied by the owner.

All requests for additional services by architects, engineers, consultants or contractors should be accompanied by a change order. A representative from the church should sign those change orders if agreeable. The proposed change order must include a detailed description of scope, cost and schedule implications. (See change order form)

It must also be understood that according to the size of the project, and your geographical location, construction estimates may not be totally "bought out." This means that all the subcontracted parts of the job have not been bid on. If all the subcontracted parts of the job have not been bid on and awarded, the final construction estimate cannot be finalized. Therefore, the owner could be paying more than what was estimated at the beginning of the project.

It should also be noted that the primary contractor, in case of unforeseen costs, should place a *contingency* in the budget. The amount of the *contingency* is based on the size of the job. The owner, with the prime contractor, will establish a standard format for the monthly pay application that is acceptable to the owner and the bank. The church will need to assign an accounting person to specifically monitor the building program. A clear paper trail must be maintained. This will ensure that everyone is paid in a timely manner thus forfeiting any liens on the project. The auditing process will be much easier. The owner along with the prime contractor will verify all work completed that is claimed on the payment application, ensure that proper backup is included, obtain certification that the contractor's subcontractors and suppliers have been paid on schedule and that the proper retainage is included. *Retainage is a holdback amount, usually 10% of the contractor's monthly pay application, which is held by the owner until "substantial completion" of the project is reached. The contractor similarly holds retainage on his subcontractors.*

Substantial completion is the point when the building can be occupied and used for it's intended purpose, but the contractor usually still has some minor work to perform. It is usually about 30 days before final completion. Substantial completion can be declared after the Certificate of Occupancy (CO) is issued by the locality. The CO is issued after all of the city building officials and city fire Marshall have made their final inspections and found the building and all systems to be functioning in compliance with building and fire codes.

CONCEPTUAL DESIGN BUDGET MEETINGS

The conceptual design budget phase is to develop a total project cost. The amount is to include cost of construction (building only), infrastructure (roads utilities, parking), landscaping, furnishings and equipment, as well as all consulting fees and permits. A budget is then put into place. A conceptual budget will be developed to include all of the facility components including:

- Cost of Planning
- Design
- Site work
- Construction
- Furnishings
- Equipment
- Landscaping

The conceptual budget is a target dollar figure based on the program data. It will be revised periodically as the design progresses and will not be a final estimate until all of the subcontractors are under contract, sometime after construction is underway.

After the architect has designed the building and the general contractor has been engaged, the bank process for the construction loan should be underway.

TASK #24

Under the **Banking /Leasing** segment review the "Bank Loan" form. This is a typical application. Fill out the total application and review.

CHANGE ORDER EXAMPLE

Date submitted:

Time submitted:

Received by: ☐ Superintendent ☐ Subcontractor

Initiator of change order: _____

_____

Description of change:

_____

_____

_____

_____

Cost of construction before change order ($) _____

Cost of construction after change order ($) _____

Actual construction increase ($): _____

When was your job to be completed _____

How long will the change order take _____

Will you add additional manpower to stay on schedule ☐ Yes ☐ No

What is the cost impact for the additional manpower ($) _____

What impact does this change order have on the other related subcontractors?

_____

_____

_____

Change order accepted   ☐ Yes   ☐ No

Additional cost to the owner ($) _____

_____

Signature of owner representative

_____

Signature of construction superintendent

CHURCH STRATEGIES
for the 21st century

Banking/Leasing

Below are actual comments from a bank loan officer that specializes in lending to churches.

"More importantly, I typically will start with a church by asking for documentation (detailed below) which I can use to pre-qualify the church for an assumed maximum loan amount based on recent financial history. In fact, I will (at the request of the church) fax the information request (shown below) immediately to the church in order to expedite."

"After we evaluate this information and make a determination that the church qualifies for a loan under our guidelines, we provide to the church a non-binding "Expression of Interest" letter which will summarize, for discussion purposes, credit accommodations which the bank would be interested in considering at that time. Each church is different, but typically the initial documentation requested is listed as follows."

1. General details of the loan request including amount, purpose and type of loan.

2. Church's financial statements for the last three years (1997, 1998, 1999) and year to date 2000 (as available). Such statements should include a balance sheet, income/expense statement and attendant financial exhibits that might be available under the circumstances.

3. Average weekly **adult** attendance for each of the last three years (1997, 1998, 1999). (Eliminate any duplication for adult attendance at multiple services.)

4. Estimate of the percentage of the congregation in each of the age groups: 0-18 years, 19-35 years, 36-55 years, and over 65 years. Your best guess at percentages will be sufficient.

5. Church's top 15 donors for year 2000. Please include donors by **amount, initials only of donor, and city of residence.**

6. Please describe any pledge drives currently in progress or planned within the next three 3 years. Include its purpose, total or pledge goal, total amount of signed pledge commitments, total amount collected to date, start (or anticipated start) date and ending date.

7. A brief description of the church's present land and facilities, and general details of the planned construction project including latest estimates of the anticipated cost to complete.

8. Please list each outstanding debt of the church including: (1) name of lender (2) original loan amount (3) current outstanding indebtedness (4) current interest rate (5) monthly payment amount (or other terms of repayment, if indicated) and (6) brief description of collateral.

9. Copy of the church's Articles of Incorporation and by-laws, and any subsequent amendments. Please list the church's Board of Directors (or other governing body)

10. Indicate if board members are part of church's pastorate/staff and/or immediate family members of the pastorate.

"In order to expedite our response time to the church, I request that they fax or mail (at their discretion) the above information to me. If it is a local church or within a two hour drive, I am more than glad to go to the church for a meeting to pick up this documentation."

"Beyond the initial "Expression of Interest" letter, if a church wants to pursue a formal loan commitment from our bank, it usually takes another week sometimes longer (assuming we have needed documentation) to issue the formal commitment letter to the church. After the commitment letter is mutually executed between parties, we try to close the loan within 30-45 days."

Please provide the following information as completely as possible; if information requested is not available, please state so.

I. GENERAL INFORMATION

A. CHURCH INFORMATION

1. Denominational Affiliation _____

2. Other Affiliation(s) _____

3. Federal Tax ID Number _____

4. School Name(s) _____

5. How long has the congregation been meeting in its present location?

6. Please include a brief narrative on the chronological history of your church as an attachment or addendum. Please include the following information:

    a. When was your Church founded?

    b. By whom was it founded?

    c. Number of people in congregation at founding?

    d. Give information as to the progress of the church?

    e. What special ministries does the Church perform?

    f. What are the future plans of the church? (new construction; acquisition of land or buildings; merger or combination with other congregations; other)

7. Please include a list of your Board of Directors and indicate their current job positions and telephone numbers.

8. Please provide a copy (including any amendments) of;
   a. Certificate and Articles of Incorporation by-laws
   b. Resolution of the Board wherein the motion for the proposed financing was approved. Included should be the tally of affirmative and negative votes.

B. MEMBERSHIP/ATTENDANCE INFORMATION

1. Please provide attendance and membership information for the current and previous five years:

   1995, 1996, 1997, 1998, 1999
   Adult Members (over 18 yr. Of age)
   Giving Units
   Average Weekly Worship Adult Attendance

2. Please provide the percentage of your present congregation in each of the following age groups: 0-18   19-30   31-65   over 65

3. Please project your anticipated membership and worship attendance for the next five years: 2000   2001   2002   2003   2004

   Adult Members
   Average Weekly Worship Adult Attendance
   Total Number of New Members Last 12 Months:

4. When did you last purge your membership roll?

C. STAFF INFORMATION

1. Senior Pastor:

   Name _____

   Residence Address _____

   Years with Church_____

   Date of Birth _____ Social Security No. _____

   Telephone No. (_____)_____ Fax No. (_____)_____

Please include a brief profile/resume of your Senior Pastor.

2. Business Administrator:

Name _____

Residence Address _____

Years with Church_____

Date of Birth _____ Social Security No. _____

Telephone No. (_____)_____ Fax No. (_____)_____

Please include a brief profile/resume of your Business Administrator.

3. Pastoral Staff:

How Many _____

D. CHURCH'S PROFESSIONAL ADVISORS

1. CPA/Accountant:

Name _____

Firm _____

Address _____

Telephone No. (_____)_____ Fax No. (_____)_____

2. Insurance Agent:

Name _____

Firm _____

Address _____

Telephone No. (_____)_____ Fax No. (_____)_____

Policy No._____ Expiration: _____

II. LOAN REQUEST INFORMATION

a. Please provide an itemized list of the anticipated use of the loan proceeds.

b. Outstanding Credit Obligations:

c. What property(ies) do you plan to use for collateral for this loan request? Please provide a description of the property (i.e. square footage, number of buildings, seating capacity, age of buildings, etc.)

d. Is this request for construction purposes? ☐ YES ☐ NO ☐ IF YES,
    1. Has construction already started?

    2. Please include a complete cost breakdown of your project. Additional construction information will be required after your request is reviewed.

    3. Architect:

      Name _____

      Residence Address _____

      Years with Church _____

      Date of Birth _____ Social Security No._____

      Telephone No. (_____)_____ Fax No. (_____)_____

    4. Building Contractor/Project Manager:
      Name _____
      Residence Address _____
      Years with Church _____
      Date of Birth _____ Social Security No._____
      Telephone No. (_____)_____ Fax No. (_____)_____

III. CHURCH FINANCIAL INFORMATION

A. What is your annual fiscal year end?

B. Please provide 5 years' fiscal year end balance sheets (blank form provided upon request).

C. Please provide 5 years' fiscal year end income and expenses, including all sources of income and all expenses. Please be sure to include special fundraising sources (blank form provided upon request).

D. Please describe any pledge drives which were initiated or completed over the past 5 years, include its purpose, amount pledged, amount collected, and percentage of pledges collected. Please describe any pledge drives currently in progress or planned within the next 5 years.

E. Please include a list of your 15 largest givers and their contribution for the last fiscal year. Individuals are to be identified by initials and city of residence.

F. If any large, unusual and/or non-recurring contributions were received within the most recent 5 fiscal years, please list the years(s) and amount(s).

G. Please provide the annual church budget for the current and prior 3 fiscal years.

H. Do you own all properties occupied by the Church? ☐ YES ☐ NO

If no, specify location(s) not owned and annual rent paid for property use:

LOCATION_____RENT_____

LOCATION_____RENT_____

IV. SCHOOL INFORMATION

A. Is there a school run by your church? ☐ YES ☐ NO ☐ IF YES,

Number of Students _____

Annual Tuition Per Student _____

B. Total number enrolled in each of the prior 4 fiscal years.

Preschool _____

Kindergarten _____

Grades 1-6 _____

Grades 7-8 _____

Grades 9-12 _____

C. What is your school's annual fiscal year end?

D. Please provide 5 years' fiscal year end balance sheets (blank form provided upon request).

E. Please provide 5 years' end income and expenses, including all sources of income and all expenses. Please be sure to include special fundraising sources (blank form provided upon request).

F. Please provide the current and prior years' school budgets.

G. Number of teachers/administrators: ☐ FULLTIME ☐ PARTTIME

H. Do you provide day care (either before or after school)? ☐ YES ☐ NO

I. Are school facilities ☐ LEASED/RENTED ☐ OWNED

If leased/rented, annual rental expense: _____

THE LEASING OPTION

There will always be some type of on going needs that your organization will have. Whether it's a new van, sound system, copy machine, television equipment etc., the needs will always be there. Usually, to get what is needed, churches, in particular, will either take the money out of operating funds, raise a special offering, which takes away from the operating funds, or increase debt and make a bank loan. Over time if the purchase, for example, was for three vans, the vehicles depreciate in value and in a few short years they start breaking down and need to be sold. You start all over again raising money for more vans.

Many pastors do business the same way they run their homes. "Let's buy it and we won't owe anything." That may be true for the homeowner where only your family uses the equipment and it lasts for 5 to 10 years. But when buying equipment, especially for a public facility like a church, the use ratio doubles and triples. The equipment is operated by numerous people, repairs are usually more expensive, demand on the equipment is higher, therefore the life expectancy is lower, and you end up needing a new piece of equipment sooner.

An alternative to outright purchasing is leasing. **Leasing is an agreement in which an owner of equipment permits another party to use the equipment for a specified period of time for a specified series of payments.** Numerous churches and faith-based organizations lease.

Why lease:

1. **Conserves working capital**

   - In most cases leasing requires a lower down payment than other types of financing.
   - Available cash can be used for other needs of the organization.
   - Decreases out of pocket expenses. Installation, software, disposables, can be included in the lease.

2. **Leasing can be flexible**

   - Lease terms can range from 12 to 60 months.
   - Special payment schedules can be arranged.
   - Specialized ownership options can be arranged.
   - Lease payments are fixed during the term of the lease.

3. **Frees bank lines of credit**

   - Leasing leaves lines of credit with banks open.

4. **Leasing is a hedge**

   - With leasing you can get 100% financing.

- **First amendment lease**
  Amendment to a lease agreement where the lessee agrees to purchase the equipment at the end of the original lease term for the fair market value or specified amount, whichever is greater. This is useful to establish off balance sheet financing on equipment with little or no residual value.

- **Capital lease**
  A lease which has the characteristics of a purchase agreement. This type of lease will have a $1.00 purchase option, and should be capitalized on the lessee's financial statements.

- **Bargain purchase option**
  A lease provision which allows the lessee to purchase the equipment at the end of the lease, for an amount below the fair market value of the equipment.

- **Lease renewal option**
  An option in a lease which gives the lessee certain rights to extend the term of the lease for an additional period of time in exchange for renewal payments.

- **Master lease**
  A lease line credit that allows the lessee to obtain additional leased equipment under the same lease terms and conditions.

- **Step-down lease**
  A lease in which the payments decline over the period of the lease term.

- **Operating lease**
  A lease in which the payments decline over the period of the lease term.

- **Present value**
  The discounted value of a payment stream to be received presently, taking into consideration a specific interest or discount rate.

- **Residual value**
  The discounted value of a payment stream to be received in the future, taking into consideration a specific interest or discount rate.

CHECKLIST OF QUESTIONS BANKS WILL ASK
WHEN CONSIDERING TO LOAN YOU MONEY

- How long has your church been in existence?

- Who prepares your financials? (it should be a credible accounting firm)

- What are your operating expenses (should be in the financials)

- Do you have an annual audit?

- What is the appraised value of your property?

- What are the annual giving units for your church?

- How many actual tithe paying members do you have?

- Can you provide at least 3 to 5 years of financials?

- Who are your largest givers?

- What is the average weekly adult attendance?

- How many worship services do you have per week?

- What is the percentage of your congregation in the following categories?
    0-18 years , 19-30 years , 31-65 years, over 65 years

- Please describe how an individual becomes a member of your church?

- How much money do you have in savings?

- How much future debt do you anticipate having?

- Please estimate the percentage of the congregation that live under 2 miles from the church, between 2 and 5 miles from the church, over 5 miles from the church.

- When do you plan to build?

Session Topic: _____

Presenter: _____

Date: _____ / _____ / _____

<u>**NOTES**</u>

_____
_____
_____
_____
_____
_____
_____
_____
_____
_____
_____
_____
_____
_____
_____
_____
_____
_____
_____
_____
_____
_____
_____
_____
_____
_____
_____
_____

IDEAS TO TAKE WITH YOU

_____
_____
_____
_____
_____
_____
_____
_____
_____
_____
_____
_____
_____
_____
_____
_____
_____
_____
_____
_____

BOOKS AND OTHER MATERIALS

_____
_____
_____
_____
_____
_____
_____
_____

Session Topic: _____

Presenter: _____

Date: _____ /_____ /_____

<u>NOTES</u>

_____

_____

_____

_____

_____

_____

_____

_____

_____

_____

_____

_____

_____

_____

_____

_____

_____

_____

_____

_____

_____

_____

_____

_____

_____

_____

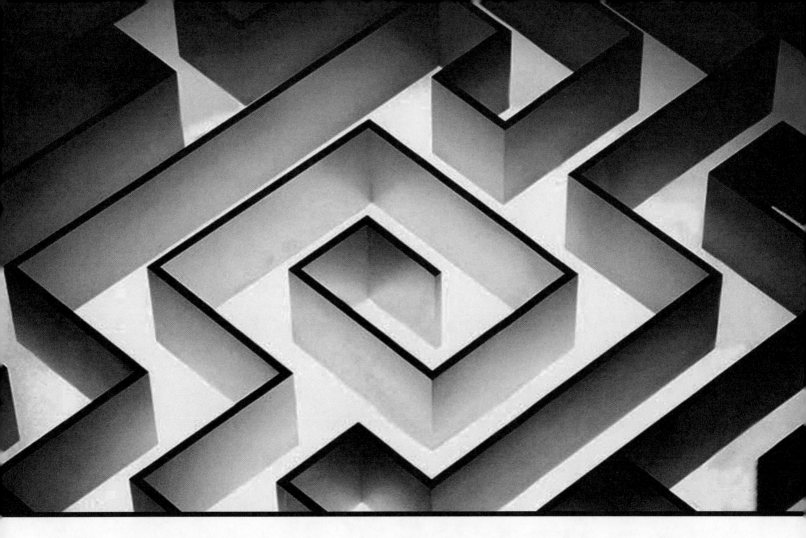

CHURCH STRATEGIES
for the 21st century

Grant Writing &
Foundations

- If the grant proposal is not in response to an RFA (request for application), first talk to the program director to find out whether the ideas and the hypothesis that you are putting forward will be welcomed with enthusiasm. This will give you more direction.

- Give yourself at least four months to write a grant proposal with the goal to have the grant ready about one month prior to submission. Use the last month to polish the writing and the style of presentation.

- Read the instructions for writing the grant carefully and strictly adhere to them.

- Write a succinct proposal that can be easily understood by those who are not necessarily experts in the field. It is best if you can get the grant reviewed by at least three individuals – one expert in the field, a non-expert scientist and an editor to proof the English grammar and the style of the proposal. Revise the manuscript according to the best suggestions of these individuals.

- If the page limit to the grant proposal is 25, try to write a proposal that fits 20-23 pages. Use the additional space for stylistic alterations.

- Use the largest size font that makes the grant easy to read and does not pose any strain to the eye.

- Separate different sections of the grant so that various pages do not look monotonous.

- Try to make some sections bold, italicize other sections and use numbering to identify sections and subsections of the grant.

- Avoid using meaningless jargon.

- Avoid using excessive abbreviations. Define abbreviations when used the first time.

- Add adequate spaces where required.

- Left justify the text but avoid the right justification of the text.

- Do not include figures that cannot be copied well. Include glossy prints in the body of the text.

- Do not try to use the appendix to present data that is not included in the original application.

- Provide the figures and tables immediately after they are cited.

- Provide clear figures and table legends.

- Write a clear hypothesis. Clearly spell out the specific aims.

- Do not offer more than two to three specific aims. More specific aims may be regarded unachievable and too ambitious.

- Avoid putting too much information in any specific section of the proposal. Putting too much detail in the method section may prevent you from putting adequate emphasis in the design section.

- For each specific aim, provide a section in the experimental design that discusses alternative strategies and ideas to test the hypothesis. Try to spell out the shortcomings and pitfalls and how to solve them.

- Do not try to impress the reviewers with too much preliminary data. Just present the relevant data. Show that the proposed ideas are sound and are achievable.

- Provide preliminary data that shows that the methodologies can be successfully accomplished.

- If necessary, call the program director to find out how to insure that the reviewers will obtain the original copies of the manuscript which includes the glossy figures.

- If the grant does not get funded, contact the program director to find out the reason why the grant was denied and what steps you must take to resubmit.

- In the revised application, try to first summarize the shortcomings indicated in the "summary statement" and then respond to each one carefully. Try to be neutral and neither antagonistic nor conciliatory.

- Spell check the document carefully before mailing.

- Always send the proposal by express mail several days prior to the due date. Call the express mail service to verify that the grant has been received by the granting agency.

- After the grant has been submitted, if a manuscript should be published or additional relevant data becomes available call the program director to see whether you can send the manuscript or a summary of findings to the reviewers.

- If the grant is funded, celebrate, but immediately afterward prepare a plan and deadlines for accomplishing the proposed project and for writing the renewal grant.

GRANT FOUNDATION LINKS
http://www.granted.org

Alphabetical listing of current links
to nationwide foundations.

AAUW Educational

American Association of University Women promotes education and equity for all women and girls.

Adobe Philanthropy Council
http://www.adobe.com/philanthrophy

Local community improvement – average award $1,500.

Aetna Foundation
http://www.aetna.com/foundation

Area of Giving – Children's health (at risk children) and education (at risk children), primarily in greater Hartford, Connecticut & National Organizations.

Allen Foundation
http://www.tamu.edu/baum/allen

Human nutrition, child development nutrition.

Alliance Healthcare Foundation
http://www.alliancehf.org

Community health, health care, substance abuse, violence prevention.

America's Charities
http://www.charities.org

Community service, cultural heritage, & economic independence.

Ameritech Corporation
http://www.ameritech.com/community

Education, economic development and quality of life, primarily in Illinois, Indiana, Michigan, Ohio, and Wisconsin.

Annenberg Foundation
http://www.whanneberg.org

Public education, K-12, early childhood education, child development & youth services.

Archstone Foundation
www2.archstone.com

Health and well beings of seniors.

ARCO Foundation
http://www.arco.com.corporate/reports/foundation

Education, Community arts and humanities, environment and public information-primarily in the West, Southwest, Alaska and the Rocky Mountain Regions.

AT&T Foundation
http://www.att.com/foundation

Non-profits helping people achieve self-sufficiency, education, arts and culture, civic & community service.

Autodesk Foundation
http://www.autodesk.com/foundation

Improving public schools and expanding education opportunities beyond the walls of the classroom.

Bank of America Corporation
http://www.bankofamerica.com/communitycommunity

Community development and the environment.

Bankers Trust Foundation
http://www.bankerstrust.com/corpcomm/community

Primarily in New York City – Community development, education, arts & humanities, healthcare, health & hospitals, and environment.

Arnold & Mabel Beckman Foundation
http://www.beckman-foundation.com

Research in chemistry & the life sciences.

Ben & Jerry's Foundation
http://www.benjerry.com/foundation

Progressive social change by addressing the underlying conditions of societal or environmental problems; 1. children & families, 2. disenfranchised groups, 3. environment.

Benton Foundation
http://www.benton.org

Communications in the public interest.

Frank Stanley Beveridge Foundation
http://www.beveridge.org

Massachusetts-Hampshire Co., Hampden Co., Florida-Hillsborough Co., Palm Beach Co., New Hampshire, Rhode Island, California-Ventura Co.

Arthur M. Blank Family Foundation
http://www.blankfoundation.org

Arts & culture, athletics, environment, fostering understanding, adolescents, young women and girls.

The Brainerd Foundation
http://www.brainerd.org

Protecting the environmental quality of the Pacific Northwest.

Brookdale Foundation
http://www.awol.com/brookdale

Needs and challenges of America's elderly population.

Burroughs Wellcome Fund
http://www.bwfund.org

Medical science research & enhancement.

Carnegie Corporation of New York
http://www.carnegie.org

Academic institutions, & national and regional non-profits for national or international projects: 1. education & healthy development of children & youth; 2. Preventing deadly conflict; 3. strengthening human resources in developing countries.

Annie E. Casey Foundation
http://www.aecf.org

Build better futures for disadvantaged children in the United States.

Casey Family Program
http://www.casey.com

Service of planned long-term family foster care.

The Commonwealth Foundation
http://www.oneworld.org/com_fnd

Inter-country exchange co-operation among non-governmental organizations, professional & cultural bodies of the 53 commonwealth countries.

Commonwealth Fund
http://www.cmwf.org

Improving health care services, minority American health, elderly well-being, children & young people capacities.

Crail-Johnson Foundation
http://www.crail-johnson.org

Children in need.

Charles E. Culpeper Foundation

Health, education, arts & culture, administration of justice.

The Charles A. Dana Foundation
http://www.dana.org

Health-brain diseases & disorder research, education-spread of well-tested innovations previously screened.

Arthur Vining Davis Foundations
http://www.jvm.com/davis

Private higher education, secondary education, religion (graduate theological education), health care (caring attitudes), public television.

Dekko Foundation
http://www.noblecan.org

Educational impact in selected counties in Alabama, Florida, Indiana, Iowa, and Texas.

Gladys Krieble Delmas Foundation
http://www.delmas.org

Cultural Heritage – humanities, performing arts, research library, Venetian research program.

Geraldine R. Dodge Foundation
http://www.grdodge.org

Elementary & secondary education, arts (New Jersey), local projects (Morris Co. New Jersey), welfare of animals, public issues (New Jersey & Northeast).

William H. Donner Foundation

U.S. Canadian relations, education, human capital development.

Do Right Foundation
http://www.doright.org

The Camille and Henry Dreyfus Foundation
http://www.dreyful.org

Community support particularly for youth & K-12 public education.

Dreyer's Charitable Foundation
http://www.dreyers.com/thecompany

Advance the science of chemistry, chemical engineering, & related sciences.

Jessie Ball Dupont Fund
http://www.dupontfund.org/guide

Limited to 350 institutions which received prior funding from Mrs. Dupont.

The Energy Foundation
http://www.ef.org

Energy efficiency and renewable energy.

▲

The Enterprise Foundation
http://www.enterprisefoundation.org

Develop affordable housing, develop community & individual assets, and enhance community safety.

The Fieldstone Foundation
http://www.netcom.com

Community & education, cultural humanitarian and Christian ministries.

The Ford Foundation
http://www.fordfound.org

Asset building & community development, education, media, arts & culture, and peace & social justice.

The Foundation for Microbiology
http://www.t.ac.net

Scientific research in microbiology.

Foundation for Seacoast Health
http://www.nh.ultranet.com

New Hampshire/Maine Seacoast Area.

Friedman-Klarreich Family Foundation

Focus on young women & family stability, education, social & culture.

Gates Library Foundation
http://www.gif.org

Multimedia computer grants and assistance to public libraries.

Gebbie Foundation
http://www.gebbie.org

Primarily in Chautauqua County, New York – children/youth/education, arts, human services, community development.

GE Fund
http://www.ge.com/fund

▲

Higher education, pre-college, arts & culture, international, public policy, matching gifts, united way.

The Global Fund for Women
http://www.lgc.apc.org

Focuses on female human rights.

The Global SchoolNet Foundation
http://www.gsn.org

Internet-based learning.

The Harry Frank Guggenheim Foundation
http://www.hfg.org

Scholarly research on problems of violence, aggression, and dominance.

John Simon Guggenheim Memorial Foundation
http://www.gf.org

Fellowships for individuals in all fields (natural sciences, social sciences, humanities, creative arts).

George Gund Foundation
http://www.gundfdn.org

Education, arts, economic development & community revitalization, human services, civic affairs, environment.

The Gunk Foundation
http://www.mhv.net

Public arts projects and scholarly/artistic publications.

Hewlett Packard Company
http://www.webcenter.hpcom/grants

University grants, national grants, U.S. education matching programs/commonly given products, U.S. local grants, European grants program.

The Whitney Houston Foundation for Children
http://www.whfoundation.com

IBM Corporation
http://www.ibm.com/ibm/ibmgives

Education, environment, health, human services, arts & culture.

Ittleson Foundation
http://www.ittlesonfoundation.org

Aids, the Environment, Mental Health.

The Japan Foundation
http://www.ipf.go.jp

Networking of Japan Specialists, access to Japan-related information.

JCPenny

Health & welfare, education, civic betterment, arts & culture.

Elton John Aids Foundation
http://www.ejaf.org

Jerome Foundation
http://www.jeromefdn.org

Arts in Minnesota & New York.

Robert Wood Johnson Foundation
http://www.rwjf.org

Health & healthcare of Americans, substance abuse.

Henry J. Kaiser Family Foundation
http://www.kff.org

W. Alton Jones Foundation
http://www.wajones.org

Global environmental protection and the prevention of nuclear war or other massive release of radioactive material.

Ewing Marion Kauffman Foundation
http://www.emkf.org

Enterpreneurship education, & youth development.

W.M. Keck Foundation
http://www.wmkeck.org

Scientific, engineering and medical research programs at accredited universities & colleges in the United States.

The W.K. Kellogg Foundation
http://www.wkkf.org

Health, philanthropy, & volunteerism, food systems & rural development, youth & education/higher education.

The Joseph P. Kennedy, Jr. Foundation
http://www.familyvillage.wisc.edu

Needs of people with mental retardation – independence, productivity, & inclusion.

Keterring Foundation
http://www.kettering.org

Political research.

John S. and James L. Knight Foundation

Journalism, education, arts & culture.

The Charles A. and Anne Morrow Lindbergh Foundation

Balance between technological advancement and environmental preservation.

The Link Foundation Fellowships

Doctoral student fellowships in advanced simulation & training.

Edward Lowe Foundation
http://www.lowe.org

Services for small business.

George Lucas Educational Foundation
http://www.glef.org

Education K-12.

Henry Luce Foundation
http://www.hluce.org

Higher education, understanding between Asia & U.S., study of religion & theology, scholarship in American art, women science & engineering, youth & public policy programs.

Robert R. McCormick Tribune Foundation
http://www.rrmtf.org

Communities, citizenship, journalism, education.

James S. McDonnell Foundation
http://www.jsmf.org

Biomedical & behavioral sciences research & related educational innovations.

John D. and Catherine T. MacArthur Foundation
http://www.macfdn.org

Human & community development, global security & sustainability.

Nellie Mae Fund for Education

New England States – disadvantaged, college potential middle & high school students at risk of not completing their high school education or pursuing a higher education.

A.L. Mailman Family Foundation
http://www.mailman.org

Children & families with a special emphasis on early childhood.

The John and Mary r. Markle Foundation
http://www.markle.org

Media & political participation, interactive communications technologies, communications policy.

MCI Communication Corporation
http://www.wcom.com

Education & technology.

R.J. McElroy Trust
http://www.cedarnet.org

Assist non-profit, tax-exempt organizations, which provide educational services to deserving youth.

Andrew W. Mellon Foundation

Higher education, cultural affairs & the performing arts, population, conservation & the environment, and public affairs.

Joyce Mertz-Gilmore Foundation
http://www.jmgf.org

Environment, human rights, peace & security, and New York City Civic and Cultural Issues.

Microsoft Corporation
http://www.microsoft.com

Puget Sound Region.

Milbank Memorial Fund
http://www.milbank.org

Support nonpartisan analyses, study, research and communication on significant issues in health policy.

Milken Family Foundation
http://www.mff.org

Public recognition & financial rewards to elementary & secondary school teachers, principals & other educational professionals who are furthering excellence in education.

Mitsubishi Electric America Foundation

Assist young Americans with disabilities through education & other means, to lead fuller & more productive lives.

J.P. Morgan
http://www.jpmorgan.com

Arts. education, environment, health & human services, international affairs, and urban affairs.

Charles Stewart Mott Foundation
http://www.mott.org

Efforts that promote a just, equitable and sustainable society.

National Foundation for the Improvement of Education
http://www.nfie.org

▲

Improve student learning in the nation's public schools.

National Geographic Society Educational Foundation
http://www.nationalgeographic.com

Geography education programs K-12.

National Heritage Foundation
http://www.nhf.org

Efforts which enhance National Heritage.

NEC Foundation of America
http://www.nec.com

National reach & impact – in science & technology education at the secondary level, and/or application of technology to assist people with disabilities.

Needmor Fund
http://www.fdncenter.org

Community organizing.

Norman Foundation
http://www.normanfdn.org

Efforts to reverse regressive social & economic policies of the last two or three decades.

Novartis Foundation for Sustainable Development
http://www.foundation.novatis.com

Poverty-alleviating programs and projects in developing countries.

Jessie Smith Noyes Foundation
http://www.noyes.org

Environment & reproductive rights.

John M. Olin Foundation
http://www.jmof.org

Public policy research, American institutions, law and legal, strategic and international studies.

Open Society Institute
http://www.soros.org

▲

Multi-dimensional.

Ottinger Foundation
http://www.funder.org/ottinger www.funder.org/ottinger

Multi-dimensional.

David and Lucile Packard Foundation
http://www.packfound.org www.packfound.org

Science, center for the future of children, population, conservation, arts & film preservation, education, community.

Allicia Patterson Foundation

Working journalists to pursue independent projects for APR Reporter.

The Pew Charitable Trusts
http://www.pewtrusts.com www.pewtrusts.com

Culture, education, environment, health & human services, public policy, religion, venture fund.

Pfizer Venture Philanthropy

Health Care, education, and community & cultural affairs.

The Prudential Foundation

Foundation grants, social investments.

Public Welfare Foundation
http://www.publicwelfare.org www.publicwelfare.org

Criminal justice, disadvantaged elderly, disadvantaged youth, environment, health, population & reproductive health, community support.

Research Corporation
http://www.rescorp.org www.rescorp.org

Advancement of science and technology.

Rex Foundation

Environment, social and community services to the arts, cultural preservation.

Rockefeller Foundation
http://www.rockfound.org

African initiatives, agricultural sciences, arts & humanities, Bellagio, health sciences, equal opportunity, global environment, population sciences, school reform, special interests.

Joseph Rowntree Charitable Trust
http://www.jrct.org.uk

U.K. Foundation – Poverty & economic justice, handling conflict & promoting peaceful alternatives, democratic process, racial justice, corporate responsibility, Quaker & other religious concerns, Ireland, South Africa.

Russell Sage Foundation
http://www.russellsage.org

Social science resource center, social science as a means of improving social policies in the U.S.

Scaife Foundation
http://www.scaife.com

Sarah Scaife Foundation, Scaife Family Foundation, Allegheny Foundation, Carthage Foundation.

Arthur B. Schultz Foundation
http://www.absfoundation.org

Empower individuals worldwide through educational opportunity, responsible economic development, & environmental conservation.

Sears-Roebuck Foundation
http://www.sears.com

Gilda's Club – Nonprofit organization providing emotional & social support services for people with cancer, their family & friends.

SEVA Foundation
http://www.seva.org

Prevent & relieve suffering, generate hope through compassionate action.

The Sierra Club Foundation
http://www.sierraclub.org

Sierra Club & other environmental endeavors.

Alfred P. Sloan Foundation
http://www.sloan.org

Science & technology, standard of living & economic performance, education & careers in science & technology, selected national issues, civic projects.

Soros Foundation
http://www.soros.org

Multi-dimensional, operates in 31 countries.

Southwestern Bell Company Foundation

Texas, Missouri, Kansas, Oklahoma & Arkansas – education, economic development.

The Spencer Foundation
http://www.spencer.org

Research which contributes to the understanding of education and improvement of its practice.

Sprint Corporation
www3.sprint.com

Education, arts &culture, community improvement, youth development.

Stern Family Fund
http://www.essential.org

Policy oriented government & corporate accountability projects.

Surdna Foundation
http://www.surdna.org

Environment, community revitalization, effective citizenry, arts, nonprofit sector support initiatives, organizational capacity building grants.

The John Templeton Foundation
http://www.templeton.org

Spiritual & moral understanding through scientific research.

Trinity Grants Program

Spiritual formation & development in the Episcopal, strengthen the church in the global south, needs of metropolitan New York, strengthen telecommunication in the Anglican Communion.

Turner Grants Program

Spiritual formation & development in the Episcopal Church, strengthen the church in the global south, needs of metropolitan New York, strengthen telecommunication in the Anglican Communion.

Turner Foundation

Energy, water/toxin, forests/habitats, population.

United States – Japanese Foundation

Japan-U.S. relations: precollege education, policy studies.

United Technologies

Education, health & human services, arts & culture, and civic & community.

United Way
http://www.unitedway.org

United ways on the internet.

Virtual Foundation
http://www.virtualfoundation.org

Creating partnerships among individuals and groups to support environment & health initiatives globally.

Wallace Global Funds

Advance globally sustainable development.

DeWitt Wallace-Reader's Digest Fund
http://www.wallacefunds.org

Education & career development opportunities for school-age youth in low-income communities.

Lila Wallace-Reader's Digest Fund
http://www.wallacefunds.org

Culture life of communities, arts & culture.

Weeden Foundation
http://www.weedenfdn.org

Adverse impact of growing human population & overuse of natural resources.

Kurt Weill Foundation
http://www.kwf.org

Kurt Weill Foundation for music.

Worldwide Education and Research Institute

Self-sufficiency, philanthropic, housing/construction, experimental.

Francois Xavier-Bagnoud Foundation

Health & human rights.

CORPORATE FUNDING LINKS

CORPORATIONS WITH NON-PROFIT FUNDING

Note – most corporations give only in those communities in which they have a presence.

Abbott Laboratories Fund
http://www.abbott.com

Within Abbott Communities (130 worldwide) human health & welfare: elementary, secondary & higher education; culture, arts & civic activities.

Adobe Systems Inc.
http://www.adobe.com/aboutadobe/philanthropy

Adobe software products, small $1,500 cash grants to nonprofit organizations which service: youth, the homeless, people with disabilities, minorities, the elderly, and victims of abuse, provide education & literacy programs, support human rights, support the arts, protect the environment, & support animal rights.

Aetna Foundation
http://www.aetna.com/foundation

Limited to proposals submitted by invitation only.

▲

American Express Company
http://www.americanexpress.com/corp

Community service, culture heritage & economic independence.

Ameritech Corporation
http://www.ameritech.com

Education, economic development and quality of life.

AMR/American Airlines Foundation
http://www.amrcorp.com/corp-fdn

Dallas/Fort Worth, Chicago, Miami, & San Juan – needs of nonprofits in the communities that American Airlines serves.

Apple Computer
http://www.apple.com/education

Special rates on Apple computers for educators.

Arvin Foundation
http://www.arvin.com/sub

Report on Arvin's philanthropic contributions you may send for.

Ashland Inc./Ashland Foundation
http://www.ashland.com

U.S. & U.K. – in Ashland Inc. Communities.

Aspect Telecommunications
http://www.aspect.com

Education K-9, nonprofits & school focusing on the education of children and youth in Aspect Telecommunication's communities.

AT & T Foundation
http://www.att.com/foundation

Invitational programs or by solicited applications from non-profit organizations – education, civic & community service, arts, & culture.

▲

Avon Products Foundation
http://www.avon.com/about/women/foundation

Women's programs in – health, education, community & social services, arts & culture.

Baltimore Gas and Electric Company
http://www.bge.com

Central Maryland service territory – early childhood development, education, health & welfare, hospitals, cultural, civic, community revitalization, & environment.

BankAmerica Corporation
http://www.bankofamerica.com/community

Community development & the environment.

Bankers Trust Corporation
http://www.bankerstrust.com/corpcomm

Bankers Trust Foundation – Community development, education, arts, & culture, health & hospitals, environment, general, international.

Bayer Foundation
http://www.bayerus.com/about/community

Bayer Communities – civic & community programs, science education & work force development, the arts, art education & culture.

Baxter Foundation
http://www.baxter.com/investors

Access to health care.

Beauticontrol – Women Helping Others Foundation
http://www.beauticontrol.com

Health, education & wellness concerns specifically for women & children.

Bechtel Foundation
http://www.bechtel.com/buildingminds

Bechtel Communities – typically youth & educational programs, grants are under $5,000.

BellSouth Foundation
http://www.bellsouthcorp.com

Improve education in the U.S. South by stimulating fundamental changes in primary & secondary education that will result in active learning & improving outcomes for all students.

Ben & Jerry's Foundation
http://www.benjerry.com/foundation

Progressive social change by addressing the underlying conditions of societal or environmental problems – children & families, disenfranchised groups, the environment.

Boston Globe Foundation
http://www.boston.com/extranet/foundation

Boston, Mass. Area only – children & youth 0-22 years.

Bristol-Myers Squibb Company
HYPERLINK http://www.bms.com

Unrestricted biomedical research, women's health education, math & science education, local/community involvement.

Ceridian Corporation
http://www.ceridian.com/whocommunity

Balance the growing demand of work & home life; health, education, & arts.

Chevron Company
http://www.chevron.com/community

Education & the environment.

CIGNA Corporation
http://www.cigna.com/corp/contributions

Organizations & activities that improve the overall climate for businesses.

Cinergy Foundation
http://www.cinergy.com/foundation

Parts of Ohio, Indiana, & Kentucky only – arts & culture, community development, education, health & social services.

Citibank/Citicorp Foundation
http://www.citicorp.com/corporate

Day to day business practices.

Clorox Company Foundation
http://www.clorox.com/company/foundation

Primarily Oakland & San Francisco area in California.

Coca-Cola Company
http://www.cocacola.com/foundation

150 scholarships to High School seniors in Coca-Cola areas.

Compaq Computer Corporation
http://www.compaq.com/corporate

Limited to Houston, Texas.

ConAgra, Inc.
http://www.conagra.com/foundation

Improve the quality of life in communities where ConAgra employees work & live – education, health & human services, arts & culture, and civic & community betterment.

James M. Cox Foundation
http://www.cox.com/school/resources

In Cox Communications communities – cable service free of charge to every elementary, junior & senior high school, (public & private).

Datatel Scholars Foundation
http://www.datatel.org/corporate

Scholarships to eligible students to attend a higher learning institution selected from Datatel's more than 400 client sites.

John Deere & Company
http://www.deere.com

Human services, community development, educational enterprises, & cultural opportunities.

Detroit Edison Foundation
http://www.detroitedison.com

Southeastern Michigan – Detroit Area.

R.R. Donnelley & Sons Company
http://www.rrdonnelley.com/public/community

Chicago, Illinois – to support the written word, to serve children & youth, to enhance the quality of life in our communities.

Dow Chemical Company
http://www.dow.com/about/charitable

Address a demonstrated need in a city/community in which the Dow Chemical Company has a presence – hands on science experience for students below the college level, supports a university project or program involving science, engineering or business which enhances the environment.

Dreyer's Foundation
http://www.dreyers.com/globals

Communities where the company has operating facilities, focused community support, youth & K-12 public education.

Dupont
http://www.dupont.com/corp/philanthropy

In communities in which they operate – community social progress and economic success, environmental excellence, education.

Eastman Kodak Company
http://www.kodak.com/us/__/corp

Primarily focused at site communities – community revitalization, environment, arts & culture, education, health & human services.

Eaton Corporation
http://www.eaton.com/corp/contribution

Communities where it has facilities – education & community improvement.

Electronic Data Systems Corporation
http://www.eds.com/community

Education outreach.

El Paso Energy Foundation
http://www.epng.com/about/involve

El Paso, Houston, Western Texas – education, youth groups, community programs, social service programs and the arts.

Entergy Corporation
http://www.entergy.com

Portions of Arkansas, Louisiana, Mississippi, & Texas – education & community involvement.

Fannie Mae Foundation
http://www.fanniemaefoundation.org

Consumer housing education, and home-buying fairs.

Farmers Insurance Group
http://www.farmersinsurance.com

Higher education & community efforts.

Fieldstone Foundation
http://www.aol.com/mmfieldsto/index

Communities where Fieldstone builds homes – community & education cultural, humanitarian & Christian ministries.

FMC Foundation
http://www.fmc.com/corp/community

In communities in which FMC operates – local civic, cultural & educational organizations.

Ford Motor Company Fund
http://www.ford.com/corporate-info/cultural

Education, health & welfare, arts, humanities, civic activities & public policy.

Freddie Mac Foundation
http://www.freddiemacfoundation.org

Metropolitan Washington D.C. Area, Maryland, Virginia, National programs-children, families of children, children's communities.

Frontier Corporation
http://www.frontiercorp.com

Rochester, New York.

Gannett Foundation
http://www.gannett.com/map/foundation

Gannett (owner of numerous newspapers) communities – qualified nonprofit organizations to improve the education, health & advancement of the people.

Gap Inc.
http://www.gapinc.com

San Francisco Bay Area, New York city, Chicago & Washington D.C. – youth & business, HIV/Aids prevention & education.

Genetech, Inc.
http://www.gene.com/company/responsibility

General Electric Fund
http://www.ge.com/fund

General Mills, Inc.
http://www.genmills.com

General Mills Foundation – General Mills communities – arts & culture, education, family life, health & nutrition.

General Motors Corporation Foundation
http://www.gm.com/philanthropy

Education, health & human services, arts & culture, civic & community, public policy, environmental & energy, cancer research.

GTE Corporation/Foundation
http://www.gte.com/aboutgte

Education, health & human services, local communities, arts.

John Hancock Company
http://www.jhancock.com

Boston – health & human services agencies: arts & cultural groups, civic and interracial organizations, school & adult education programs, and job training and economic development programs.

Hannaford Bros. Company
http://www.hannaford.com/community

Hannaford communities – education & children, environmental programs, food donations, cultural & civic activities, health programs.

HEI Charitable Foundation
http://www.hei.com

Hawaii – community development, education, environment, family services.

Hewlett-Packard Company Foundation
http://www.webcenter.hp.com/grants

Education, arts, health & human services, civic groups, & environmental organizations.

Home Depot Inc.
http://www.homedepot.com

Housing projects, youth, environmental.

Humana Foundation, Inc.
http://www.humanafoundation.org

Charitable organizations and institutions that promote education, health and human services, community development and the arts.

IBM Corporation
http://www.IBM.com/ibm/ibmgives

Local, national, international – cutting across such societal needs as education, the environment, health, human services, arts and culture.

Inland Paperboard and Packaging Inc.
http://www.iccnet.com

Health & welfare, education, art & culture, civic.

Intel Corporation
http://www.intel.com/intel/community

National grants, local communities (Arizona, Folsom Ca., Santa Clara Ca., New Mexico, Oregon, Washington, Ireland) – Education, technology improving life, protecting the environment.

Intimate Brands, Inc.
http://www.intimatebrands.com

Women, children, & education in our communities.

International Paper Company Foundation
http://www.internationalpaper.com/ourworld

Education & charities in communities where they do business.

Ipalco Enterprises
http://www.palco.com

S.C. Johnson Wax Fund
http://www.scjohnsonwax.com

KN Energy Foundation
http://www.kne.com/pages/community

Lincoln Financial Group
http://www.lfg.com

Fort Wayne, Indiana area & communities where Lincoln National Employees live and work – art & culture, education, human services.

Lucent Technologies
http://www.lucent.com

Education & needs of communities where their employees live & work.

Mallinckrodt Community Partnership Program
http://www.mallinckrodt.com

Communities where they have facilities – philanthropic efforts that enhance the quality of life.

McDonald's Corporation
http://www.mcdonalds.com/community

Help children – health & medical research, education, & social responsibility, includes Ronald McDonald Houses.

MCI Communications Corporation
http://www.wcom.com/marcopolo

Education technology programs (note: not reviewing proposals at this time.)

McKesson Corporation
http://www.mckesson.com

San Francisco Bay Area – Youth, health, human services, culture and the arts.

Medtronic Foundation
http://www.medtronic.com/foundation

Health, education & community in areas where they have facilities.

Merrill Lynch & Co., Inc.
http://www.ml.com/wou_l/phil

New York metro area & national organizations – major colleges & universities, cultural arts, environmental, human services, health, & civic organizations.

Metropolitan Life Foundation
http://www.metlife.com/companyinfo

Educational, health and welfare, civic and cultural activities in communities which Metlife has a major presence.

Micron Technology, Inc.
http://www.micron.com

Only in Idaho & Utah – education and nonprofits.

Microsoft Corporation
http://www.microsoft.com/giving

Pudget Sound & National Initiatives – education, community support, software donations.

Millipore Foundation
http://www.millipore.com/corporate/foundation

Education & research, social development, public policy, community & employee relations – in communities where the company resides.

Minnesota Mining & Manufacturing Co.
http://www.mmm.com/profile/community

Higher education in science, technology & business, health & human services, arts, civic & community initiatives.

Mitsubishi Electric America Foundation
http://www.meaf.org

Helping young people with disabilities through technology, to maximize their potential and participation in society.

Monsanto Fund
http://www.mousanto.com

Science education, environment, young people in inner cities, health & wellness.

J.P. Morgan & Co., Inc.
http://www.jpmorgan.com/corpinfo

Arts, education, environment, health & human services, international & urban affairs.

Morton International, Inc.
http://www.morton.com/comm/

Chicago, Illinois area.

Nalco Foundation
http://www.nalco.com/about

Non-profits services for education, community & civic affairs, health & cultural & arts – in company areas.

NEC Foundations of America
http://www.nec.com/company/foundation

Organizations & programs of national reach & impact in science & technology education or technology to assist people with disabilities.

New England Financial
http://www.nefn.com/content/aboutus

Boston, Massachusetts area non-profits.

Newport News Shipbuilding
http://www.nns.com/overview

In Virginia, educational, cultural arts, civic & health, human services organizations.

Owens-Corning Foundations Inc.
http://www.owenscorning.com/owens

Education, fine & performing arts, habitat for humanity.

Oxford Health Plans Foundation
http://www.oxhpfoundation.org

Health research.

Pacific Bell Foundation
http://www.sbc.com

Education, arts & culture, community, United Way.

Pacific Gas & Electric Company
http://www.pge.com/aboutus/community

Northern & Central California – employment program training.

J.C. Penny Company
http://www.jcpennyinc.com

Health & welfare, education, civic betterment, arts & culture.

Pentair Foundation
http://www.penair.com/profile/contribution

Communities in which Pentair operates – education & community.

Pfizer Inc.
http://www.pfizer.com/pfizerinc/philanthropy

Health care, education, community & cultural affairs.

Pillsbury Company Foundation
http://www.pillsbury.com/community/foundation

In Pillsbury communities – caring adults and kids & skills for self-sufficiency.

Piper Jaffray Companies
http://www.piperjaffray.com

Communities where they live and work – civic & nonprofit organizations.

Polaroid Foundation
http://www.polaroid.com/polinfo/foundation

Massachusetts communities – disadvantaged children & adults, develop measurable skills.

Proctor & Gamble Fund
http://www.pg.com/docCommunity

Prudential Insurance Co.
http://www.prudential.com/community

Prudential communities – community resources.

Raytheon Company
http://www.raytheon.com

Info only – Defense Products & Services.

Reynolds & Reynolds Company Foundation
http://www.reyrey.com/about

Dayton & Celina, Ohio – arts & culture, education K-12, community betterment, health & human services.

Rite Aid Corporation
http://www.riteaid.com/community

In Rite Aid Drugstore communities – health & medical, social service, education, arts, civic services.

Rockwell International Corporation Trust
http://www.rockwell.com/commaffairs

Education, culture & arts, civic, health & human services – in Rockwell Communities.

Sara Lee Foundation
http://www.saraleefoundation.org

Nonprofit organization in the Chicago, Illinois area.

SBC Foundation
http://www.sbc.com/foundation

Arkansas, California, Kansas, Missouri, Nevada, Oklahoma, Texas – education, community economic development, health & human services (primarily United Way), and cultural and arts.

Sega Foundation
http://www.sega.com/cenral/foundation

Not accepting any unsolicited requests through March 31, 1999.

SmithKline Beecham
http://www.sb.com/company/community

Healthcare issues, local community partnership in our communities.

Sonoco Products Company
http://www.sonoco.com/grant

Education, health & welfare, arts & culture, and the environment – in communities where Sonoco has operations.

Southwire Company
http://www.southwire.com/community

Education & grass roots programs in our communities.

Sprint Corporation
www3.spring.com/overview/community

Education, arts & culture, community improvement, youth development – in those communities in which the corporation has a major presence.

State Farm Companies Foundation
www2.statefarm.com/foundation

Higher education & limited grants to community, human service, and health agencies in locations with large State Farm employee populations.

Sun Microsystems
http://www.sun.com/corporateoverview

Southern San Francisco Bay Area & Merrimack Valley in Mass.

Tesoro Foundation
http://www.tesoropetroleum.com/community

Tesoro in Hawaii – community, education, & environment.

Texaco Foundation
http://www.texaco.com/corporate/foundation

Highest programs that prepare children for the study of math & science.

Texas Instruments Foundation
http://www.ti.com/corp/docs.company

Education & research institutions engaged in advancing knowledge and to organizations & projects in communities where TI has major facilities.

Textron Charitable Contributions Program
http://www.textron.com/profile/community

360 Communications
http://www.360.com/cc

In communities in which they operate – community organizations & projects.

Toshiba America Foundation
http://www.toshiba.com

Science & math education.

Toyota USA Foundation
http://www.toyota.com

K-12 math & science education.

TRW Foundation
http://www.trw.com/foundation

United Airlines Foundation
http://www.ual.com

Education & careers, health – cities where we do business.

United Technologies
http://www.utc.com

Civic, culture, education, health & human services, international programs.

United Missouri Bancshares Foundation
http://www.umb.com/smb/community

Missouri, Kansas.

U.S. Bank
http://www.usbank.com/communityrelations

U.S. West Foundation
http://www.usx.com/grant

Arts & culture, civic & community improvement, education,
& human services.

USX Foundation
http://www.usx.com/grant

Education, health & human services, and public, cultural and scientific affairs.

Wal-Mart Foundation
http://www.wal-mart.com/community

Children, education, community.

Wells Fargo & Company
http://www.wellsfargo.com/cra.contrib

Community development, pre & k-12, education, human services, benefit low & moderate income individuals.

Westinghouse Foundation
http://www.westinghous.com/corp

Weyerhauser Company Foundation
http://www.weyerhaeuser.com/who/foundation

Whirlpool Foundation
http://www.whirlpoolcorp.com/ics/foundation

Women & family life issues.

Williams Companies Foundations Inc.
http://www.twc.com

In towns & cities where we live & work – United Way, Project Jason.

Wisconsin Power and Light Foundation
http://www.wpi.com/ewpl/who/foundation

Health, education, cultural & community development activities that will benefit the citizens of the communities we serve.

Xerox Foundation
http://www.xerox.com/community

Zeneca
http://www.zeneca.com
Charitable, educational, & environment initiatives which help promote understandings of Zeneca and benefit Zeneca's local communities.

LINKS TO GOVERNMENT SERVERS
AND INFORMATION

U.S. Senate: www.senate.gov/
From this site you can find all senators and e-mail them directly.

U.S. House of Representatives: www.house.gov/
From this site you can find all congresspeople and e-mail them directly.

White House: www.whitehouse.gov/WH/Welcone
This is a handy page and has links to other parts of the executive branch.

The Congressional Internet Caucus: www.netcaucas.org Those in Congress who should have the most interest and knowledge of the net.

To write a senator or representative you can go to the EFF web page: www.eff.org/congress/ where you can generate e-mails directly or find out who is your representative if you know your address and zip code.

Govbot The University of Massachusetts has a service which lets you search many government data bases: www.ciir2.cs.umass.edu/govbot. This has a fairly sophisticated search engine and can be very helpful.

THE PROPOSAL ELEMENTS OF A GRANT PROPOSAL

A proposal must convince the prospective donor of two things:

1. That a problem need of significant magnitude exists, and

2. That the applicant agency has the means and the imagination to solve the problem or meet the need.

When no specific format or guidance is given by the funding source, it is safe to generally assume that the proposal should be no more than 15 pages in length (single-spaced) and should include the following sections:

- Qualifications of the Organization

- Problem Statement of Needs Assessment

- Program Goals and Objectives

- Methodology

- Evaluation

- Future Funding

- Budget

- Appendices

Letter of Inquiry/Intent

Some foundations/corporations prefer a letter of inquiry to determine whether the applicant falls within the foundation's guidelines. In this case, an inquiry letter is used instead of a cover letter and proposal. It is very succinct, and attachments are not included. If the funder determines that your request falls within their guidelines the organization will be directed to submit a complete proposal. If not, a decline letter is usually issued at that time. A letter of inquiry should meet the following criteria:

- Includes funder's name, title, and address

- Is directed to the individual responsible for the funding program

- Provides a brief overview of the organization and its purpose

- Includes the reason for the funding request

- Includes the amount requested (if required by funder)

- Describes the need the project intends to meet (including target population, statistics, example)

- Provides a brief description of the project

- Includes a thank you and next step to be taken
- Does not exceed two pages (one page is recommended)
- Includes name and phone number of contact at the organization
- Is signed by the person who can speak with authority on behalf of the organization

FULL PROPOSAL

Cover Letter

The cover letter serves as the organization's introduction and should always accompany a proposal. A cover letter should meet the following criteria:

- Includes funders name, title, and address
- Is directed at the individual responsible for the funding program (is not addressed "To Whom It May Concern", "Dear Sirs", etc.)
- Provides a brief overview of the organization and its purpose
- Includes the amount requested (if required by funder)
- Does not exceed two pages (one page is recommended)
- Includes name and phone number of contact at the organization
- Is signed by the person who can speak with authority on behalf of the organization

Summary (1/2 page)

This section clearly and concisely summarizes the request. It should provide the reader with a framework that will help him/her visualize the project. The remainder of the proposal will then serve to deepen and amplify the "vision" presented in the summary section at the beginning. A summary should meet the following criteria:

- Appears at the beginning of the proposal
- Identifies the grant applicant
- Includes at least one sentence on credibility
- Includes at least one sentence on problem
- Includes at least one sentence on objectives
- Includes at least one sentence on methods
- Includes total cost, funds already obtained and amount requested in this proposal
- Is brief (limited to several paragraphs, half page at most)
- Is clear
- Is interesting

Qualifications of the Organization (1-2 pages)

This section describes the applicant agency and its qualifications to receive funding and establishes its credibility. The programs and accomplishments of the organization will be examined in light of how they address current demographics, social issues, specific constituencies, etc. In addition to convincing the funder of the extent of the need for the proposed project, the agency must also demonstrate that theirs is the appropriate agency to conduct the project. In this section, the organization should demonstrate that it has the means and the imagination to solve the particular problem or meet the need.

A proposal will often sink or swim based on the need for the project and the project methodology, not on the accomplishments of the overall organization. Therefore, an agency should not make the mistake of devoting half of its proposal to the history or programs of the agency.

The proposal should address the projects and programs the organization intends to undertake over the next twelve to fifteen months. If growth is projected in the program, anticipated goals should be stated, as should any new projects to be undertaken. If a detailed program description or annual report exists, it should be included as the first item in the proposal appendices. The qualifications of the organization section should meet the following criteria:

- Clearly establishes who is applying for funds

- Briefly addresses the rationale for the founding of the organization

- Describes applicant agency's purposes and long-range goals

- Describes applicant's current programs and activities

- Describes applicant's client or constituents

- Provides evidence of the applicant's accomplishments

- Offers statistical support of accomplishments

- Offers quotes/endorsements in support of accomplishments

- Supports qualifications in area of activity in which funds are sought (e.g. research, training)

- Describes qualifications of key staff members

- Provides other evidence of administrative competence

- Leads logically to the problem statement

- Is as brief as possible

- Is interesting

Problem Statement or Needs Assessment (3-4 pages)

When seeking funds, a specific problem area or need should be addressed. This is a critically important section of the proposal. Information based on objective research, not subjective impressions, should be provided to justify the need or problem. This data, however, should not be voluminous, but sufficient to demonstrate that a problem or need exists. A problem statement or needs assessment should meet the following criteria:

- Describes the target population to be served
- Defines the community problem to be addressed and the need in the geographical area where the organization operates
- Is related to the purposes and goals of the applicant agency
- Is of reasonable dimensions – not trying to solve all the problems of the world
- Is supported by relevant statistical evidence
- Is supported by statements from the authorities
- Is stated in terms of clients' needs and problems – not the applicant's
- Is developed with input from clients and beneficiaries
- Makes no unsupported assumptions
- Is as brief as possible
- Is interesting to read
- Is free of jargon
- Makes a compelling case

Program Goals and Objectives (1-2 pages)

This section of the proposal describes the outcomes of the grant in measurable terms. It is a succinct description of what the organization hopes to accomplish. In this section be sure to clarify the following:

- At least one objective for each problem or need committed to in the problem statement
- Your objectives are outcomes and not just methods
- The population that will benefit from the program
- The time by which objectives will be accomplished
- Your objectives will be measurable and quantifiable (if at all possible)

ELEMENTS

There are at least seven elements to include in your explanation of how you will meet the need.

1. Behavioral – At the end of the program a measurable change in behavior is expected.

Example: Children/youth will learn conflict resolution.

2. *Performance* – A behavior or learned skill will occur, at an expected proficiency level, within a specific time.

Example: Fifty of the seventy children will learn to swim within six months and will pass a basic swimming proficiency test administered by a Red Cross-certified lifeguard.

3. *Process* – The manner in which something occurs is an end in itself.

Example: We will document the teaching methods utilized, identifying those with the greatest success.

4. *Product* – A tangible item results.

Example: A manual will be created to be used in teaching swimming to this age and proficiency group in the future.

5. *Methodology* **(4+Pages)**

This section describes the activities to be conducted to achieve the desired objectives. It also includes the rationale for choosing a particular approach. Generally, a straightforward, chronological description of the operations of the proposed project works most effectively. The methodology section should meet the following criteria:

- Flow naturally from problems to objectives
- Clearly describe program activities
- State reasons for the selection of activities
- Describe staffing of program
- Describe clients and client selection
- Present a reasonable scope of activities that can be accomplished within the time and with the resources of the program
- Provide a timeline of activities (if possible)

6. *Evaluation* **(1 – 2 Pages)**

Proposals must include a plan for determining the degree to which objectives are met and methods are followed. This section is extremely important as funders pay particular attention to evaluation methods since they need help determining whether a proposed project represents an intelligent investment for them. The evaluation section should meet the following criteria:

- Present a plan for evaluating accomplishment of objectives
- Present a plan for evaluating and modifying methods over the course of the program
- Tell who will be doing the evaluation and how they were chosen
- Clearly state evaluation criteria

- Describe how data will be gathered

- Explain any test instruments or questionnaires to be used

- Describe the process of data analysis

- Show how evaluation will be used for program improvements

- Describe any evaluation reports to be produced

Future Funding (1/2 **page**)

This section describes a plan for continuation beyond the grant and/or the availability of other resources necessary to implement the grant. In equipment/capital requests, many funders require organizations to demonstrate how the on-going cost of operations and equipment maintenance will be met. A statement about future funding sources is also advisable for the maintenance equipment. The section on future funding should meet the following criteria:

- Present a plan for evaluating accomplishment of objectives

- Present a plan for evaluating and modifying methods over the course the program

- Tell who will be doing the evaluation and how they were chosen

- Clearly state evaluation criteria

- Describe how data will be gathered

- Explain any test instruments or questionnaires to be used

- Describe the process of data analysis

- Show how evaluation will be used for program improvements

- Describe any evaluation reports to be produced

Budget

All proposals should include a budget which clearly delineates costs to be met by the funding source and those provided by other parties and outlines both *administrative* and *program* costs. If a proposal is for a specific project, separate budgets for the general operating budget and the special project budget should be included. Budgets should show income as well as expenses and should be structured in columnar form, listing the expense on the left and the dollar amount in the right column, according to general accounting/bookkeeping principles. Budgets should not be submitted in narrative form.

Budget expense information should delineate personnel costs such as salary and benefit information, and non-personnel expenses such as facility costs (rent/mortgage, utilities, maintenance, taxes), fundraising expenses, travel, postage, equipment costs, supplies, and insurance. These should be reflected in both the expense and income columns.

Sources of income should be listed separately as part of budget information. Sources should be actual funders, not merely prospects. However, pending proposals may be listed separately, if desired. Sources for funding may include fees for service, government funds, corporate/private grants, individual donations, etc. A budget should meet the following criteria:

- Tell the same story as the proposal narrative
- Is detailed in all aspects
- Includes project costs that will be incurred at the time of the program's implementation
- Contain no unexplained amounts for miscellaneous or contingency
- Include all items asked of the funding source
- Include all items paid for by other sources
- Include all volunteers
- Include all consultants
- Detail fringe benefits, separate from salaries
- Separately detail all non-personnel costs
- Include separate columns for listing all donated services
- Include indirect costs where appropriate
- Is sufficient to pay for the tasks described in the narrative

Appendices

Some attachments are recommended in all proposals, while others may be included at the author's discretion. If a recent article or endorsement has been written about your organization, and if it is germane, it may be included as an attachment to the proposal. Generally funders will look at only one or two articles/endorsements. Therefore, your organization must carefully select the best recent article/endorsement to submit. Additional attachments can be included at the author's discretion. Appendices may include:

- Verification of tax-exempt status (generally the IRS determination letter)
- Names and affiliation of officers and Board of Directors members
- Financial statements for last completed fiscal year (audited, if available)
- Current general operating budget and special project budget (if applicable)
- Lists of clients served (if appropriate)
- List of other current funding sources
- Biographies of key personnel (only if requested)
- Article/endorsements (no more than two)
- Diagrams for equipment or building requests
- Organization's by-laws

Format and Appearance

There are different forms and formats for proposals. Sometimes these formats are at the author's discretion. However, the author should research the prospective funding source to know the funder's usual requirement.

Funders often have specific requirements for the format of the proposal they will consider. It is the responsibility of the organization to submit the proposal in the required form, if there is one. Some funders issue specific grant applications which organizations must submit as the proposal. These are typically discussed in the funder's published guidelines or in research directories. A proposal should always be concise, no more than 15 pages single-spaced. (Consider the page length indicated after each section the recommended <u>maximum</u> length.)

In addition to the contents of the proposal, its appearance is important. Foremost, a proposal should be presented neatly. The cover letter should be typed on the nonprofit organization's letterhead, followed by the proposal and attachments, respectively. Since proposals are not voluminous, it is not necessary to include an index or table of contents.

Proposals should not be submitted with binding (like a book), as funders often dismantle the proposal to make copies of it when referring it to a review committee for consideration. To assemble a proposal, an organization should consider using staples or a folder to contain the proposal and attachments. Funders do not judge a proposal on its weight, but on its contents and presentation. Thus, it is important to assemble the proposal in an organized, concise, and attractive manner.

Conclusion

In summary, a proposal should reflect planning, research and vision. The importance or research cannot be overemphasized, both in terms of the funders solicited and the types of funds requested. The appropriate format should be used, and the required attachments should be included.

The most successful proposals are those which clearly and concisely state the community's and organization's needs and are targeted to donors which fund that field, a reflection of careful planning and research.

In writing and/or evaluating a proposal , the following conclusions drawn from the University of Pennsylvania study may be useful. A study team investigated the criteria foundations and government agencies consider most important when reviewing proposals for community-based projects. They concluded that there are five factors all funders consider "highly important":

- Project purpose
- Feasibility
- Community need for the project
- Applicant accountability
- Competence

Other factors also considered important include:

- Project logic
- Probable impact
- Language
- Money needed
- Community support

Although there is some disagreement about the factors which are considered unimportant, funders generally agreed that the least important factors in assessing a proposal are:

- Working relationships
- Advocates
- Minority status
- Social acceptability
- Prior funding
- Influence of acquaintances

▲

Session Topic: _____

Presenter: _____

Date: _____ / _____ / _____

<u>NOTES</u>

_____

_____

_____

_____

_____

_____

_____

_____

_____

_____

_____

_____

_____

_____

_____

_____

_____

_____

_____

_____

_____

_____

_____

_____

_____

_____

_____

_____

_____

▲

IDEAS TO TAKE WITH YOU

_____
_____
_____
_____
_____
_____
_____
_____
_____
_____
_____
_____
_____
_____
_____
_____
_____
_____
_____
_____

BOOKS AND OTHER MATERIALS

_____
_____
_____
_____
_____
_____
_____
_____

▲

Session Topic: _____

Presenter: _____

Date: _____ /_____ /_____

<u>**NOTES**</u>

_____

_____

_____

_____

_____

_____

_____

_____

_____

_____

_____

_____

_____

_____

_____

_____

_____

_____

_____

_____

_____

_____

_____

_____

_____

_____

_____

_____

▲

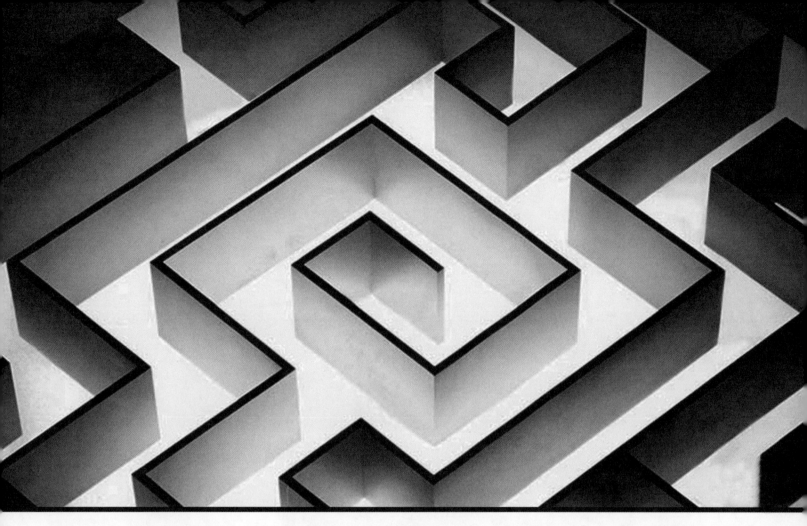

CHURCH STRATEGIES
for the 21st century

Starting A Business

The purpose of this segment is to help the administrator or lay person to assist members in the church who may be interested in going into business. This segment will help the potential entrepreneur answer the important questions that need to be addressed in order to make the right decision. "Is having my own business for me?" Owning a business is the dream of many people. Converting that dream into reality calls for careful planning. As a business owner, one has to plan to avoid drastic mistakes. If you are working with potential entrepreneurs, have the individuals take some of the worksheets home and answer each question thoroughly. The response should be typed and well written.

Listed below are guidelines that can help you develop a comprehensive business plan.
Make copies of the worksheets and let the potential entrepreneur fill out all the forms and return them to you for discussion. There are also discussion sheets which will aid in thinking through the business process. This is a starting point to help a church member make an educated decision.

There are many reasons for a person to go into business Listed below are some of the most common reasons *not* to go into business.

- **"We are not making ends meet."**
- **"The kids need braces."**
- **"We need money to save for college."**
- **"I'm tired of working for someone else."**
- **"I want to stay home with my family."**

All of the above reasons are legitimate, but the future entrepreneur must realize that a business takes time to grow. One must plan to invest a tremendous amount of time, and in some cases large amounts of money.

Operating a successful small business will depend on:

1. A practical plan with a solid foundation.

2. Dedication and willingness to sacrifice to reach your goal.

3. Technical skills.

4. Knowledge of management, finance, record keeping and market analysis.

WHY DO YOU WANT TO GO INTO BUSINESS?

Introspection is important and you need to ask the "why" question. Check the reasons that apply to you.

- ☐ I want freedom from a 9-to-5 job.

- ☐ I want to be my own boss.

- ☐ I want to do what I want to do, when I want to do it!

- ☐ I want to improve my standard of living.

- ☐ I am bored with my job.

One must understand that there are tradeoffs. You may quit your 9 to 5 job but end up working 6am to 9pm six days a week.

SELF–EXAMINATION # 1

Going into business requires self-examination; a business owner must have certain personal characteristics. Review the information below. These questions require serious thought, so try to be objective.

Personal Characteristics (answer each question yes or no)

Are you a leader? ☐ yes ☐ no

Do you like to make your own decisions? ☐ yes ☐ no

Do others turn to you for help in making decisions? ☐ yes ☐ no

Do you enjoy competition? ☐ yes ☐ no

Do you have willpower and self-discipline? ☐ yes ☐ no

Do you plan ahead? ☐ yes ☐ no

Do you like people? ☐ yes ☐ no

Do you get along well with others? ☐ yes ☐ no

SELF – EXAMINATION # 2

Please answer the following questions to assess your business skills in more detail

Do you like being around people? ☐ Yes   ☐ No   ☐ Sometimes

Do you have difficulty putting in long hours? ☐ Yes   ☐ No

Do you work well alone? ☐ Yes   ☐ No   ☐ Most of the time

Do you enjoy giving presentations? ☐ Yes   ☐ No

Do you get upset easily when things don't go your way? ☐ Yes   ☐ No   ☐ Sometimes

Do you understand what you want from your business? ☐ Yes   ☐ No   ☐ Not clear yet

Do you have physical limitations or an illness? ☐ Yes   ☐ No

Do you like to travel? ☐ Yes   ☐ No

Do you have difficulty with your personal finances? ☐ Yes   ☐ No   ☐ Being addressed

Do you have a good plan to market your business? ☐ Yes   ☐ No   ☐ I need help in this area

Will you have a partner? ☐ Yes   ☐ No

Can you deal with rejection? ☐ Yes   ☐ No   ☐ Sometimes

Are you in need of money personally now? ☐ Yes   ☐ No   ☐ It would be helpful

Do you enjoy talking to strangers? ☐ Yes   ☐ No

Turn to the next page for results

▲

SELF – EXAMINATION # 2 ANSWER SHEET

Do you like being around people? [X] Yes   [ ] No   [ ] Sometimes

Do you have difficulty putting in long hours? [ ] Yes   [X] No

Do you work well alone? [X] Yes   [ ] No   [ ] Most of the time

Do you enjoy giving presentations? [X] Yes   [ ] No

Do you get upset easily when things don't go your way? [ ] Yes   [X] No   [ ] Sometimes

Do you understand what you want from your business? [X] Yes   [ ] No   [ ] Not clear yet

Do you have physical limitations or illness? [ ] Yes   [X] No

Do you like to travel? [X] Yes   [ ] No

Do you have difficulty with your personal finances? [ ] Yes   [X] No   [ ] Being addressed

Do you have a good plan to market your business? [X] Yes [ ] No [ ] I need help in this area

Will you have a partner? [X] Yes   [X] No

Can you deal with rejection? [X] Yes   [ ] No   [ ] Sometimes

Are you in need of money personally now? [ ] Yes   [X] No   [ ] It would be helpful

Do you enjoy talking to strangers? [X] Yes   [ ] No

▲

The above answers are the ideal. If you answer more than 4 questions differently, you should reevaluate whether or not you are ready to go into business for yourself. Review those four questions. List additional reasons below why you want to be in business.

_____

_____

_____

_____

_____

_____

_____

_____

_____

_____

_____

_____

_____

_____

_____

_____

_____

_____

_____

_____

_____

_____

_____

_____

_____

▲

YOUR PERSONAL CONDITIONS

This next group of questions, though brief, is very important to the success of your business plan. It covers the physical, emotional and financial strains you will encounter in starting a new business.

- Are you aware that running your own business may require working 10 to 16 hours a day, six days a week, maybe even Sundays and holidays? ☐ Yes ☐ No

- Do you have the physical stamina to handle the workload and schedule? ☐ Yes ☐ No

- Do you have the emotional strength to withstand the strain? ☐ Yes ☐ No

- Are you prepared, if needed, to temporarily lower your standard of living until your business gets on its feet? ☐ Yes ☐ No

- Are you prepared to lose your savings? ☐ Yes ☐ No

Write a paragraph on one of the questions above that you feel is most important and needs more consideration

_____

_____

_____

_____

_____

_____

_____

_____

_____

_____

_____

_____

_____

_____

_____

▲

YOUR SKILLS AND EXPERIENCE

There are particular skills and experiences that are essential to the success of a business. In most cases one who opens a business usually lacks many of the skills needed to be successful. It is important to know what skill-sets one possesses and what skills are needed to get the job done. The skills inventory below will help you evaluate what skills you have and those that need reinforcing.

- What basic skills do you need in order to have a successful business?

- Do you possess those skills?

- Have you ever worked in any type of supervisory position?

- Have you ever worked in a business similar to the one you want to start?

- Have you ever had any business training in college or high school?

- If you find out that you lack the skills needed for the business, are you willing to wait until you have developed those skills? – This question will be most difficult especially for those who have already made up their mind.

If you answered "yes" to any question, that's good. But if you answered "no" to any question, you may have a difficult time.

FINDING THE RIGHT NICHE

A tremendous amount of time and money will be spent starting the business. If there is no real niche, success will not be attainable. It would be like selling water skis in the desert. Do you have a good idea? To help you find out, answer the questions below.

- Can you describe in detail the business you plan to start?

- What are you planning to sell? A product or service? Describe.

- Does the product or service satisfy an unfulfilled need in the community?

- Is there a high demand for your product or service? How do you know?

- Will your product or service be price competitive?

If you answered "yes" to any question, that's good. But if you answered "no" to any question, you may have a difficult time.

IS THERE A MARKET FOR THE BUSINESS?

"The market" basically means what type of people will buy your product or service -- the age, gender, where they live, when will they buy, what are their buying habits, etc. The questions below will help with these issues.

- Do you know who your customers are?

- What do they want?

- Where are they located in town?

- Are you selling a product or service that people will purchase?

- Based on the competition, will your prices be competitive?

- What type of advertising and promotion is planned?

- How will your business compare with the competition?

- Where will the business be located -- what part of town? Will your market niche be reachable from your location?

- Will you need lots of parking space?

PREPARING FOR LAUNCHING OF YOUR NEW BUSINESS

- What will be the name of the business?
  Make sure the business name describes what you do, but doesn't limit you if other services are added. For example, if the business is called Classic Cakes, one would assume that all you do is cakes, when in reality it caters banquets as well.

- Will your business be a sole proprietorship, partnership, or corporation?
  You will need to consult an attorney to address this question.

- Do you know what local or state laws you will have to be in compliance with?

- Do you have a lawyer?

- Are there any occupational or safety requirements?

- Will you be able to have a large sign or will local ordinances prohibit it?

- Are there tax breaks for start-up businesses?

- If you are hiring staff, what are the Workmen's Compensation issues?

Risk management is an essential part of a running a business. The issues that need to be addressed in this area are:

- Accident liability

- Vandalism

- Robbery

- Theft

- Fire

- Workmen's Compensation

- Key-man insurance

- Inventory insurance

LOCATION, LOCATION, LOCATION

- Have you found an acceptable location? Will your customers be able to reach you easily?
- Can the location you are renting be remodeled to fit your needs at a reasonable cost?
- Has a lawyer checked the zoning regulations?
- Is renting or leasing a better option with an option to purchase later on?

BUSINESS LOCATION EVAUATION SHEET

"A" for excellent, "B" for good, "C" for fair, and "D" for poor

The location is centrally located to reach my market. ☐ A ☐ B ☐ C ☐ D

The building physically suits what I need. ☐ A ☐ B ☐ C ☐ D

The lease is within my range. ☐ A ☐ B ☐ C ☐ D

The location has room to grow if needed. ☐ A ☐ B ☐ C ☐ D

Overall estimate of quality of site in 5 to 10 years. ☐ A ☐ B ☐ C ☐ D

The location has suitable utilities -- sewer, water, power, gas. ☐ A ☐ B ☐ C ☐ D

There is adequate parking now and as the business grows. ☐ A ☐ B ☐ C ☐ D

Public transportation is near the location. ☐ A ☐ B ☐ C ☐ D

Competition is nearby which can help draw customers to the location. ☐ A ☐ B ☐ C ☐ D

The traffic flow is beneficial. ☐ A ☐ B ☐ C ☐ D

Taxation burden. ☐ A ☐ B ☐ C ☐ D

Quality police and fire protection. ☐ A ☐ B ☐ C ☐ D

The community is healthy -- schools, community activities, business people other healthy businesses. ☐ A ☐ B ☐ C ☐ D

Quality and quantity of available employees. ☐ A ☐ B ☐ C ☐ D

Quality of businesses nearby. ☐ A ☐ B ☐ C ☐ D

Adequate delivery areas. ☐ A ☐ B ☐ C ☐ D

Heating and air in the building are operational. ☐ A   ☐ B   ☐ C   ☐ D

Good visibility. ☐ A   ☐ B   ☐ C   ☐ D

Adequate signage. ☐ A   ☐ B   ☐ C   ☐ D

WHAT ARE YOU GOING TO SELL?

When considering the product you will sell, make sure that your local distributor explains to you what sells and what does not. A grave mistake can be made if you only pick out the products that you like. What you like and what sells are two different issues. Be prepared to sell inventory that is slow to move by putting it "on sale at ___% off." The following should also be kept in mind.

- Have you decided how much merchandise needs to be purchased? How much will you sell per week, per month?

- Will your supplier help you with the start-up purchase?

- Will the supplier give you at least 30 to 40% discount on your merchandise?

GETTING THE CAPITAL

- How much money do you have personally to contribute to the business?

- How much money do you need from the bank?

- How much money can you borrow from friends or relatives?

- How much money do you need to stay in business for at least six months without making a red cent?

START-UP EXPENSES

DESCRIPTION	COST	TIME LINE
Installation of fixtures	$	
Supplies		
Inventory		
Attorneys fees		
Utility deposit		
Telephone deposit		
Rent deposit		
Insurance		
Advertising		
Signs		
Wages		
Taxes		
Remolding		
Fixtures		
TOTAL COST		

HOW MUCH WILL IT COST TO OPERATE FOR THE FIRST MONTH?

When the doors open, you should start making money. But in order to run your business you will have operating expenses. Listed below are some of the fixed and variable expenses that are part of the operating cost.

- Your salary
- Wages for staff
- Rent
- Utilities
- Supplies
- Insurance
- Taxes
- Gas

List other expenses that you think may arise

DESCRIPTION	$

Now take the total of all the expenses for the month and multiply by 3 months or 6 months. Take that amount of money, and put it in a short-term interest-bearing instrument. Use the money for those expenses listed above if you have a short fall for a particular month. Businesses that don't do this often end up closing their doors soon after they open.

By adding the total "start-up expenses" to the total "operating expenses" for 3 or 6 months you can get a good idea of what the estimated costs will be to start and operate your business for 3 to 6 months. By subtracting the totals of the charts from what cash you have available, you can determine how much additional money you will need to borrow or secure from some other source.

SELL, SELL, SELL

The primary source of money in your business will be in the form of sales of your product or service. Based on what you are selling, there will be times of the year when sales will be lower than others. You need to be able to project what your "cash flow" will be which is dependent on how much cash comes in and what your expenses are. Careful planning and budgeting will keep you from getting behind.

There are many mistakes that are made which adversely affect cash flow. Four of the most common are:

1. Withdrawal of large amounts of business funds for personal use.
2. Carrying non-paying customers for long periods of time.
3. Growing too fast - overextending.
4. Poor planning for slow or down time.

Use the following space to outline your plans to keep your cash flow even.

_____

BUSINESS MISTAKES

- **Getting locked in on an idea and sticking with it too long.**
  The worst thing that an entrepreneur can do is hold on to an idea too long. You end up beating a dead horse, and in the end losing a tremendous amount of money. A smart entrepreneur keeps a portfolio of ideas going and whatever makes money, that's the one you spend your time on.

- **Being something else.**
  If you are an entrepreneur, that's what you should be. Your greatest asset is who you are.

- **Believing your own hype.**
  Entrepreneurs are usually optimistic. Keep your optimism in focus, becoming too overly optimistic can cause you to make mistakes. Stay optimistic with a touch of reality.

- **Attract smart people.**
  Do not hire people to work for you that are not smarter than you.

- **Pushing too hard.**
  If you find yourself trying to sell what no one wants to buy, start listening to why your potential customers do not want to buy what you're selling.

- **Get help.**
  Get skilled people who can support you. Your time should be used in building your business and not the everyday details of running the office.

- **Don't give up.**
  Failure will happen and, in most cases, it does several times. If you fail ...so what? Don't give up. Try again until you win. DON'T GIVE UP.

▲

▲

ANSWER THE FOLLOWING QUESTIONS IN DETAIL BELOW

WHO

Are you going to work alone? With a friend or relative? Do you have all the knowledge needed to work alone?

_____

_____

_____

WHAT

What type of business is it? Do you have the knowledge needed?

_____

_____

_____

_____

WHERE

Are you going to rent a store, or will it be a home-based business, franchise, or partnership?

_____

_____

_____

_____

WHEN

Is this business season related? Is this the best time to open your business? Who else has the same type of business?

_____

_____

_____

_____

HOW

How will you financially get started? Bank loan? Borrow money from relatives? Savings? Do you have enough money to take you through at least six months?

_____

_____

_____

_____

▲

DISCUSSION SHEET
THE NEXT STEP – PART 1

It is very important that you investigate the type of business you're considering. Does the business fit your personality and the amount of time that you can invest? The following questions need to be answered as you move to the next step.

- **Is there a niche?**
  Is there a market for the business? For example, if there are five hair salons in a three- block radius there really is no new niche for your business. On the other hand, there may not be five salons in a three-block radius but the female population may be limited; therefore, there really is still no market for your business.

- **How much money can you make?**
  One of the primary objectives for being in business is to make a profit. Preparing a business plan will help you get a good idea of how much money you will make and how much time you will have to invest to get a return.

- **Does the business have a future?**
  For many years video stores were extremely popular. You could get any type of movie you wished. Technology has changed the way the public views movies. You can now receive some 500 channels via digital cable TV in your home. Because of this innovation video sales at video stores have dropped. The future in buying a video store franchise is limited. Will the business you are going into be around three years from now or is it a fad?

- **Do you have to depend on other people's performance?**
  Multilevel-marketing has been touted as a "business." In the classic sense it is a business but in most cases is dependent on the down-line performance. If your down-line is weak, it affects your profits. You end up having to rally the troops, push them to sell more water filters. You end up losing down-line partners and recruiting more; it's a never-ending circle.

- **Is a large capital investment needed?**
  There is a misconception that if you invest huge dollars into a business, you'll get a huge return. There are businesses that have started on a shoestring ($1,000 or less) and have become multimillion dollar businesses. Microsoft and Bill Gates started in a small shop; Macintosh computers started in a garage space. Try to avoid investing a large amount of money in an untested business.

- **Do you believe in the business?**
  The big mistake made by many entrepreneurs is that they go into the business with the wrong motive. They want to make money; they want to be rich. Another important motive for going into business should be to provide quality service and provide a quality product. If those two elements are provided the money will come.

DISCUSSION SHEET CONTINUED

• **Your spouse**

Does your spouse want to go into business? Is your spouse willing to take the risk with you? If your wife or husband is really against going into business, this could create a tremendous problem. As the money problems occur from time to time and the work hours increase, it can add undue stress on the family. One approach is to start as a home-based business for at least one year part-time, then consider going into full-time business.

THE NEXT STEP – PART 2

List 7 things you do best.

_____

_____

_____

_____

_____

_____

_____

List how people can benefit from what you do best.

_____

_____

_____

_____

_____

Based on the above 7 items, how can you give the customer what he or she wants.

_____

_____

_____

_____

_____

Who is the competition? Why do you think they are successful?

_____

_____

_____

_____

_____

Who do you think is a successful businessperson and why do you think he or she is successful?

_____

_____

_____

_____

_____

<u>THE NEXT STEP – PART 3</u>

Will you enjoy doing this business, will you have fun?

_____

_____

_____

_____

_____

_____

_____

_____

_____

Are there spin-offs or related businesses?

_____

_____

_____

_____

_____

_____

_____

_____

_____

_____

Are you willing to make mistakes?

_____

_____

_____

_____

_____

_____

_____

_____

_____

_____

DISCUSSION SHEET

THE NEXT STEP – PART 3

- **Do you really understand the business that you're going into?**
  This is a big problem with new entrepreneurs. Many look at the illusive money they can make, without taking into consideration whether or not they really understand the business. Not understanding the business makes you vulnerable to losing money and losing the business completely.

- **Do you understand the customer and know what he or she wants?**
  Have you done your homework? How many businesses like yours are in the area? How many have closed? How many have expanded? What type of patrons can you expect?

- **Do you know the law?**
  Are there legal constraints that should be taken under consideration, such as zoning, licensing, noise restrictions, signage, traffic, waste disposal, amount of square feet, the list goes on.

- **Added value**
  What are you offering that is better than everyone else or adds additional value to your service? What gives your products and service more "worth?"

- **What are your personal assets?**
  Skills, knowledge, experience, money, time. Write below about each one of the 5 areas and explain how they are assets.

Session Topic: _____

Presenter: _____

Date: _____ /_____ /_____

NOTES

_____

_____

_____

_____

_____

_____

_____

_____

_____

_____

_____

_____

_____

_____

_____

_____

_____

_____

_____

_____

_____

_____

_____

_____

_____

IDEAS TO TAKE WITH YOU

_____
_____
_____
_____
_____
_____
_____
_____
_____
_____
_____
_____
_____
_____
_____
_____
_____
_____
_____
_____

BOOKS AND OTHER MATERIALS

_____
_____
_____
_____
_____
_____
_____

IDEAS TO TAKE WITH YOU

_____
_____

Session Topic: _____

Presenter: _____

Date: _____ /_____ /_____

<u>NOTES</u>

_____
_____
_____
_____
_____
_____
_____
_____
_____
_____
_____
_____
_____
_____
_____
_____
_____
_____
_____
_____
_____
_____
_____
_____
_____
_____
_____
_____
_____

IDEAS TO TAKE WITH YOU

_____

_____

_____

_____

_____

_____

_____

_____

_____

_____

_____

_____

_____

_____

_____

_____

_____

_____

_____

_____

_____

_____

_____

BOOKS AND OTHER MATERIALS

_____

_____

_____

_____

_____

_____

_____

_____

CHURCH STRATEGIES
for the 21st century

Job Descriptions

POSITION TITLE: PASTOR
DEPARTMENT:
REPORT TO: Church board
STATUS: Exempt
GENERAL SUMMARY: To serve the church by providing a balanced ministry of preaching, teaching, pastoral care and organizational leadership to the congregation, and to enable the church to grow to its full potential in membership and spiritual vitality.

ESSENTIAL JOB FUNCTIONS:

1. Provide a solid Biblically-based preaching and teaching ministry to meet the needs of the congregation and attract new members.

2. Lead in worship and administer the sacraments.

3. Encourage and nurture the spiritual development and beliefs of the congregation through regular teaching of the Bible.

4. Lead and inspire the church board(s) and congregation in the development and effective operation of a wide range of program activities.

5. Recruit, motivate and train youth and adult leadership.

6. Administer the programs of the church by leading volunteers and paid staff members and conducting regular staff meetings for planning and informational purposes.

7. Provide pastoral counseling in times of crisis and minister to the sick, dying and bereaved.

8. Conduct weddings and funerals, providing appropriate preparation and support.

9. Instruct classes of new members at least twice a year.

10. Moderate the church board(s) in developing reasonable goals, communicating a clear sense of direction and equipping the leadership for ministry.

11. Develop and administer the budget and lead financial drives and giving programs as needed.

12. Work with the Personnel Committee in developing job descriptions, personnel policies and procedures and performance evaluations.

13. Represent the church by serving on appropriate committees of the denomination and organizations in the community.

14.   Schedule necessary time for study, preparation and planning in order to develop and maintain a deep level of spiritual growth.

KNOWLEDGE SKILLS AND ABILITIES:
- Leadership skills
- Preaching skills
- Ability to delegate tasks
- Mentoring skills
- Strong spiritual background

EDUCATIONAL EXPERIENCE:
- Based on churches needs

Note: The statements herein are intended to describe the general nature and level of work being performed by employees assigned to this classification. They are not intended to be construed as an exhaustive list of all responsibilities, duties and skills required of personnel so classified.

POSITION TITLE: CHURCH ADMINISTRATOR
DEPARTMENT:
REPORT TO: Senior Pastor
STATUS: Exempt
GENERAL SUMMARY: To serve the church by running the day-to-day operation of the facility; supervising all support staff members and volunteers, overseeing church finances, coordinating the scheduling and communication of programs, assist the Senior Pastor in strategic planning.

ESSENTIAL JOB FUNCTIONS:

1. Coordinate the administrative functions of the church including staffing, purchasing, budgeting, short and long term planning
   - Printing
   - Telephone operators
   - Secretarial pool
   - Purchasing supplies and equipment

2. Supervise all support staff members.

3. Develop budgets for all departments.

4. Ensure that buildings and grounds are well maintained and repairs are completed on a timely basis.

5. Maintain inventory of equipment and supplies and ensure that office equipment is well maintained and serviced.

6. Coordinate and schedule the outside use of facilities.

7. Establish and maintain the master program and facilities calendar(s) and coordinate the total program of the church.

8. Serve as a resource person on appropriate committees and boards.

9. Research new business procedures, computer techniques, financial programs and salary surveys.

10. Establish and maintain complete and up-to-date personnel files.

11. Coordinate the recruitment of volunteers, as necessary.

12. Work closely with the Pastor to plan and implement his vision for the church.

13. Attend staff meetings, retreats, and any other committee or board meetings necessary to carry out the administrative function of the church.

KNOWLEDGE SKILLS AND ABILITIES:
- Leadership skills
- Time management skills
- Able to clearly delegate
- Strong computer management background
- Public speaker
- Mentoring skills
- Team developer

EDUCATIONAL EXPERIENCE:
- Minimum 4 year degree in management
- Understand the church culture
- Some biblical training
- Management training

Note: The statements herein are intended to describe the general nature and level of work being performed by employees assigned to this classification. They are not intended to be construed as an exhaustive list of all responsibilities, duties and skills required of personnel so classified.

POSITION TITLE: PASTOR - PASTORAL CARE
DEPARTMENT:
REPORT TO: Senior Pastor, Pastor of Family Ministries
STATUS:
GENERAL SUMMARY: To serve the church by developing an effective ministry of visitation for the hospitalized and homebound of the church. Establish a caring ministry to meet the needs of senior adults and supervising staff members and volunteers involved in this ministry.

ESSENTIAL JOB FUNCTION:

1. Make regular visits to the sick, hospitalized and homebound of the church.

2. Serve communion to the sick, hospitalized and homebound.

3. Plan, develop and implement a counseling ministry that includes:
   • Training lay biblical counselors
   • Providing professional pastoral counseling for those in need
   • Referring those with deeper needs, or those requiring long-term counseling, to a counseling center.

4. Plan, develop and initiate support groups that include:
   • 12-step programs
   • Divorce recovery workshops
   • Grief groups

5. Bring seniors with common needs together to comfort and minister to each other.

6. Develop a tele-visitation program for homebound seniors.

7. Develop a strategy for effective personal communication with the congregation, including birthday cards, newsletters and follow-up calls on anniversaries of the death of loved ones and home visits to recovering hospital patients.

8. Maintain a resource list of qualified retired people who are available to give assistance to senior members in such areas as preparing wills, estate planning, banking, real estate, legal service and home repairs.

9. Assist in worship and preach at the request of the Senior Pastor.

10. Conduct weddings and funerals, providing appropriate preparation and support.

11. Work with appropriate committees, officers and leaders in carrying out the pastoral care of the church.

12. Attend staff meetings and retreats.

13. Attend board(s) meetings as a resource and for informational purposes.

14. Represent the church by serving on appropriate committees in the community.

15. Cooperate with the Senior Pastor by performing any other duties when asked to do so.

KNOWLEDGE SKILLS AND ABILITIES:
- Strong theological training
- Biblical counseling skills
- Leadership skills
- Public speaker

EDUCATION EXPERIENCE:
- At least 2-4 years of pastoral leadership
- 4 year college degree in theology

Note: The statements herein are intended to describe the general nature and level of work being performed by employees assigned to this classification. They are not intended to be construed as an exhaustive list of all responsibilities, duties and skills required of personnel so classified.

POSTION TITLE: DIRECTOR OF CHILDREN'S MINISTRIES
DEPARTMENT:
REPORT: Associate Pastor
STATUS: Exempt
GENERAL SUMMARY: To serve the church by developing a comprehensive educational ministries program for children (infant through 6th grade) in the church and the surrounding community. Supervising staff members and volunteers involved in this ministry.

ESSENTIAL JOB FUNCTION:

1. Recruit, train, coordinate and supervise the adult leaders to operate dynamic children's ministry programs, such as:
    - Teachers
    - Superintendents
    - Coordinators
    - Volunteer committee members

2. Review and select curriculum and educational tools for the Sunday school program.

3. Recruit, train, coordinate and supervise staff members of the church nursery.

4. Plan and coordinate activities, such as:
    - Backyard Bible clubs
    - Latchkey programs
    - Day care for low-income families

5. Plan and coordinate summer activities, camps and conferences for children.

7. Offer various parenting classes for families in the church and community.

9. Maintain an inventory of equipment and supplies; purchase supplies as needed.

10. Develop and maintain a children's library containing audio, video and Internet materials.

11. Work with appropriate committees, officers and leaders in carrying out the children's ministries of the church.

KNOWLEDGE SKILLS AND ABILITIES:
- Able to clearly delegate
- Child development background
- Leadership skills
- Good communication skills
- Team builder
- Knowledgeable in the area of child law

▲

▲

EDUCATIONAL EXPERIENCE:
- Church literate
- Minimum 4 year degree in child development
- Strong Biblical background

Note: The statements herein are intended to describe the general nature and level of work being performed by employees assigned to this classification. They are not intended to be construed as an exhaustive list of all responsibilities, duties and skills required of personnel so classified.

▲

POSITION TITLE: CHURCH MUSICIAN
DEPARTMENT:
REPORT TO: Director of Music Department
STATUS: Gratis
GENERAL SUMMARY: Provide professional quality, appropriate musical accompaniment for worship services and other programs.

ESSENTIAL JOB FUNCTIONS:

1. Support the Director of Music.

2. Provide appropriate music for worship services and other programs of the church.

3. Rehearse for optimum performance.

4. Accompany choirs and soloists during rehearsals, worship services and other programs.

5. Provide for authorized substitute when not able to be present.

6. Cooperate with the audio department.

KNOWLEDGE SKILLS AND ABILITIES:
- Able to read music
- Able to play a variety of music by ear
- Experience in playing before the public
- Provide your own instrument

EDUCATIONAL EXPERIENCE:
- Music studies

Note: The statements herein are intended to describe the general nature and level of work being performed by employees assigned to this classification. They are not intended to be construed as an exhaustive list of all responsibilities, duties and skills required of personnel so classified.

▲

POSITION TITLE: CUSTODIAN (Lead)
DEPARTMENT:
REPORT TO: Church administrator
STATUS: Exempt
GENERAL SUMMARY: To serve the church by providing custodial services for the total facility, including the grounds. Supervising all facilities maintenance staff.

ESSENTIAL JOB FUNCTIONS:

1.   Keep buildings clean and well maintained on the inside.

2.   Clean, vacuum, dust and empty wastebaskets in church offices and rest rooms at least twice a week.

3.   Vacuum carpets and dust sanctuary prior to weekend services.

4.   Clean nursery and rest rooms prior to weekend services.

5.   Vacuum carpets, sweep and mop floors of Sunday school rooms weekly.

6.   Clean kitchen after each event, ensuring that all equipment is clean and well maintained.

7.   Maintain inventory of paper products and cleaning supplies.

8.   Set up and clean up for weddings, funerals, receptions and other special events.

9.   Set up and tear down chairs and tables as needed.

10.   Make minor repairs to masonry, electrical system, plumbing, painting, and immediate temporary repairs in an emergency.

11.   Strip and polish floors and shampoo carpets a minimum of 4 times per year.

12.   Wash windows in heavily trafficked areas weekly and all other windows at least twice a year.

14.   Cooperate with the Senior Pastor and Church administrator by performing any other duties when asked to do so.

KNOWLEDGE SKILLS AND ABILITIES:
• Management skills
• General repair skills in:
    • Plumbing
    • Air conditioning
    • Heating

▲

- Basic carpentry
- Electrical repairs

EDUCATIONAL EXPERIENCE:
- Vocational training
- At least 2 years of maintenance experience (based on size of facility additional years may be needed.)

Note: The statements herein are intended to describe the general nature and level of work being performed by employees assigned to this classification. They are not intended to be construed as an exhaustive list of all responsibilities, duties and skills required of personnel so classified.

POSITION TITLE: CUSTODIAN (Outside)
DEPARTMENT:
REPORT TO: Custodian -lead
STATUS: Non-exempt
GENERAL SUMMARY: To serve the church by providing custodial services for the grounds and exterior areas of church buildings.

ESSENTIAL JOB FUNCTIONS:

1. Maintain landscaping by:
   - Cutting grass
   - Shoveling snow
   - Watering;
   - Pruning shrubs
   - Caring for flower beds

2. Maintain and repair sprinkler systems as needed.

3. Remove litter (paper, cans, and bottles) in parking areas and from slopes and/or banks on church property.

4. Ensure that outside lighting is working properly, replacing light bulbs as necessary.

5. Sweep or blow walkways and patio areas prior to weekend services and large mid-week events.

6. Maintain and make minor repairs to masonry, electrical system, plumbing and painting.

7. Be available to make immediate temporary repairs in an emergency.

8. Work with the Inside Custodian when necessary in setting up rooms, moving furniture, stripping floors and washing windows.

KNOWLEDGE SKILLS AND ABILITIES:
- Landscaping
- Horticulture

EDUCATIONAL EXPERIENCE:
- High school diploma

Note: The statements herein are intended to describe the general nature and level of work being performed by employees assigned to this classification. They are not intended to be construed as an exhaustive list of all responsibilities, duties and skills required of personnel so classified.

POSITION TITLE: PROGRAM/ PUBLIC RELATIONS COORDINATOR
DEPARTMENT:
REPORT TO: Pastor, Church Administrator
STATUS: Exempt, Non-exempt
GENERAL SUMMARY: To serve the church by coordinating programs and facilities of the church, and being the major information source for planning and developing publicity for the church.

ESSENTIAL JOB FUNCTION:

1. Assist staff members in facilitating the efficiency and effectiveness of church events.

2. Develop and maintain the master program and facilities calendar of the church.

3. Communicate the program of the church to the congregation by:
   • Preparing weekly bulletins
   • Editing and overseeing production of newsletters
   • Preparing the annual report
   • Developing visitor brochures
   • Coordinating with staff members in the design and production of brochures and flyers.
   • Writing press releases
   • Coordinating church mailings
   • Establishing public relations contacts with community groups, local officials and newspapers.

4. Coordinate production and sale of cassette and videotapes and other marketable materials generated by the church.

5. Arrange for appropriate facilities and sites for conferences, retreats and off-campus events.

6. Work with the Church Hostess in planning special events and receptions at the church.

7. Work with the Coordinator of Weddings in providing appropriate facilities for church weddings.

8. Function as the major information source for staff members and congregation.

9. Work with staff members and committees, assisting them in the preparation of printed materials for the congregation.

KNOWLEDGE SKILLS AND ABILITIES:
- Good writing skills
- Good communication skills
- Ability to do newsletter layouts
- Public speaking skills

EDUCATIONAL SKILLS:
- Public relations experience
- Degree in communications

Note: The statements herein are intended to describe the general nature and level of work being performed by employees assigned to this classification. They are not intended to be construed as an exhaustive list of all responsibilities, duties and skills required of personnel so classified.

POSITION TITLE: PASTOR OF COLLEGE/ YOUNG ADULTS MINISTRIES
DEPARTMENT:
REPORT TO: Senior Pastor
STATUS: Exempt
GENERALSUMMARY: To serve the church by developing, coordinating and administering an effective and comprehensive college ministry.

ESSENTIAL JOB FUNCTION:

1. Develop and implement the college ministry young adult ministry of the church, including:
    - Sunday morning adult education
    - On-campus Bible studies
    - On-campus sharing groups
    - Fellowship events
    - Music concerts (in cooperation with the music department)

2. Encourage college-age adults to develop healthy relationships with other members of the congregation in conjunction with the singles fellowship.

3. Provide support and guidance to college-age adults as they mature in their faith.

4. Disciple and nurture college-age adults to cope with life experiences such as: abstinence, relationships, career development, ministry.

5. Identify, develop and disciple college-age leaders.

6. Preach at the request of the Senior Pastor. Teach in the education program, as requested.

7. Establish departmental goals and objectives by prioritizing related programs, managing the use of facilities, planning an appropriate budget, delegating tasks and evaluating progress regularly.

8. Represent the church by serving on appropriate committees of the denomination and organizations in the community.

9. Cooperate with the Senior Pastor and Church Administrator by performing any other duties when asked to do so.

KNOWLEDGE SKILLS AND ABILITY:
- Strong Biblical background
- Biblical counseling skills
- Leadership skills
- Public speaker

EDUCATIONAL EXPERIENCE:
- 4 year degree in theology
- Christian counseling experience
- Assistant pastor background (optional)

Note: The statements herein are intended to describe the general nature and level of work being performed by employees assigned to this classification. They are not intended to be construed as an exhaustive list of all responsibilities, duties and skills required of personnel so classified.

POSITION TITLE: PASTOR OF CONGREGATIONAL CARE
DEPARTMENT:
REPORT TO: Senior Pastor
STATUS: Exempt
GENERAL SUMMARY: To serve the church by providing pastoral care to the congregation through the oversight and coordination of caring ministries of the church, and providing leadership to and supervision of staff members and volunteers involved in this ministry.

ESSENTIAL JOB FUNCTION:

1.   Develop a comprehensive pastoral care ministry by:
     • Enabling people who have the gifts of helps, hospitality and caring to identify and understand those gifts
     • Providing those people with appropriate equipping for effective use of those gifts
     • Send those that are trained into the ministry of helps

2.   Organize and develop the small group ministry of the church, training leaders, providing materials.

3.   Coordinate a discipleship ministry for Christians desiring a deeper relationship with God and their brothers and sisters, including faith development/enrichment classes.

4.   Care for the needy of the church and community who seek food and financial assistance.

5.   Assist in worship and preach at the request of the Senior Pastor. Teach in the adult education program, as requested.

6.   Provide short-term pastoral counseling to those in crisis.

7.   Develop a strategy for effective personal communication with the congregation, including birthday cards, newsletters and follow-up calls on anniversaries of the death of loved ones and home visits to recovering hospital patients.

8.   Develop, coordinate and participate in the Pastor-on-call ministry.

9.   Administer the work of the Department of Congregational Care by encouraging teamwork and mutual support and providing leadership and nurture to staff members who work in the department.

10. Attend staff meetings and retreats.

11. Cooperate with the Senior Pastor or his designate by performing any other duties when asked to do so.

KNOWLEDGE SKILLS AND ABILITY:

- Strong Biblical background
- Biblical counseling skills
- Leadership skills
- Public speaker

EDUCATIONAL EXPERIENCE:

- Former Assistant Pastor
- Christian counseling experience
- 4 year degree in theology

Note: The statements herein are intended to describe the general nature and level of work being performed by employees assigned to this classification. They are not intended to be construed as an exhaustive list of all responsibilities, duties and skills required of personnel so classified.

POSITION TITLE: PASTOR OF COUNSELING
DEPARTMENT:
REPORT TO: Senior Pastor, Pastor of Family Ministries
STATUS: Exempt
GENERAL SUMMARY: To provide Biblically-based counseling to church members..

ESSENTIAL JOB FUNCTIONS:

1. Screen clients and assign to appropriate counselors or support group.

2. Develop and maintain a counseling ministry, including:
    Providing Biblically-based counseling to those in need
    Referring those with deeper needs, to an outside professional counseling center.

3. Develop short-term counseling to church members only.

4. Provide appropriate support for the bereaved.

5. Work with appropriate committees, officers and leaders in carrying out the counseling ministry of the church.

6. Cooperate with the Pastor and his designates by performing any other duties when asked to do so.

KNOWLEDGE SKILLS AND ABILITIES:
- Strong people relationship builder
- Capable of working with diverse groups of people
- Strong Biblical background in counseling
- Familiar with counseling and the law

EDUCATIONAL EXPERIENCE:
- Graduate degree in Faith-based counseling
- A member of professional counseling associations
- Counseling experience in a Faith-based environment (3 to 5 years)

Note: The statements herein are intended to describe the general nature and level of work being performed by employees assigned to this classification. They are not intended to be construed as an exhaustive list of all responsibilities, duties and skills required of personnel so classified.

▲

POSITION TITLE: PASTOR OF EVANGELISM
DEPARTMENT:
REPORT TO: Senior Pastor or designate
STATUS: Exempt
GENERAL SUMMARY: To serve the church by developing, coordinating and administering an effective and comprehensive evangelism ministry for the church.

PRIMARY DUTIES AND RESPONSIBILITIES:

1.   Develop and implement a comprehensive Christ-centered evangelism program for the church.

2.   Recruit, train and motivate church members to get involved.

3.   Develop a "sharing your faith" initiative.

4.   Form teams of members to evangelize unbelievers in the local community.

5.   Recruit and train church leaders in basic evangelistic counseling techniques for use at the close of morning worship and following special events and conferences.

6.   Promote participation in evangelistic crusades in the community.

7.   Administer the work of the Department of Evangelism by encouraging teamwork and mutual support and providing leadership.

8.   Establish departmental goals and objectives for evangelizing.

9.   Cooperate with the Senior Pastor or his designate by performing any other duties when asked to do so.

KNOWLEDGE SKILLS AND ABILITIES:
- Strong Biblical background
- Train the trainer skills
- Public speaker
- Organizer
- Teaching skills
- Ability to relate to constituents

EDUCATIONAL EXPERIENCE:
- Evangelism training
- Some formal bible school training

▲

Note: The statements herein are intended to describe the general nature and level of work being performed by employees assigned to this classification. They are not intended to be construed as an exhaustive list of all responsibilities, duties and skills required of personnel so classified. ▲

▲

POSITION TITLE: PASTOR OF EDUCATIONAL MINISTRIES
DEPARTMENT:
REPORT TO: Senior Pastor or designate
STATUS: Exempt
GENERAL SUMMARY: To serve the church by developing, coordinating and administering a comprehensive educational program for the church and providing leadership.

ESSENTIAL JOB FUNCTIONS:

1. Develop and supervise the educational ministries of the church, with direct responsibility for:
    • Adult education, Sunday school classes, conferences and retreats
    • Weekday Bible studies.
    • First Principles classes

2. Supervise the recruiting, training of the volunteer staff to carry out the educational ministries of the church.

3. Teach the congregation, including:
    • Church conferences
    • Mid-week programs
    • Video and written media.

4. Conduct regular staff meetings for the Department of Educational Ministries.

5. Develop new members into the educational life of the church.

6. Administer the work of the Department of Educational Ministries by encouraging teamwork and mutual support.

7. Establish departmental goals and objectives by prioritizing related programs, managing the use of facilities, planning an appropriate budget, delegating tasks and evaluating progress regularly.

8. Cooperate with the Senior Pastor and designates by performing any other duties when asked to do so.

KNOWLEDGE SKILLS AND ABILITIES:
    • Curriculum development skills
    • Leadership ability
    • Public speaker
    • Team development skills

▲

EDUCATION AND EXPERIENCE:
- 4 year college degree
- Education background
- Classroom experience
- Train the trainer experience

Note: The statements herein are intended to describe the general nature and level of work being performed by employees assigned to this classification. They are not intended to be construed as an exhaustive list of all responsibilities, duties and skills required of personnel so classified.

▲

POSITION TITLE: PASTOR OF FAMILY MINISTRIES
DEPARTMENT:
REPORT TO: Senior Pastor or designate
STATUS: Exempt
GENERAL SUMMARY: To serve the church by developing, an effective and comprehensive program of restoring, uplifting, educating and equipping families for their ministries and spiritual development in the church.

ESSENTIAL JOB FUNCTION:

1. Develop and coordinate classes for parents on topics, such as:
    • Positive parenting
    • Self-esteem
    • Caring for troubled children
    • Caring for children with special needs
    • Healing hurts
    • Step-parenting
    • Communicating
    • Divorce

2. Provide nurturing to parents of young children through:
    • Special programs
    • Fellowship
    • Bible studies
    • Bible based counseling

3. Develop family events such as:
    • Family picnics
    • Adopt-a-grandparent program
    • Weekend conferences and retreats

4. Develop and coordinate specialized ministries, such as:
    • Women's ministries
    • Men's ministries

5. Ensure that a balanced program is available for the entire family.

6. Establish departmental goals and objectives by prioritizing related programs.

7. Cooperate with the designated departments and Pastor by performing any other duties when asked to do so.

KNOWLEDGE SKILLS AND ABILITIES:
    • Strong Biblical counseling background
    • Public speaker

▲

- Train the trainer skills
- Able to counsel married couples

EDUCATIONAL EXPERIENCE:
- Biblically based counseling degree preferred
- 4 year counseling degree (minimum)

Note: The statements herein are intended to describe the general nature and level of work being performed by employees assigned to this classification. They are not intended to be construed as an exhaustive list of all responsibilities, duties and skills required of personnel so classified.

▲

POSITION TITLE: DIRECTOR OF MUSIC
DEPARTMENT:
REPORT TO: Pastor, Church Administrator
STATUS: Exempt
GENERAL SUMMARY: To serve the church by developing a well-rounded music program for services of worship and special events and supervising staff members and volunteers involved in this ministry.

ESSENTIAL JOB FUNCTIONS:

1. Consult with the Senior Pastor regarding theme of each service of worship, special programs. selection of hymns and choral music.

2. Train choirs in choral techniques, appreciation of sacred music, leadership and participation in worship

3. Organize and supervise recruitment of church members into the music program.

4. Supervise all musicians.

5. Organize and direct instrumental groups.

6. Select and purchase music, worship and music resources, services of outside instrumentalists and orchestras.

7. Coordinate purchasing of musical instruments and equipment.

8. Schedule and rehearse soloists.

9. Develop seasonal musical programs.

10. Prepare appropriate music for special services.

11. Organize and maintain music library of musical instruments.

12. Supervise the maintenance of musical instruments.

11. Participate with other professional organizations to gain new ideas and to share expertise in music.

KNOWLEDGE SKILLS AND ABILITIES:
- Ability to read music
- Ability to direct vocal as well as instrumental groups
- Leadership ability
- A good understanding of the religious music industry

▲

- Knowledge of sound systems
- Strong leadership ability

EDUCATION AND EXPERIENCE:
- Minimum 5 years of experience as music director
- Preferably a 4 year music degree
- Understand church culture

Note: The statements herein are intended to describe the general nature and level of work being performed by employees assigned to this classification. They are not intended to be construed as an exhaustive list of all responsibilities, duties and skills required of personnel so classified.

▲

POSITION TITLE: DIRECTOR OF MUSIC (optional)
DEPARTMENT:
REPORT TO: Pastor, Church Administrator
STATUS: Exempt
GENERAL SUMMARY: To serve the church by developing a well-rounded music program for services of worship and special events and supervising staff members and volunteers involved in this ministry.

ESSENTIAL JOB FUNCTIONS:

1.	Consult with the pastor regarding theme of each service of worship, special programs, selection of hymns and choir music.

2.	Recruit church members into the music program of the church.

3.	Direct the choir and accompanist in rehearsal and presentation of selected music.

4.	Supervise the organist, pianist and all musicians.

5.	Organize and maintain music library of the church.

6.	Maintain musical instruments.

7.	Recruit gifted volunteers to form and direct children's choirs and musical activities.

8.	Develop the musical gifts and talents of the congregation, inviting members to use them as special music, in seasonal programs and occasional musicals.

9.	Attend staff meetings and any other committee or board meetings necessary to carry out the music program of the church.

10.	Provide for a substitute when not able to be present.

11.	Cooperate with the Pastor and Church Administrator by performing any other duties when asked to do so.

KNOWLEDGE SKILLS AND ABILITIES:
- Music arrangement skills
- Leadership skills
- Ability to delegate
- Ability to provide a wide variety of music

EDUCATION AND EXPERIENCE:
- At least 5 -10 years experience in music ministry

▲

Note: The statements herein are intended to describe the general nature and level of work being performed by employees assigned to this classification. They are not intended to be construed as an exhaustive list of all responsibilities, duties and skills required of personnel so classified.

▲

POSITION TITLE: MEMBERSHIP AND NEW CONVERTS DIRECTOR
DEPARTMENT:
REPORT TO: Church Administrator
STATUS: Non-exempt
GENERAL SUMMARY: To manage an effective and comprehensive membership development program for the church.

ESSENTIAL JOB FUNCTIONS:

1. Develop and oversee a system for recording visitors and prospective members, processing of registration information and the mailing of follow-up letters.

2. Train and motivate members for calling and follow-up on prospective members.

3. Develop and coordinate a sponsorship program for blending new members into the life of the church.

4. Train and motivate members for recruit inactive members.

5. Administer the work of the Department of Membership Development by encouraging teamwork and mutual support and providing leadership.

6. Establish departmental goals and objectives by prioritizing related programs..

7. Work with appropriate committees, officers and leaders in carrying out the membership development ministry of the church.

8. Cooperate with the Senior Pastor or Church Administrator by performing any other duties when asked to do so.

KNOWLEDGE SKILLS AND ABILITIES:
*   Record keeping skills
*   Telephone skills
*   Organizational skills
*   Team building skills
*   Train the trainer skills
*   Strong Biblical background

EDUCATIONAL EXPERIENCE:
*   Some teaching experience
*   Some training experience in area of people development

Note: The statements herein are intended to describe the general nature and level of work being performed by employees assigned to this classification. They are not intended to be construed as an exhaustive list of all responsibilities, duties and skills required of personnel so classified.

▲

POSITION TITLE: PASTOR OF SILVER EAGLES
DEPARTMENT:
REPORT TO: Senior Pastor or designate
STATUS: Exempt
GENERAL SUMMARY: To lead an effective and comprehensive ministry to senior adults of the church.

ESSENTIAL JOB FUNCTIONS:

1. Engage and train senior adults for home visitation, teaching basic lay skills, and spiritual counseling techniques.

2. Provide a social and recreational program for senior adults, including crafts, exercise classes, trips and luncheons.

3. Bring seniors together who have common needs, to comfort and minister to each other.

4. Organize and coordinate volunteer service opportunities for senior adults, such as reading to shut-ins and adopt-a-grandparent programs.

5. Develop a tele-visitation program for homebound seniors.

6. Develop a strategy for effective personal communication with the congregation, including birthday cards, newsletters and follow-up calls on anniversaries of the death of loved ones and home visits to recovering hospital patients.

7. Maintain a resource list of qualified retired people who are available to give assistance to senior members in such areas as preparing wills, estate planning, banking, real estate, legal service and home repairs.

8. Teach Bible studies and lead worship services in local retirement homes.

9. Conduct weddings and funerals, providing appropriate preparation and support.

10. Establish departmental goals and objectives by prioritizing related programs.

11. Represent the church by serving on appropriate Senior citizen committees and organizations in the community.

12. Cooperate with the Senior Pastor by performing any other duties when asked to do so.

KNOWLEDGE SKILLS AND ABILITY:
- Strong pastoral leadership
- Biblical counseling experience
- A silver eagle

EDUCATIONAL EXPERIENCE:

- Former Pastor

Note: The statements herein are intended to describe the general nature and level of work being performed by employees assigned to this classification. They are not intended to be construed as an exhaustive list of all responsibilities, duties and skills required of personnel so classified.

POSITION TITLE: PASTOR OF SINGLE ADULTS
DEPARTMENT:
REPORT TO: Senior Pastor
STATUS: Exempt
GENERAL SUMMARY: To develop a comprehensive singles ministry for the church.

ESSENTIAL FUNCTIONS:

1. Create and maintain a single adults ministry for the church, including:
    - Sunday morning adult education
    - Mid-week educational opportunities
    - Small groups for caring, sharing and nurturing
    - Support groups for divorce recovery, grief recovery and 12-step programs
    - Parties and fellowship

2. Encourage single adults to develop healthy relationships with all members of the church family.

3. Provide support and guidance to singles as they mature in their faith.

4. Develop classes and groups as needed, by age definition, career, gender and interests.

5. Identify, develop and disciple single adult leaders.

6. Administer the work of the Department of Single Adults by encouraging team work and mutual support and providing leadership and nurture to staff members who work in the department.

7. Establish departmental goals and objectives by prioritizing related programs.

8. Work with appropriate committees, officers and leaders in carrying out the single adult ministry of the church.

9. Cooperate with the Senior Pastor or designate by performing any other duties when asked to do so.

KNOWLEDGE SKILLS AND ABILITY:
- Ability to deal with singles
- Biblical counseling skills
- Public speaker
- Leadership ability

EDUCATIONAL EXPERIENCE:
- 4 year theology degree
- Former pastor

▲

- Former evangelist
- Prior leadership position

Note: The statements herein are intended to describe the general nature and level of work being performed by employees assigned to this classification. They are not intended to be construed as an exhaustive list of all responsibilities, duties and skills required of personnel so classified.

▲

POSITION TITLE: PASTOR OF SPIRITUAL DEVELOPMENT
DEPARTMENT:
REPORT TO: Senior Pastor
STATUS: Exempt
GENERAL SUMMARY: Create a program to deepen the spiritual maturity of the congregation, enabling the building of Christian community.

ESSENTIAL FUNCTIONS:

1. Provide mentoring and spiritual direction to those seeking a deeper level of spirituality.

2. Develop and coordinate a comprehensive small group ministry with emphasis on study, sharing, caring, prayer and fasting.

3. Develop curriculum and teach discipling to adults of the church.

4. Encourage and nurture the individual and corporate prayer life of the congregation.

5. Assist in worship and preach at the request of the Senior Pastor.

6. Establish departmental goals and objectives by prioritizing related programs..

7. Cooperate with the Senior Pastor by performing any other duties when asked to do so.

KNOWLEDGE SKILLS AND ABILITY:
- Teaching skills
- Strong biblical background
- Leadership ability

EDUCATIONAL EXPERIENCE:
- 4 year theology degree
- Former key church leader

Note: The statements herein are intended to describe the general nature and level of work being performed by employees assigned to this classification. They are not intended to be construed as an exhaustive list of all responsibilities, duties and skills required of personnel so classified.

▲

POSITION TITLE: DIRECTOR OF CHRISTIAN EDUCATION
DEPARTMENT:
REPORT TO: Senior Pastor, Church Administrator
STATUS: Exempt
GENERAL SUMMARY: To serve the church by developing a comprehensive Christian education program to meet the needs of the congregation and supervising staff members and volunteers involved in this ministry.

ESSENTIAL JOB FUNCTION:

1. Coordinate and unify the educational activities of the church into an integrated and effective ministry of Christian education.

2. Keep abreast of the educational needs of all age groups in the church.

3. Review, develop, order and implement curriculum for all age groups in the church.

4. Recruit and train teachers.

5. Supervise the nursery, ensuring that it is clean, staffed and available when needed.

6. Work with appropriate committees and volunteers to carry out the educational program of the church.

7. Plan and coordinate special educational events for the church, such as:
    • Conferences
    • Camps
    • Teacher appreciation events.

8. Provide parenting classes, intergenerational activities and other activities and classes designed to strengthen the family unit.

9. Attend staff meetings and any other committee or board meetings necessary to carry out the Christian education program of the church.

10. Cooperate with the Senior Pastor and Church administrator by performing any other duties when asked to do so.

KNOWLEDGE SKILLS AND ABILITIES:
    • Curriculum development
    • Leadership ability
    • Team development skills
    • Public speaker
    • Ability to clearly delegate

▲

EDUCATION AND EXPERIENCE:
- 4 year college degree (minimum)
- Education background
- Classroom experience

Note: The statements herein are intended to describe the general nature and level of work being performed by employees assigned to this classification. They are not intended to be construed as an exhaustive list of all responsibilities, duties and skills required of personnel so classified.

▲

POSITION TITLE: PASTOR OF VISITATION

DEPARTMENT:

REPORT TO: Senior Pastor or designate

STATUS: Exempt or Non-exempt

GENERAL SUMMARY: To serve the church by developing an effective ministry of calling on the sick, hospitalized and homebound of the church.

ESSENTIAL FUNCTIONS:

1. Call on members and friends of the church at home or in hospitals including the handi-capped, elderly, grieving, troubled or those celebrating a special occasion.

2. Serve communion to the sick, hospitalized and homebound.

3. Visit hospital patients not associated with the church who request a clergy call.

4. Recruit, train and motivate members of the congregation for hospital calling and caring for the sick.

5. Develop a strategy for effective personal communication with the congregation, including birthday cards, newsletters and follow-up calls on anniversaries of the death of loved ones and home visits to recovering hospital patients.

6. Assist in worship and preach at the request of the Senior Pastor. Teach in the adult educa-tion program, as requested.

7. Work with appropriate committees, officers and leaders in carrying out the visitation min-istry of the church.

8. Represent the church by serving on appropriate committees of the denomination and orga-nization in the community.

9. Cooperate with the Senior Pastor or his designate by performing any other duties when asked to do so.

KNOWLEDGE SKILLS AND ABILITIES:
• Strong ministry background
• Biblical counseling skills
• Leadership skills
• Public speaker

EDUCATIONAL EXPERIENCE:
• At least 2-4 years in pastoral leadership
• Christian counseling degree preferred

▲

Note: The statements herein are intended to describe the general nature and level of work being performed by employees assigned to this classification. They are not intended to be construed as an exhaustive list of all responsibilities, duties and skills required of personnel so classified.

POSITION TITLE: DIRECTOR OF DRAMA AND FINE ARTS
DEPARTMENT:
REPORT TO: Church Administrator
STATUS:
GENERAL SUMMARY: To serve the church by developing, coordinating and administering an effective drama and fine arts ministry of the church and providing leadership to and supervision of staff members and volunteers involved in this ministry.

ESSENTIAL JOB FUNCTIONS:

1. Recruit and work with drama teams for participation in drama and fine arts ministry.

2. Write and direct brief cameos for sermon illustrations.

3. Plan and implement drama programs for the congregation for special occasions such as:
   • Christmas
   • Easter
   • New Years
   • Conferences
   • Special events

4. Coordinate costuming, props and staging for drama programs.

5. Recruit and rehearse people participating in the drama ministry.

6. Expose the congregation to a broad cross-section of theater, music and fine arts.

7. Establish departmental goals and objectives by prioritizing related programs, managing the use of facilities, planning an appropriate budget, delegating tasks and evaluating progress regularly.

8. Cooperate with the Senior Pastor or his designate, by performing any other duties when asked to do so.

KNOWLEDGE SKILLS AND ABILITIES:
   • Theatrical background
   • Musical training
   • Live production experience
   • Must understand church culture

EDUCATIONAL EXPERIENCE:
   • At least 4 year college degree in theater or minimum of 5 years of theater experience.

Note: The statements herein are intended to describe the general nature and level of work being performed by employees assigned to this classification. They are not intended to be construed as an exhaustive list of all responsibilities, duties and skills required of personnel so classified.

POSITION TITLE: DIRECTOR OF FOOD SERVICE
DEPARTMENT:
REPORT TO: Church Administrator
STATUS: Non-exempt
GENERAL SUMMARY: To serve the church by providing appropriate food service for church programs and special events.

ESSENTIAL JOB FUNCTIONS:

1.   Coordinate with other staff members to ensure that appropriate food service is provided for church programs, church school and special events.

2.   Train and supervise kitchen volunteers to ensure proper food preparation, sanitation and service.

3.   Develop creative, nutritious and cost-effective menus.

4.   Ensure that kitchen and equipment are clean and well-maintained.

5.   Obtain required health and fire permits.

6.   Order food and supplies to maintain appropriate inventory levels.

7.   Coordinate with other staff members regarding special set-up requirements.

8.   Provide information about food service options for receptions, including:
       • Room capacities
       • Menus
       • Estimated costs

9.   Coordinate with caterers and other outside services.

10.   Prepare and distribute a monthly hot lunch menu to school parents and staff members.

11.   Secure money collected and turn it in along with accurate accounting to the church business office on a weekly basis.

12.   Attend regular staff meetings and retreats.

13.   Cooperate with the Church Administrator by performing any other duties when asked to do so.

KNOWLEDGE SKILLS AND ABILITIES:
       • Dietary skills
       • Ability to train
       • Management skills

EDUCATION EXPERIENCE:

- Restaurant or Catering background

Note: The statements herein are intended to describe the general nature and level of work being performed by employees assigned to this classification. They are not intended to be construed as an exhaustive list of all responsibilities, duties and skills required of personnel so classified.

▲

POSITION TITLE: DIRECTOR OF MEN'S MINISTRIES
DEPARTMENT:
REPORT TO: Senior Pastor
STATUS: Gratis
GENERAL SUMMARY: To serve the church by developing, coordinating and administering an effective and comprehensive ministry to meet the needs of men in the church and providing leadership to and supervision of staff members and volunteers involved in this ministry.

ESSENTIAL JOB FUNCTIONS:

1. Develop and coordinate men's small group Bible studies.

2. Recruit, train and motivate leaders and teachers for men's ministries.

3. Develop and coordinate a weekly businessmen's lunch.

4. Mentor and disciple men of the church, helping them to grow spiritually.

5. Develop and coordinate programs for men of the church, such as:
    • Career transition
    • Preparing for retirement
    • Job search
    • Single dads
    • Addictive behavior

6. Plan and coordinate men's conferences, prayer breakfasts, golf tournaments, service projects and trips.

7. Establish departmental goals and objectives by prioritizing related programs, managing the use of facilities, planning an appropriate budget, delegating tasks and evaluating progress regularly.

KNOWLEDGE SKILLS AND ABILITIES:
    • Strong Biblical background
    • Leadership skills

EDUCATIONAL EXPERIENCE:
    • Assistant pastor background
    • At least 2 - 4 years Biblical studies

Note: The statements herein are intended to describe the general nature and level of work being performed by employees assigned to this classification. They are not intended to be construed as an exhaustive list of all responsibilities, duties and skills required of personnel so classified.

▲

POSITION TITLE: DIRECTOR OF VOLUNTEERS
DEPARTMENT:
REPORT TO: Senior Pastor
STATUS: Exempt
GENERAL SUMMARY: To develop and coordinate a comprehensive volunteer ministry in the church and provide leadership to volunteers involved in this ministry.

ESSENTIAL FUNCTIONS:

1. Survey the congregation for skills, gifts, experience, abilities and interests for use in volunteer ministry.

2. Develop and maintain a comprehensive volunteer database.

3. Plan and coordinate use of volunteers with other staff members.

4. Utilize a "ministry gifts" assessment test.

5. Develop and implement a recognition program for volunteers.

6. Establish departmental goals and objectives by prioritizing program needs with availability of volunteers.

8. Work with appropriate committees, officers and leaders in carrying out the ministry of the church.

9. Cooperate with the Senior Pastor and Church Administrator by performing any other duties when asked to do so.

KNOWLEDGE SKILLS AND ABILITY:
  • Strong leadership ability
  • Organizational skills
  • Train the trainer skills
  • Good communication skills

EDUCATION EXPERIENCE:
  • Basic management training
  • Must understand church culture

Note: The statements herein are intended to describe the general nature and level of work being performed by employees assigned to this classification. They are not intended to be construed as an exhaustive list of all responsibilities, duties and skills required of personnel so classified.

▲

POSITION TITLE: WOMEN'S MINISTRIES COORDINATOR
DEPARTMENT:
REPORT TO: Senior Pastor or designate
STATUS: Exempt
GENERAL SUMMARY: To serve the church by developing, coordinating and administering an effective and comprehensive ministry to meet the diverse needs of women in the church and providing leadership to and supervision of staff members and volunteers involved in this ministry.

ESSENTIAL JOB FUNCTIONS

1. Develop and coordinate women's group Bible studies.

2. Recruit, train teachers for women's ministries.

3. Develop ministry to meet the needs of career women in the church.

4. Mentor and disciple women in the church.

5. Develop and coordinate programs for young mothers in the church, such as:
    • Aerobics classes
    • Parenting
    • Single mothers

6. Plan and coordinate women's conferences, luncheons, service projects and trips.

7. Provide short-term counseling for women in the church.

8. Plan and coordinate special interest classes, such as:
    • Cooking
    • Needlework
    • Crafts
    • Gardening
    • Interior decorating.
    • Budgeting
    • Investments
    • Home maintenance
    • Auto repair

9. Administer the work of the Department of Women's Ministries by encouraging teamwork and mutual support and providing leadership and nurture to staff members who work in the department.

10. Cooperate with the Senior Pastor or the Church Administrator by performing any other duties when asked to do so.

▲

KNOWLEDGE SKILLS AND ABILITIES:
- Strong Biblical background
- Leadership skills
- Public speaking skills
- Biblical counseling background
- Pastor's wife (helpful)

EDUCATIONAL EXPERIENCE:
- Formal Biblical training (optional)
- Biblical counseling training recommended

Note: The statements herein are intended to describe the general nature and level of work being performed by employees assigned to this classification. They are not intended to be construed as an exhaustive list of all responsibilities, duties and skills required of personnel so classified.

POSITION TITLE: BUSINESS ADMINISTRATOR (Chief financial officer)
DEPARTMENT:
REPORT TO: Senior Pastor, Church Administrator
STATUS: Exempt
GENERAL SUMMARY: To serve the church by providing overall direction to the property, legal, financial and business affairs of the church.

ESSENTIAL FUNCTIONS:

1. Ensure that appropriate and accurate tithing, offering, membership records and special fund raising accounting records are maintained including:
    • Accounts payable and receivable
    • Payroll
    • General ledger
    • Monthly income statement and balance sheet
    • Bank accounts
    • Investment and tax reporting
    • Individual contribution records
    • Membership statistics

2. In cooperation with Senior Pastor, Church Administrator and department heads coordinate development and preparation of the church budget.

3. In conjunction with the Church Administrator coordinate and monitor purchasing of equipment, furniture, supplies and other items.

4. With the Senior Pastor assist in developing an ongoing stewardship program.

5. Research new business procedures, computer techniques, financial programsand salary surveys.

6. Research, evaluate and sign all financial commitments and contracts.

7. Ensure that appropriate and adequate insurance coverages are in place including:
    • Workers' compensation
    • Property/casualty
    • Liability

8. Oversee the development program of the church including:
    • Bequests/memorials
    • Deferred giving
    • Trust funds

9. Supervise and manage off-campus real estate

10. In conjunction with the Senior Pastor and Church Administrator anticipate and plan for future facilities development, based on projected space needs and program plans.

11. Coordinate with appropriate committees, contractors and architects, as needed, to facilitate renovation or relocation of facilities.

12. Supervise support staff members in the following areas:
    - Custodial
    - Maintenance
    - Grounds keeping
    - Security
    - Accounting
    - Membership records
    - Food service
    - Print shop
    - Media ministry
    - Sound and lighting
    - Transportation
    - Book store

13. Work with Personnel Committee to implement personnel policies and procedures of the church.

14. Recruit, screen and recommend candidates for support staff positions.

15. Administer the work of the Administration Department by encouraging teamwork and mutual support and providing leadership and nurture to staff members who work in the department.

16. Establish departmental goals and objectives by prioritizing related programs.

17. Work with appropriate committees, officers and leaders in carrying out the business affairs of the church.

18. Attend board(s) meetings as a resource and for informational purposes.

19. Cooperate with the Senior Pastor and Church Administrator by performing any other duties when asked to do so.

KNOWLEDGE SKILLS AND ABILITIES:
- Accounting background (3 to 5 years)
- Organizational skills
- Professional business attitude
- Strong faith

▲

EDUCATIONAL EXPERIENCE:
- 4 year business degree (minimum)
- MBA preferred

Note: The statements herein are intended to describe the general nature and level of work being performed by employees assigned to this classification. They are not intended to be construed as an exhaustive list of all responsibilities, duties and skills required of personnel so classified.

▲

POSITION TITLE: CHURCH ADMINISTRATIVE SECRETARY (optional)
DEPARTMENT:
REPORT TO: Senior Pastor, Church administrator
STATUS: Exempt
GENERAL SUMMARY: To serve the church by providing secretarial and administrative services for the senior pastor.

ESSENTIAL JOB FUNCTIONS:

1. Provide secretarial services for the senior pastor as needed, such as:
    - Typing
    - Filing
    - Correspondence.
    - Data entry

2. Receive incoming calls, answer questions and provide information whenever possible. Take complete and accurate messages and route calls to appropriate staff member.

3. Greet and offer assistance to all office visitors.

4. Sort and distribute incoming mail. Seal, stamp and sort outgoing mail.

5. Reproduce, fold, address and prepare bulk mailings.

6. Maintain inventory of equipment and supplies and ensure that office equipment is well maintained and serviced.

7. Maintain membership statistics of the church, keeping staff members apprised of changes.

8. Maintain accurate and up-to-date church roles and mailing lists and produce a church directory annually.

9. Order all office supplies.

10. Prepare minutes from committee and board meetings upon request.

11. Prepare bulletins, announcements, letters, newsletters to the congregation

12. Maintain church calendar and permanent records.

13. Attend staff meetings.

14. Cooperate with the assistant pastors by performing any other duties when asked to do so.

KNOWLEDGE SKILLS AND ABILITIES:

- Power Point
- Excel
- Outlook
- Schedule +
- Access
- Accounting software (optional)
- Dictation skills (optional)
- Able to operate large phone systems
- Multi-Task Capable
- Must be able to read reports and computer 75-100%
- Must be able to hear and communicate well 75-100%

EDUCATION AND EXPERIENCE:

- Minimum 2 years of college
  or 3 years of Administrative Secretary experience
- Exhibits leadership ability
- Able to deal with all types of people
- Good math skills

Note: The statements herein are intended to describe the general nature and level of work being performed by employees assigned to this classification. They are not intended to be construed as an exhaustive list of all responsibilities, duties and skills required of personnel so classified.

POSITION TITLE: COORDINATOR OF DAY CARE
DEPARTMENT:
REPORT TO: Church Administrator
STATUS: Non-exempt
GENERAL SUMMARY: To serve the church by directing, coordinating and guiding the day care program of the church.

ESSENTIAL JOB FUNCTIONS:

1. Supervise day care staff members.

2. Train competent substitute teachers and caregivers to ensure continuity of program.

3. Review and select curriculum and educational tools for day care.

4. Develop and implement procedures for admission and appropriate placement of children.

6. Create a comprehensive training program for staff, including:
    • New staff orientation
    • In-service programs
    • Continuing education
    • Teaching demonstrations

7. Ensure that classrooms and facilities reflect a professional and Christian environment.

8. Serve as lead teacher for one class and model appropriate teaching techniques.

9. Counsel with parents as necessary.

10. Develop a parent handbook to communicate program policies and procedures.

11. Communicate the day care program to the congregation.

12. Establish departmental goals and objectives by prioritizing related programs.

13. Cooperate with the Church Administrator by performing any other duties when asked to do so.

KNOWLEGDE SKILLS AND ABILITIES:
    • Able to clearly delegate
    • Child development background
    • Leadership skills
    • Good communication skills
    • Team builder
    • Knowledgeable in the area of child law

▲

EDUCATION AND EXPERIENCE:
- Church literate
- Minimum 4 year degree in child development
- Strong Biblical background

Note: The statements herein are intended to describe the general nature and level of work being performed by employees assigned to this classification. They are not intended to be construed as an exhaustive list of all responsibilities, duties and skills required of personnel so classified.

▲

POSITION TITLE: DIRECTOR OF YOUTH MINISTRIES

DEPARTMENT:

REPORT TO: Senior Pastor, Church Administrator

STATUS: Exempt

GENERAL SUMMARY: To serve the church by developing a comprehensive spiritual, educational and social ministries for the junior high and senior high youth of the church and supervising staff members and volunteers involved in this ministry.

ESSENTIAL JOB FUNCTION:

1. Plan and develop creative programs for junior and senior high youth.

2. Review and develop curriculum to meet the educational needs of junior high and senior high youth, through group and mentoring programs.

3. Develop one-on-one relationships with junior and senior high youth by being a friend and positive role model.

5. Recruit and train essential people to work as youth advisors.

6. Oversee and teach junior high and senior high Sunday school.

7. Work with other staff and volunteers to provide a well-rounded program of teaching, music and recreation for the junior and senior high youth of the church.

8. Plan youth camps and retreats.

9. Identify, develop and disciple youth leaders.

10. Attend staff meetings.

11. Cooperate with the Senior Pastor and Church Administrator by performing any other duties when asked to do so.

KNOWLEDGE SKILLS AND ABILITIES:
- Strong Biblical background
- Public speaker
- Leadership ability
- Youth appeal
- Biblical counseling skills

EDUCATIONAL EXPERIENCE:
4 year college degree (Theology degree preferred)

▲

Note: The statements herein are intended to describe the general nature and level of work being performed by employees assigned to this classification. They are not intended to be construed as an exhaustive list of all responsibilities, duties and skills required of personnel so classified.

▲

POSITION TITLE: CHURCH SECRETARY (Senior)
DEPARTMENT:
REPORT TO: Senior Pastor
STATUS: Exempt
GENERAL SUMMARY: To serve the church by providing secretarial services for the Senior Pastor and be the initial contact person and source of general information for church members and the general public.

ESSENTIAL JOB FUNCTIONS:

1. Provide secretarial services for the Senior Pastor:
    - Maintain Pastors schedule
    - Typing
    - Filing
    - Correspondence
    - Screen telephone calls
    - Computer literate
    - Internet literate

2. Answer questions and provide information whenever possible. Take complete and accurate messages and route calls to appropriate staff members.

3. Greet and offer assistance to visitors and members.

4. Sort and distribute incoming mail.

5. Maintain inventory of equipment and supplies and ensure that office equipment is well-maintained and serviced.

6. Notify staff members and volunteers of committee meetings and prepare committee minutes as needed.

7. Lay-out and produce church newsletters.

8. Maintain minutes for all church board meetings.

KNOWLEDGE SKILLS AND ABILITIES:
- Accurate in all secretarial skills
- Professional phone skills
- Advanced record keeping skills
- Good communicator
- Team builder
- Advanced computer literacy

▲

EDUCATIONAL EXPERIENCE:
- Minimum 2 year degree in Secretarial Science or Office Administration
- Spiritually mature

Note: The statements herein are intended to describe the general nature and level of work being performed by employees assigned to this classification. They are not intended to be construed as an exhaustive list of all responsibilities, duties and skills required of personnel so classified.

POSITION TITLE: PASTOR OF YOUTH MINISTRIES
DEPARTMENT:
REPORT TO: Senior Pastor, Church Administrator
STATUS: Exempt
GENERAL SUMMARY: To serve the church by developing a comprehensive spiritual, educational and social ministries for the junior high and senior high youth of the church and supervising staff members and volunteers involved in this ministry.

ESSENTIAL JOB FUNCTIONS:

1. Plan and develop a creative program for junior high and senior high youth.

2. Review and develop curriculum to meet the educational needs of junior high and senior high youth, through group and mentoring programs

3. Develop one-on-one relationships with junior and senior high youth by being a friend and positive role model.

4. Plan and coordinate programs with other staff members, committees and boards to provide a well-rounded program for spiritual growth through teaching, music and recreation.

5. Recruit, train and equip essential people to work as youth advisors.

6. Meet regularly with lay leadership for team building and planning purposes.

7. Oversee and teach the junior high and senior high Sunday school.

8. Develop service and international mission projects for youth to grow in service to the Lord.

9. Plan and coordinate camps, conferences, retreats, and trips.

10. Attend staff meetings and any committee or board meetings necessary to carry out the youth ministries of the church.

11. Cooperate with the Senior Pastor, Church Administrator by performing any other duties when asked to do so.

KNOWLEDGE SKILLS AND ABILITIES:
- Strong biblical background
- Public speaker
- Leadership ability
- Youth appeal
- Biblical Counseling skills

EDUCATION EXPERIENCE:

- 4 year college degree (theology degree preferred)
- Pastor

Note: The statements herein are intended to describe the general nature and level of work being performed by employees assigned to this classification. They are not intended to be construed as an exhaustive list of all responsibilities, duties and skills required of personnel so classified.

POSITION TITLE: WEDDING COORDINATOR
DEPARTMENT:
REPORT TO: Pastor in-charge of church wedding
STATUS: Non-exempt
GENERAL SUMMARY: To serve the church by coordinating weddings.

ESSENTIAL JOB FUNCTIONS:

1. Coordinate wedding arrangements with couples, including:
    • Initial planning
    • Scheduling pastor and counseling dates
    • Wedding expenses
    • Reception plans

2. Develop and provide a comprehensive packet of information about weddings.

3. Develop a resource list of recommended outside services, including:
    • Florists
    • Printers
    • Photographers/video
    • Caterers
    • Musicians

4. Supervise musicians, sound/lighting technicians, photographers and florists.

5. Conduct wedding rehearsals, providing comprehensive instruction to the entire wedding party.

6. Direct receptions, ensuring that food is served on time, assist with cake cutting and clean up.

7. Work with appropriate staff, committees, officers and leaders in coordinating the weddings for the church.

8. Cooperate with the Pastor performing the wedding by performing any other duties when asked to do so.

KNOWLEDGE SKILLS AND ABILITY:
    • Ability to work with people
    • Able to work under stressful situations
    • Decorating skills
    • Skills in coordinating large social functions
    • Maintain a large vendor list

EDUCATION AND EXPERIENCE:
    • Experience with planning weddings

▲

Note: The statements herein are intended to describe the general nature and level of work being performed by employees assigned to this classification. They are not intended to be construed as an exhaustive list of all responsibilities, duties and skills required of personnel so classified.

POSITION TITLE: PASTOR OF MISSIONS AND OUTREACH
DEPARTMENT:
REPORT TO: Senior Pastor
STATUS: Exempt
GENERAL SUMMARY: To develop and coordinate an effective and comprehensive program of missions and community outreach and providing leadership to and supervision of staff members and volunteers involved in this ministry.

ESSENTIAL JOB FUNCTIONS:

1. Develop, coordinate and administer a comprehensive missions program for the church, focusing on the community, the nation and the world.

2. Supervise missions programs and strategize and communicate an expanding missions and community outreach vision.

3. Teach the congregation a Biblical understanding of world missions and encourage involvement through prayer, correspondence, friendship and financial support.

4. Evaluate and monitor mission organizations and missionaries sponsored by the church, on a regular basis.

5. Develop, supervise and coordinate the local community outreach activities of the church.

6. Recruit, train and deploy people into local, national and foreign mission.

7. Develop and administer the mission and outreach budget.

8. Conduct weddings and funerals, providing appropriate preparation and support.

9. Administer the work of the Department of Mission and Outreach by encouraging teamwork and mutual support and providing leadership and nurture to staff members who work in the department.

10. Cooperate with the Senior Pastor or his designate by performing any other duties when asked to do so.

KNOWLEDGE SKILLS AND ABILITIES:
- Must have some missionary experience
- Leadership ability
- High communications skills

EDUCATIONAL EXPERIENCE:
- Strong biblical background
- Social sciences background

Note: The statements herein are intended to describe the general nature and level of work being performed by employees assigned to this classification. They are not intended to be construed as an exhaustive list of all responsibilities, duties and skills required of personnel so classified.

POSITION TITLE: FINANCE SECRETARY
DEPARTMENT:
REPORT TO: Senior Pastor, Church Administrator
STATUS: Exempt
GENERAL SUMMARY: To serve the church by providing accurate accounting records for the church.

ESSENTIAL JOB FUNCTIONS:

1. Maintain appropriate and accurate accounting records such as:
    *   Accounts receivable and payable
    *   Payroll
    *   General ledger
    *   Monthly income statement and balance sheet
    *   Bank accounts
    *   Tax reporting
    *   Individual contribution records

2. Coordinate the counting of offerings and tithes

3. Prepare and make appropriate weekly bank deposits.

4. Receive, record and acknowledge memorial gifts to the church.

5. Cooperate with the Church Administrator by performing any other duties when asked to do so.

KNOWLEDGE SKILLS AND ABILITIES:
*   Capable of using the most up to date accounting procedures.
*   Strong computer skills

EDUCATION EXPERIENCE:
*   4 year college degree or equivalent experience

Note: The statements herein are intended to describe the general nature and level of work being performed by employees assigned to this classification. They are not intended to be construed as an exhaustive list of all responsibilities, duties and skills required of personnel so classified.

POSITION TITLE: FINANCE AND MEMBERSHIP SECRETARY
DEPARTMENT:
REPORT TO: Senior Pastor, Church Administrator
STATUS: Non-exempt, Exempt
GENERAL SUMMARY: To serve the church by maintaining accurate accounting and membership records for the church.

ESSENTIAL JOB FUNCTIONS:

1. Maintain appropriate and accurate accounting records such as:
   - Accounts payable and receivable
   - Payroll
   - General ledger
   - Monthly income statement and balance sheet
   - Bank accounts
   - Tax reporting
   - Individual contribution records.

2. Coordinate the counting of offering income.

3. Prepare and make appropriate weekly bank deposits.

4. Receive, record and acknowledge memorial gifts to the church.

5. Maintain membership statistics, keeping staff members apprised of any changes.

6. Maintain mailing lists, produce mailing labels and annual church directory.

7. Cooperate with the Senior Pastor, Church Administrator and Accounting department by performing any other duties when asked to do so.

KNOWLEDGE SKILLS AND ABILITIES:
   - Accounting background (2 to 4 years)
   - Organizational skills
   - Ability to delegate

EDUCATIONAL BACKGROUND:
   4 year business degree

Note: The statements herein are intended to describe the general nature and level of work being performed by employees assigned to this classification. They are not intended to be construed as an exhaustive list of all responsibilities, duties and skills required of personnel so classified.

CHURCH STRATEGIES
for the 21st century

Sample Policies

PERSONNEL POLICIES

Copy No. _____

(When no longer required by the holder, or upon termination,
this copy must be returned to the Human Resources Department)

Issued To: _____

Date: _____

Department: _____

Supervisor: _____

Employee's signature: _____

*Note: To be removed and placed in the employee's file
in the Human Resource Department.*

TO ALL EMPLOYEES

WELCOME

As you begin your employment with the (Church), I would like to welcome you to our organization and invite you to read and become familiar with the contents of this policy manual. I hope that you find it full of helpful and valuable information about the policies, benefits, procedures and opportunities available to guide and assist you in performing to the best of your abilities, developing and realizing your personal potential as one of our employees.

The (church) is becoming a leading provider of christian ministry to our community. With your help, we are looking forward to continuing growth as we serve the body of Christ.

The policies, procedures and programs outlined in this handbook are designed to serve as guidelines to keep you informed of relevant facts about your employment. As the (Church) continues to grow, conditions may change that will affect your employment. Additionally, federal, state and local statutes and rulings may alter the policies described herein. The (Church) reserves the right to revise, supplement, or rescind any policies or portions of the handbook from time to time as it deems appropriate in its sole and absolute discretion and without prior notice. THE ONLY MATTERS NOT SUBJECT TO CHANGE ARE THE (CHURCH) AT-WILL EMPLOYMENT POLICY AND ALTERNATIVE DISPUTE RESOLUTION AGREEMENT BETWEEN YOU AND THE CHURCH.

While the policies and procedures outlined in this manual should give you answers to most of the general questions you might have about your job and the (Church) programs and procedures, it cannot cover every situation that might arise. If you have questions about these guidelines or need further information about any subject, please consult with your supervisor or The Human Resources Department. We also welcome your suggestions for improvements either to policies or procedures covered in this handbook or in job-related areas or subjects. Your ideas on ways to improve our operation and procedures are important to us, and, along with your effort and performance, are an ideal way to contribute to the (Church) future growth and your development. Please read this handbook carefully and retain it for future use. Try to familiarize yourself with it as soon as possible as it will answer many of your initial and ongoing questions about your employment with the (Church). We want you to be informed and understand our policies and procedures completely. You should read, understand and comply with all provisions of this handbook.

This handbook does not constitute an express or implied contract between the (Church) and any of its employees. Every employee is employed "At-Will" by the (Church). All employees are free to resign or leave their employment at any time for any or no reason. Likewise, the (Church) is free to terminate the employment relationship of any employee for any or no reason, with or without notice.

Once again, I welcome you and wish you success as we turn to face the numerous challenges, opportunities and potential rewards ahead.

Sincerely,

_____

Pastor

ACKNOWLEDGEMENT OF RECEIPT

I, _____, hereby acknowledge that I have received and read a copy of the (Church) Employee Handbook. The Handbook provides guidelines for the policies, procedures and programs affecting my employment with this organization. Since the information contained within this handbook is necessarily subject to change, I understand that the (Church) can, at its sole discretion, modify, eliminate, revise or deviate from the guidelines and information in this handbook as circumstances or situations warrant, at any time, with or without notice.

I also understand that changes made by the (Church) with respect to its policies, procedures or programs can supersede, modify or eliminate any of the policies, procedures or programs outlined in this handbook. I accept responsibility for familiarizing myself with the information in this handbook, to comply with the provisions contained in this handbook and any revisions made to it while in the ministry's employ, and I will seek verification or clarification of its terms or guidance where necessary.

Furthermore, I acknowledge that this handbook is neither a contract of employment nor a legal document and nothing in the handbook creates an expressed or implied contract of employment. I understand that I should consult my supervisor or a representative of the Human Resource Department if I have any questions that are not answered in this handbook.

I also understand that a church is employing me and that churches are exempt from unemployment insurance regulations. Therefore, I will not be eligible to draw unemployment benefits for the period I am employed by the (Church).

Employee's Signature: _____

Date: _____

Note: *To be removed and placed in the reemployee's file in the Human Resource Department.*

AT-WILL EMPLOYMENT ACKNOWLEDGEMENT FORM

I, _____, acknowledge that my employment with the (Church), is an "at-will employment" relationship that has no specific duration. This means that I can resign my employment at any time, with or without reason or advance notice and that the (church) has the right to terminate my employment at any time, with or without reason or advance notice, so long as there is no violation of applicable state or federal law as applied to churches and religious organizations.

I also acknowledge that no officer, supervisor, or employee of the (Church), other than the Pastor or Church Administrator, has the authority to promise or agree to any substantive terms or conditions of employment different from those stated in the written guidelines and policies contained in the Employee Handbook I received from the (Church). I also understand that any different employment agreement or arrangement entered into by the Pastor or Church Administrator must be clearly stated in writing and signed by both the Pastor and the Church Administrator prior to my reliance on such agreement.

Furthermore, I acknowledge that the Employee Handbook I received from the (Church) is for informational purposes and is neither a contract of employment nor a legal document and nothing in the handbook creates an expressed or implied contract of employment. I understand that I should consult my supervisor or a representative of the Human Resource Department if I have any questions that are not answered in this handbook.

In consideration for my employment, I agree to be bound by the terms set forth in this acknowledgement.

Employee's Signature: _____

Date: _____

Note: To be removed and placed in the employee's file in the Human Resource Department.
christian alternative dispute resolution agreement

CHRISTIAN ALTERNATIVE DISPUTE RESOLUTION AGREEMENT

Christian Alternative Dispute Resolution: In keeping with 1 Corinthians 6:1-8, all disputes which may arise between any employee and the (Church) shall be resolved in accordance with the Rules of Procedure for Christian Conciliation, Institute for Christian Conciliation. If efforts to conciliate or mediate the dispute fail, then the matter shall be resolved through binding arbitration. The decision of the arbitrators shall be binding on both parties and both parties submit themselves to the personal jurisdiction of the court of both state and federal for the entry of a judgment confirming the arbitrators' award. Each party shall bear their own costs, including attorney's fees related to any mediation, conciliation or arbitration proceedings.

If a dispute results in an award or monetary damages, then use of the conciliation mediation and arbitration procedure is conditioned on acceptance of the procedure by the liability insurer of the (Church) and their agreement to honor any mediation, conciliation or arbitration award up to any applicable policy limits. The mediation, conciliation and arbitration process is not a substitute for any disciplinary process set forth in the employee handbook of the (Church) and shall in no way affect the authority of the (Church) to investigate reports of misconduct, conduct hearings or administer discipline of employees up to and including termination of employment.

Employee's Signature: _____

Date: _____

Note: *To be removed and placed in the employee's file in the Human Resource Department.*

CHRISTIAN STANDARDS OF LIVING

It shall be the (Church) policy to employ staff members capable of meeting our high standards of character, education and occupational qualifications. In addition, staff members shall be congenial with fellow staff members, capable of occupational growth and must have made a commitment to Jesus Christ as their Lord and Savior as indicated in the Application for Employment and consistent with the Church's Statement of Faith, doctrinal tenets and teachings.

It is imperative that all staff members conduct themselves in a manner that reflects favorably upon the (Church). All staff members are expected to maintain a consistent attitude of friendliness, teachability and a love and concern for others. Critical or negative attitudes, gossip and conduct not consistent with Christian Biblical standards cannot be tolerated and are grounds for discipline up to and including termination of employment. Employees are expected to be courteous and helpful to the public, to partners of the Ministry, and those doing business with the Ministry. Should a staff member's conduct, whether on or off the premises, be criminal, dishonest, immoral in nature, unbiblical or detrimental to the best interest of the Ministry, then it may subject the staff member to discipline or dismissal, depending upon the nature and extent of the conduct. The Board of Directors, as the highest ecclesiastical tribunal of the (Church), shall be the sole arbiters of whether an employee's conduct is in violation of this policy.

Employee's Signature: _____

Date: _____

Employee identification number: _____

Note: To be removed and placed in the employee's file in the Human Resource Department.

DISCLOSURE TO CANDIDATES CONCERNING DRUG AND ALCOHOL TESTING

Dear_____

(Name of candidate)

You have been offered a position as a _____.
Your refusal to submit to a drug test or failure to pass such a test means, you will not be employed by the (Church). As a Christian Ministry, illegal drug use by employees of the Church is not tolerated.

Drug testing will be conducted in a manner that affords maximum privacy to the individual being tested. Neither the collector of specimens nor the medical professional that reviews the test results will be an employee of the (Church) The test results will be analyzed by an independent laboratory and all test results will be kept confidential. The individual undergoing testing will not be directly observed while providing the specimen, unless there are reasonable grounds to believe the individual may alter or substitute the specimen.

After you have read this disclosure, please acknowledge that you have received and reviewed this notice by signing this letter and returning it to the Human Resources Department. Your signature is an acknowledgment that you consent to pre-employment drug testing as a condition of employment. You should keep the second copy of this letter, which has been provided for your convenience.

If you have any questions concerning this letter, please contact the Human Resources Department.

_____

(Signature)

_____

(Printed name)

_____

(Date)

Note: To be removed and placed in the employee's file in the Human Resource Department.

<u>REFUSAL BY CANDIDATE TO SUBMIT TO DRUG TESTING</u>

I have been offered a position with the (Church). As a Christian Ministry, illegal drug use by employees of the (Church) is not tolerated. I acknowledge that the (Church) is concerned about my ability to perform all of the essential functions for the position for which I am being considered, with or without reasonable accommodation. Whether I am able to perform those functions is based on whether I do or do not use drugs illegally. The (Church) has therefore requested that I submit to drug testing.

I understand that the testing is voluntary on my part and that I may refuse to submit to testing. I acknowledge that such refusal will result in the (Church) withdrawing its offer of employment.

With full knowledge of the foregoing, I hereby refuse to submit to drug testing.

DATE: _____

_____
Candidate's signature

_____
Candidate's printed name

Note: To be removed and placed in the employee's file in the Human Resource Department.

PHYSICAL EXAMINATION AND EMPLOYEE DRUG TESTING CONSENT

I, _____, hereby give my consent and express my willingness to undergo a physical examination as requested by the (Church). I also consent to the release of the results of the physical examination to the (Church). I understand that this physical examination may also include a drug test. With this agreement, I am also consenting to the collection of any urine sample collected from me by the (Church's) designated physician or testing representative. I understand that if such a sample is collected, it is sent to a laboratory selected by the (Church) which conducts screening tests to detect the presence of illegal narcotics, including marijuana and other drugs, as well as signs of abuse of legal drugs. I consent to the release to the (Church) of all my medical records related to this physical examination and any drug test that contains relevant information about my fitness and ability to perform the essential functions of the position in which I am employed or being considered for.

I acknowledge and understand that if I do not satisfactorily complete this examination or drug test, or if the examination results indicate that I cannot physically perform the essential functions of the position in which I am working, with or without reasonable accommodations, the (Church) has the right to decide whether my continued employment is in the overall best interests of the organization. I understand it is not the intent of the (Church) to investigate my health or physical condition for any purpose other than my suitability for employment in my position. I understand that the Church complies with all the requirements of the Americans with Disabilities Act (ADA), as it applies to churches, and the (Church) will only request medical examinations, other than drug tests, when the examination is job-related and consistent with the (Church's) business needs as an employer. When medical examinations are required for employees doing a particular job, all said medical examinations or inquiries should be administered in a nondiscriminatory, uniform, even-handed manner to all such employees.

In exchange for the (Church's) scheduling and paying for these medical examinations and tests, I release and discharge the (Church) and any of its designated medical personnel, agents or authorized test laboratories from any claims or potential liability arising out of or related to any physical or medical examination or the results of such examinations or tests. I also agree not to file or pursue any complaints, claims or legal actions of any kind against the (Church) or any of its employees, representatives or agents arising out of their activities or actions performed in connection with these physical or medical examinations.

DATE: _____

_____
Candidate's signature

_____
Candidate's printed name

Note: *To be removed and placed in the employee's file in the human resource department.*

SAMPLE STATEMENT OF FAITH

The Statement of Faith of the (Church) shall serve as the cornerstone of all the policies in this handbook. It is required that all of the Administrators, Directors, Officers and Employees of the (Church) subscribe to this statement, either orally or in writing.

A.   We believe that the Holy Bible is the inspired, infallible and authoritative source of Christian doctrine and precept and serves as our standard for Christian living.

B.

C.

D.

E.

F.

SAMPLE MISSION STATEMENT

The mission of the (Church) is to prepare our community for the coming of Jesus Christ and the establishment of the Kingdom of God on earth. Our ultimate goal is to achieve a time in history when "the knowledge of the Lord will cover the earth as the waters cover the sea."

In achieving our mission, our chief method is the strategic use of mass communication, especially radio, television, literature and education that will train the young and old to understand how the principles of God relate to those spheres of human endeavor which play a dominant role in our world.

In achieving our mission, nothing should be done that does not glorify God and His son Jesus Christ.

Three words should characterize the execution of our mission. First, we will be <u>innovative</u>...Our task is not to duplicate or copy other men's labors. Second, we will be <u>excellent</u>...Our work must either be of lasting value and the highest quality or it should not be done at all. Third, we will demonstrate *integrity* in our work, our public relations and our internal and external communications. There will be an abiding commitment to truth. Integrity must characterize all of our dealings with others.

In staffing for our mission, we must insist on securing the best possible Christian men and women for each task and we will make every reasonable effort to see that people and tasks are matched appropriately. Our policy will be to secure a staff of outstanding people and to compensate them for their labors. Our staff should be "filled with the Holy Spirit and wisdom." God's work must be done by people equipped and chosen.

As part of our goals we continually endeavor to give generous assistance to the relief of human need and suffering and donate to other organizations that share our basic objectives as well. We believe that God's work done according to the principles of His kingdom will prosper financially. We cannot serve God and money, so service to God and His call always takes precedence over conflicting considerations of money. Nevertheless, we recognize that only those activities which are economically viable can continue in our present society, so planning must take into account economic viability. We also categorically state that the payment of accounts when due is a key ingredient of integrity. We work to finance our activities by all lawful and morally correct means, including but not limited to, contributions, sales and investment income. In planning, we will endeavor to project adequate income for current activities, plus generous surpluses from which we can build and expand.

PREFACE TO THE MANUAL

The historical tenets of the Christian faith, in general, and the principles of the Scriptures in particular, are the guiding principles upon which human resources are managed at the (Church).

Rather than attempt to "proof text" each policy, a process that could violate accepted practices of Biblical exegesis and hermeneutics, emphasis has been placed upon the general principles of God's Kingdom as revealed through the Bible. One of the most important principles, foundational to the life and ministry of Jesus Christ, is the concept of "servant leadership." This principle, modeled by Jesus himself, undergirds all that we do in interpersonal relationships. As we seek to do unto others, as we would have them do to us, a quality of love emerges that validates our relationship to Christ.

The (Church) has been called to conduct its ministry within the context of and in compliance with duly constituted civil authority. These regulations have been carefully considered in the formulation of human resource management procedures.

This manual represents the dedicated efforts of individuals committed to the integration of the Christian faith with the best of human resource policy and practice. The result is a framework within which each individual employee of the (Church) might achieve the highest potential for Christ's purpose and glory.

CODE OF EMPLOYER-EMPLOYEE RELATIONS

1.   POLICY

It is the policy of the (church) to announce to employees the fundamental principles and the relationship between the (church) and its personnel.

2.   GUIDELINES OF THE POLICY:

A.   The (Church) expects all employees:

(1) To give a productive day's work to the best of their ability and skill.

(2) To arrive at their department and begin work on time.

(3) To demonstrate a considerate, friendly and constructive attitude toward fellow employees.

(4) To adhere to the policies adopted by the (Church).

(5) To concur with and subscribe to the (Church's) Statement of Faith and Mission Statement.

(6) To live a lifestyle consistent with Biblical tenets as espoused by the ministry.

B.   The (Church) retains the right to exercise customary managerial functions including, but not limited to the right:

(1) To dismiss, assign, supervise, or discipline employees, with or without notice.

(2) To determine and change starting times, quitting times and shifts, with or without notice.

(3) To transfer employees within a department or into another department and/or classification, with or without notice.

(4) To determine and change the size of and qualifications of the work force, with or without notice.

(5) To establish, change or abolish its policies, practices, rules and regulations, with or without notice.

(6) To determine or change methods by which its operations are to be carried out, with or without notice.

(7) To assign duties to employees in accordance with the (Church's) needs and requirements.

(8) To carry out all ordinary administrative and managerial functions.

EQUAL EMPLOYMENT OPPORTUNITY

1.   POLICY:

It is the policy of the (Church) to provide equal opportunity in employment to all employees and applicants for employment consistent with the (Church's) Statement of Faith, Mission Statement, and corporate purpose. No person shall be discriminated against in employment because of such individual's race, color, sex, age, veteran status or national origin. Persons with handicaps will be evaluated in terms of their ability to perform their present or prospective jobs. It is required that each employee subscribe to the (Church's) *STATEMENT OF FAITH* and *MISSION STATEMENT.*

As a church, the (Church) takes full advantage of the exemption for Title VII "religious discrimination" afforded religious organizations. In so doing so, the (Church) reserves all rights allowed by law to base employment action on the grounds of religious beliefs and doctrine. Any decision made by the Ministry in this regard is not subject to review. The (Church) encourages any concerned employee to report discrimination issues to the Human Resources Department without fear of reprisal.

The (Church) is committed to employing only United States citizens and aliens who are authorized to work in the United States and does not unlawfully discriminate on the basis of citizenship or national origin.

Employees with questions on immigration law issues are encouraged to contact the Human Resources Department. Employees may raise questions or complaints about immigration law compliance without fear of reprisal, subject to our stated goal to comply with all employment laws.

The (Church) is committed to complying fully with the Americans with Disabilities Act (ADA), as it applies to churches, and ensuring equal opportunity in employment for qualified persons with disabilities. All employment practices and activities are conducted on a nondiscriminatory basis as it relates to persons with disabilities.

All employment decisions are based on the merits of the situation in accordance with defined criteria, not the disability of the individual. The Ministry is also committed to not discriminating against any qualified employees or applicants because they are related to, or associated with, a person with a disability. The Ministry will follow state or local laws that provide individuals with disabilities greater protection than the ADA. This policy is neither exhaustive nor exclusive. The Ministry is committed to taking all other actions necessary to ensure equal employment opportunity for persons with disabilities in accordance with the ADA and all other applicable federal, state and local laws.

2.   GUIDELINES OF THE POLICY:

     A.   This policy applies to all terms, conditions and privileges of employment including hiring, probation, training and development, promotion, transfer, compensation, benefits, educational assistance, layoff, social and recreational programs, termination and retirement.

     B.   The Director of Human Resources has been appointed director of equal employment opportunity programs for the (Church) and will be responsible for formulating, implementing, coordinating and monitoring all efforts in the area of equal employment opportunity. His or her duties shall include, but not necessarily be limited to:

         (1)   Assisting management in ADA compliance.

         (2)   Developing policy statements and internal and external communication techniques regarding the equal employment policies of the (Church).

         (3)   Designing and implementing record keeping and reporting systems to ensure compliance with legal requirements and posting of notices as required by law.

HARASSMENT-FREE, PRODUCTIVE WORK ENVIRONMENT

1.   POLICY:

It is the policy of the (Church) to provide its employees with a pleasant environment, which encourages efficient, productive and creative work.

Verbal, physical, visual and sexual harassment of co-workers, co-employees and members of the public is absolutely forbidden. Harassment can take many forms. You must be sensitive to the feelings of others and must not act in a way that might be considered as harassment by someone else. A few examples of prohibited harassment (for illustrative purposes only) are:

A.   Verbal (racial, sexual or ethnic jokes, insults).

B.   Physical (sexually suggestive or unwelcome touching, pinching, brushing against another's body or obscene gestures).

C.   Visual (insulting cartoon, sexually suggestive or lewd pictures or photographs).

D.   Retaliation for complaints of harassment.

Prohibited sexual harassment does not always require a promised exchange for sex or threat if sex is withheld. Sexual harassment may take the form of unwelcome sexual advances, deprecating sexual remarks, references to women as "honey," "doll," "dear" or any environment demeaning of women. Sexually oriented teasing, kidding, jokes, foul language, or any verbalization of sexually suggestive language in the work environment is a violation of our Christian Code of Conduct, and will subject you to discipline up to and including termination.

If you think that you or one of your co-workers has been the victim of harassment, you must report the incident and the names of the persons to your Administrator, supervisor or Pastor immediately. The incident will be investigated. If you do not report harassment, it cannot be investigated. Your cooperation is crucial. There will be no retaliation against you by management for making a complaint of sexual harassment or any other type of harassment. Your failure to fully and completely cooperate in an investigation of any employee misconduct will subject you to discipline up to and including termination.

If you are afraid to report harassment to your supervisor, you should report it to the Church Administrator or the Pastor.

2.   GUIDELINES OF THE POLICY:

A.   The (Church) will not tolerate conduct by any employee that harasses, disrupts or interferes with another's work performance or which creates an intimidating, offensive or hostile environment.

B.   While all forms of harassment are prohibited, it is the (Church's) policy to emphasize that sexual harassment is specifically prohibited. Each supervisor should maintain his workplace free of sexual harassment. This duty includes discussing this policy with all employees and assuring them that they are not required to endure insulting, degrading or exploitative treatment because of their gender. Specifically, no supervisor shall threaten or insinuate, either explicitly or implicitly, that an employee's refusal to submit to sexual advances will adversely affect the employee's employment, evaluation, wages, advancement, assigned duties, shifts or any other condition of employment or career development; or that their willingness to submit to sexual advances will enhance their employment.

C.   Other sexually harassing conduct in the workplace, whether committed by supervisors or non-supervisory personnel, is also prohibited. Such conduct includes, but is not limited to:

    (1)   Unwelcome sexual flirtations, advances or propositions.

    (2)   Verbal abuse of a sexual nature or profanity.

    (3)   Graphic verbal comments about an individual's body.

    (4)   Sexually degrading words used to describe an individual.

    (5)   The display in the workplace of sexually suggestive objects or pictures.

D.   Any employee who believes that he/she has been the subject of sexual harassment should report the alleged act immediately to his/her supervisor. Supervisors should make every effort to insure that complaints of sexual harassment are resolved promptly and effectively.

E.   If the employee is not satisfied with the action taken by the supervisor, the supervisor should advise the employee to bring the complaint to the attention of the Administrator, Pastor or Director of Human Resources and the employee will be advised of the findings and conclusion. Employees should bring their complaint to the Church Administrator, Pastor or Director of Human Resources when they deem necessary, even if they were not instructed to do so by their supervisor.

F. The Administrator, Pastor or Human resource department will attempt to resolve complaints of harassment through confidential internal investigations.

G. Any supervisor, agent or other employee who is found, after appropriate investigation, to have engaged in harassment of another employee will be subject to appropriate sanctions depending on the circumstances, up to and including termination.

HIRING

1. POLICY:

It is the policy of the (Church) to hire individuals who are qualified for employment based on their aptitude, capability, spiritual maturity and character. All decisions regarding the recruitment, selection, placement and advancement of employees are made on the basis of job-related criteria and spiritual maturity. Every effort will be made to hire new employees for positions that best utilize their abilities and in which they will be able to achieve both personal satisfaction and opportunity for growth. In no event shall the hiring of an employee be considered a contractual relationship between the employee and the (Church), and such relationship shall be defined as "employment-at-will," where either party may dissolve the relationship with or without notice.

It is the intent of the (Church) to clarify the definitions of employment classification so that employees understand their employment status and benefit eligibility. These classifications are not guaranteed for any specified period of time. Accordingly, the right to terminate the employment relationship AT WILL at any time is retained by both the employee and the (Church).

Each employee is designated as either NON-EXEMPT or EXEMPT from federal and state wage and hour laws. NON-EXEMPT employees are entitled to overtime pay under the specific provisions of federal and state laws. Vacation, holidays, lunch and sick days do not count as hours worked for purposes of computing overtime pay. EXEMPT employees are excluded from specific provisions of federal and state wage and hour laws. An employee's EXEMPT or NON-EXEMPT classification may be changed only upon written notification by the Administration Office or the Administrator. By law, all employees who do not meet the criteria for EXEMPT are NON-EXEMPT. Direct any questions regarding your employment classification to the Administrator or Director of Human Resources.

2. GUIDELINES OF THE POLICY:

A. Job openings will be filled by promoting personnel from within the (Church) when possible and when it is in the Ministry's best interest as determined by the Human Resources Department. When it is necessary to recruit applicants for employment from outside the (Church), all available sources of qualified personnel shall be utilized.

B. As a general matter, the (Church) will not pay any employment agency fees for unsolicited referrals of individuals to fill job openings.

C. When a department manager or other manager or supervisor determines that there is a requirement for one or more new employees, he shall submit an Employment Requisition form signed by the Administrator to the Human Resources Department. Requisitions to fill existing jobs that are being vacated will be processed routinely.

The Human Resources Department before approval and processing will review all other requisitions with the Administrator or Pastor.

D.   To aid the process of selecting those most qualified for employment, the (Church) utilizes employment tests as a part of normal hiring procedures.

E.   Job openings will be posted in accordance with procedures contained in the PRO-MOTION policy.

F.   If it is determined that additional personnel should be hired from outside the (Church), the following procedures shall be adhered to:

(1)   The initial interview of applicants for employment shall be conducted by the Human Resources Department. The selection process shall include, but not be limited to, an employment application, a determination as to whether the applicant has the legal right to work in the United States, applicable employment tests and applicable reference investigations (credit, personal, criminal, etc.).

(2)   If the Human Resources Department determines that the applicant is eligible for employment, the department manager shall be notified. If the department manager considers the applicant eligible, an interview shall be arranged between the applicant and the department manager by the Human Resources Department. When necessary, the Human Resources Department shall initiate and coordinate all applicant travel arrangements.

(3)   It is the department manager's responsibility to determine if an applicant is technically qualified for the position and if the applicant can work compatibly within the department and is otherwise qualified. The decision whether to hire the applicant shall be made by the department manager and the Human Resources Department.

(4)   Offers of employment shall be approved and authorized only by the Human Resources Department prior to extending an offer of employment to a prospective employee. No other division or employee is authorized to approve offers of employment. Any and all unauthorized offers of employment will not be processed by the Human Resources Department.

(5)   Prior to a decision to hire the applicant, a medical examination may be arranged by the Human Resources Department, if the Ministry determines that need for an examination exists for the job position applied for to determine if the applicant is capable of performing the job tasks.

(6)   If the medical examination or background investigation reveals any misrepresentation on the application form or information indicating that the individ-

ual is not suited for employment, the applicant shall be refused employment or, if already employed, shall be terminated as an employee of the Church.

(7)   Orientation and training of a new employee shall be conducted by the Human Resources Department and the employee's supervisor in accordance with the Human Resources Department's orientation, training and development program.

G.   All representatives of the (Church) should be aware that employment with the (Church) is "at-will." Therefore, during the recruitment, hiring, and orientation process, no statement shall be made promising permanent or guaranteed employment. No document shall be called a contract unless, in fact, an employment contract, approved by the Administrator and Human Resources Department is to be used.

*H.   RELATIVES: The (Church) may employ a relative of an employee provided the individual possesses the particular qualifications for employment. However, those persons shall not be given work assignments which require one relative to direct, review or process the work of the other, or where there is substantial compromise or conflict. "Relatives" in this restriction include: parents, grandparents, children, brothers, sisters, parents-in-law, brothers-in-law, sisters-in-law, uncles, aunts, nieces, nephews, and first cousins, but shall not include spouses who are subject to Item I of this Policy. Any questions regarding the interpretation of this policy should be directed to the Human Resources Division for resolution.

*I   SPOUSES: Provided there is no other compromise or conflict, spouses may be hired only under one of the following conditions:

(1)   Spouses are not employed in the same department or they are not under the supervision of the same department head.

(2)   If one employee marries another employee, and both have been employees for a minimum of six (6) months, both may continue to be employed, provided they are in different divisions and they are not in the same chain of supervision. If a specific instance would necessitate a job transfer in order to be in compliance, a vacant position, for which the subject employee is a qualified candidate, must be available within ( ) days of the marriage in order for both to remain employed.

NOTE: Items H and I apply to all categories of employment: Regular, temporary, full-time, part-time, on-call and contract personnel. Exceptions must be approved in writing by the Pastor or Administrator.

J.   FORMER EMPLOYEES: The general policy is not to hire any former employees whether they have been discharged or they have resigned, unless they are recommended for rehire when the employment relationship is terminated. Exceptions will be considered only after careful review by the former supervisor, Administrator, the Human Resources Division and other applicable supervisors. The final decision to hire will be made by the hiring manager in concurrence with the Administrator and Human Resources Department.

K.   NOTIFICATION OF UNSUCCESSFUL CANDIDATE: Once the best qualified candidate for a position has accepted an employment offer, the Human Resources Department is responsible for notifying unsuccessful candidates that the position has been filled. The Human Resources Department is responsible for compiling and maintaining all legally required documentation relating to the (Church's) efforts to fill the open position.

SKILLS TESTING

NOTE: *Testing of any kind should be handled correctly. A final decision whether or not to hire an individual should be based on all the gathered information: the interview, application information, references and career history. Testing should be one of the factors.*

1. POLICY:

    It is the policy option of the (Church) to test employees prior to hiring and during any placement or evaluation procedure to assist in the decision-making process.

2. GUIDELINES OF POLICY:

    A. The (Church) shall use a variety of tests and measurement tools deemed appropriate for assisting employees in defining current interests, performance skills and future potential. The goal of such evaluation shall be to assist the (Church) and the employee in making maximum use of employee resources in a way that benefits both the employee and the (Church).

    B. All testing will be managed by the Human Resources Department and no test shall be used without approval of the Human Resources Department.

    C. The (Church) reserves the right to determine whether test results will be shared with the employee being tested, or any other person.

ORIENTATION, TRAINING AND DEVELOPMENT

1. POLICY:

It is the policy of the (Church) to conduct orientation programs and provide training and development for all employees within the (Church) enabling them to personally incorporate the mission of the (Church) and master their assigned jobs and to develop skills for both effective and efficient job performance.

2. GUIDELINES:

A. An orientation program shall be provided for all new employees to introduce them to the mission of the (Church), its related ministries, and the role of each employee in helping to accomplish that mission. It also provides important information about structures, systems and procedures in place to help the employee serve effectively.

B. All employees shall receive on-the-job training which will aid the employee to successfully perform his tasks. The supervisor will explain the mission of their unit and the importance of the new employee's contribution.

C. Employees may be given the opportunity to participate in on going corporate sponsored training and development programs designed to enhance their skills and prepare them for future opportunities that may exist within the organization.

D. All supervisory and management personnel are encouraged to participate in scheduled training and development activities designed to improve their skills in corporate and personnel management.

E. In cases where the (Church) is unable to offer direct support for requisite training, the (Church) may make on-site programs available.

MEDICAL TESTING

1. POLICY:

    It is the Policy of the (Church) to require its employees to be examined by a physician when-ever warranted for the protection of other employees of the (Church). Medical examinations or inquiries concerning health will only be requested as they are related to your ability to perform your job and are consistent with the Church's business needs.

2. GUIDELINES OF THE POLICY:

    A. Employees may be required to have a physical examination at the (Church's) expense on occasions such as transfer, promotion or when management determines that the interests of the (Church) and the employees will be served.

    B. The (Church) provides annual physical examinations for the (Church) executives, with a physician selected by the (Church). The Human Resources Department is responsible for advising individuals of their eligibility for this exam and for schedul-ing appointments with the physician's office. The (Church) will pay the cost of the examination and tests that are routinely scheduled as part of the examination. Any additional action or medical treatment recommended or required will be the respon-sibility of the individual.

    C. Any physical examinations administered at the request of the (Church) or medical report requested by the (Church) shall be paid by the (Church). The physician or other examiner shall be selected by the (Church).

    D. Medical examinations paid for by the (Church) are the property of the (Church). Records of such examination will be made available to public agencies if required by law or regulation, and may be made available for use within or outside the (Church), as the need arises.

    E. Employees returning from sick leave or other leave of absence may be required to have a physical examination to determine their capability to perform their regular work without endangering themselves or their fellow employees.

    F. Any expenses incurred or time lost as a result of occupational injury or illness by an employee will be handled as required through Workman's Compensation by the Human Resources Department.

    G. The Security department, Administrator and the Human Resources Department shall be informed immediately if an employee requires medical attention during the course of his employment.

EMPLOYEE CLASSIFICATION

1.   POLICY:

It is the policy of the (Church) to establish standardized terminology and provide common understanding in reference to the classification of its employees. The (Church) shall have the following categories for individuals performing services to the (Church). All services the church receives are from the following three basic sources:

A.   EMPLOYEES: An individual who works for salary/wages and performs services, of which the details and means are subject to the direction of the (Church).

B.   FOREIGN NATIONALS: Employees of the (Church) who work in foreign offices and who are not United States citizens or are unable to provide appropriate documentation permitting employment in the United States.

C.   INDEPENDENT CONTRACTORS: (Includes: CONSULTANTS, FREELANCE, TALENT): One who, in the course of an independent occupation, contracts to render services to the (Church) according to his own means and methods, without being subject to the control of the (Church), except as to the result of the work. An Independent Contractor Agreement and Contractor Authorization Form, approved by the Administrator, the Church's General Counsel and Human Resources Department, are required prior to enlisting the services of an independent contractor.

2.   GUIDELINES OF THE POLICY:

A.   Classifications- Exempt and Nonexempt. These terms refer to an employee's coverage or exemption under federal and state wage-hour laws. The (Church) is required to pay nonexempt employees a rate at least equal to federal minimum wage. The (Church) must also pay nonexempt employees overtime pay of at least one-and one-half times their regular rate for hours worked in excess of 40 in any workweek.

B.   In addition to the Exempt and Non-Exempt categories, each employee will belong to one other employment category.

(1)   REGULAR FULL-TIME EMPLOYEES. Those who are not in a temporary or introductory status and who are regularly scheduled to work at least forty (40) hours per week on a regular basis. Generally, regular full-time employees are eligible for the Ministry's benefit package, subject to the terms, conditions and limitations of each benefit program.

(2)   REGULAR PART-TIME EMPLOYEES. Those who are not assigned to a temporary or introductory status and who are regularly scheduled to work less than forty (40) hours per week. Regular part-time employees receive all legally mandated benefits such as Medicare and workers' compensation insurance.

They are ineligible for all other benefit programs.

(3)   INTRODUCTORY EMPLOYEES: Those whose performance is being evaluated to determine whether further employment in a specific position with the Ministry is appropriate. Please refer to the Ministry's policy

(4)   INDEPENDENT CONTRACTORS: (Includes: CONSULTANTS, FREELANCE, TALENT) Encompasses a wide range of individuals who provide services for the (Church) but who are not employees. Contractors can include self-employed individuals as well as employees of firms with which the (Church) has contracted for services. Using contractors allows the (Church) to respond flexibly to changing work demands and can cut costs since contractors are not provided with employee benefits.

(5)   TEMPORARY EMPLOYEES: Temporary personnel hired when the need arises. When necessary, the Human Resources Division will contact and arrange for the needed manpower upon receipt of a Temporary Employee Requisition form with proper signatures from the Administrator. Individual departments are not to contact agencies or make any arrangements concerning temporary help or their salaries. It is the policy of the (Church) to supplement the regular work force with temporary or on-call employees when necessitated by periods of peak workload, employee absences, or other situations as may be determined by management.

(6)   MINORS: Those under the age of eighteen shall only be hired upon presentation of proof of age. The (Church) shall verify that they are age sixteen or older prior to employment. In doing so, the (Church) may seek a federal certificate of age from the Wage and Hour Division of the U.S. Department of Labor and/or an age certificate from the (state) Department of Labor prior to the commencement of employment. A birth certificate may be requested from prospective employees, in addition to state identification, who appear to be under the age of eighteen. Certificates of age should be kept in the individuals personnel file.

(7)   ALIENS: A requirement for employment in the United States is evidence of United States employment authorization and proof of personal identification. This evidence is required by the Immigration Reform and Control Act of 1986 and applies to all employees.

INTRODUCTORY PERIOD AND PROBATION

1. POLICY:

It is the policy of the (Church) that all new employees hired to fill regular status jobs, and all employees transferred or promoted to new regular status jobs shall be placed on introductory status for a period of ( ) to ( ) months. Upon successful completion of the introductory period, the employee will be given regular status.

2. GUIDELINES OF THE POLICY:

A. INTRODUCTORY PERIOD:

(1) During the introductory period, the supervisor will carefully observe the employee's job performance. Weaknesses in performance or attitude shall be brought to the employee's attention in a manner appropriate for understanding and self-correction.

(2) At some time after the ( ) months of the introductory period, the supervisor shall prepare a written evaluation of the introductory employee's job performance. The evaluation should include a recommendation as to granting the introductory employee regular employee status. Copies of the evaluation shall be forwarded to the department manager and the Human Resources Department for inclusion in the introductory employee's personnel file.

(3) The department manager may grant regular status to the introductory employee at any time between the ( )and ( ) months of the introductory period if the employee's job performance is satisfactory. An introductory employee may be granted an extension of one ( ) to ( ) months of introduction if there is need for additional time to achieve satisfactory job performance.

(4) Introductory employees, as all other employees, may be terminated at any time during the introductory period.

(5) Employees who are terminated during or at the end of the introductory period are not eligible for severance pay.

(6) Introductory employees during their introductory period shall not be eligible for paid absences, vacation or educational assistance.

(7) An introductory employee will be granted regular status only after the period of introduction has been satisfactorily completed.

B. PROBATION:

(1) Any regular employee may be placed on probation for up to ( ) months when his or her performance has deteriorated and the supervisor believes it is necessary to impress upon the employee the need for improvement. Employees who improve satisfactorily during the probation period may be restored to regular employee status. Failure to gain a performance rating of "satisfactory" or better during probation may result in a transfer to another job more suited to the employee's capabilities or other action up to and including termination.

(2) Regular employees who have been placed on probation are eligible for paid holidays but may not take any vacation days during the probation period.

SALARY AND WAGE ADMINISTRATION

1.   POLICY:

It is the policy of the (Church) to pay wages and salaries that are based upon the nature of the job performed. Economic conditions affecting the (Church) may also determine compensation levels.

2.   GUIDELINES OF THE POLICY:

A.   A compensation program has been designed to provide guidance for management with compensation-related responsibilities. This compensation program consists of the following basic elements:

    (1)   Written job descriptions

    (2)   Formal job evaluation system

    (3)   Wage and salary structures

    (4)   Compensation surveys

    (5)   Performance evaluation program

    (6)   Written administrative policies and procedures

B.   New employees generally are hired between the minimum and midpoint range assigned to their job. Supervisors may recommend higher starting rates based on the employee's experience or education. The appropriate department managers and the Human Resources Department will review these recommendations.

C.   Salary increases are intended to reward excellent job performance and are not given on the basis of length of service. Supervisors may recommend salary increases for their employees in accordance with the guidelines published annually by the Human Resource Department.

D.   Employees are paid bi-weekly. All salaries and wages are subject to all applicable taxes.

E.   Overtime compensation will be paid to nonexempt employees who work in excess of ( ) hours during a normal workweek at one and one-half time their regular hourly rate.

F.   Definitions of Overtime:

(1) Requested Overtime:

    a.   Employees are requested to work overtime with or without prior notice.

    b.   Employees that are requested to work overtime will not be counted absent if they do not report to work during overtime hours.

    c.   Employees that are requested to work overtime who report to work after the designated work time will not be considered tardy during overtime hours.

(2) Mandatory Overtime:

    a.   Mandatory overtime is for serious backlog or critical time-sensitive situations only.

    b.   Employees are not required to work mandatory overtime except in unavoidable circumstances that must be approved by the Administrator or Department Supervisor.

    c.   Employees should be so advised at least ( ) week before, but not less than ( ) days before scheduled mandatory overtime.

    d.   Any employee that does not report to work during mandatory overtime will be counted absent for the overtime period.

    e.   Employees reporting to work after the designated work time will be considered tardy.

    f.   Consistently refusing to work when mandatory overtime is called will affect your appraisal rating or may result in disciplinary action.

(3) Overtime Pay

    a.   Overtime shall not be paid until the actual hours worked exceeds ( ) hours per week regardless of the number of hours worked per day or the number of days per week.

    b.   As required by federal law, overtime is paid at the rate of one and one-half times the regular rate of pay.

    c.   Until actual hours worked exceeds ( ) hours per week, all compensation shall be at the regular rate of pay.

    d.   All categories of leave, such as paid personal time, vacation, jury duty, funeral leave and on-the-job injury compensated hours will not be considered as time worked for the purposes of overtime pay.

g.   All overtime must be pre-approved by the Administrator or Department Supervisor.

e.   It is the responsibility of the department supervisor to verify that overtime hours worked by the employee are accurate.

TIMEKEEPING

1.   POLICY:

It is the policy of the (Church) to require employees to keep their time as accurately as possible.

2.   GUIDELINES OF THE POLICY:

Accurately recording time worked is the responsibility of every nonexempt employee. Time worked is all the time actually spent on the job performing assigned duties. Nonexempt employees should accurately record the time they begin and end their work, as well as the beginning and ending time of each meal period. They should also record the beginning and ending time of any split shift or departure from work for personal reasons. Overtime work must always be approved before it is performed.

Altering, falsifying, tampering with time records or recording time on another employee's time record may result in disciplinary action, up to and including termination of employment.

Nonexempt employees should report to work no more than seven minutes prior to their scheduled starting time nor stay more than seven minutes after their scheduled stop time without prior authorization from their supervisor.

Each employee is responsible for signing his or her time record to certify the accuracy of all time recorded before submitting it for payroll processing.

HOURS OF OPERATION

1. POLICY:

    It is the policy of the (Church) to establish working hours as required by workload, production flow, and the efficient management of personnel resources.

2. GUIDELINES OF THE POLICY:

    A. The Ministry is open to the public (weekday) to (weekday).

    B. The official workweek begins at midnight on Sunday and ends at midnight the following Sunday. A workweek shall consist of (   ) days of work totaling (   ) hours. Business, economic, or other conditions may warrant greater or lesser numbers of hours or days; therefore, this policy is not to be construed as a guarantee of your particular hourly or daily assignment.

    C. The workday begins at (   ) a.m. and ends at (   ) p.m. The lunch period is (   ) minutes for full time staff and (   ) minutes for part time staff. Break times are at the department supervisor's discretion in keeping with demands and schedules.

ATTENDANCE AND PUNCTUALITY

1. POLICY:

    It is the policy of the (Church) to require its employees to have good attendance and be punctual. Management recognizes that circumstances beyond an employee's control may cause absence from work for all or part of a day. However, unauthorized absences or tardiness will not be tolerated and will result in disciplinary action, up to and including termination of employment.

2. GUIDELINES OF THE POLICY:

    A. Employees are expected to report to work on time. If an employee is unable to come into work or will be late, he/she is expected to notify the supervisor no later than (   ) minutes before the employee's regular starting time. However, as much advance notice as possible should be given to permit scheduling a replacement. If an employee's supervisor or manager is not available, employees should contact the Human Resources Department. Failure to notify the (Church) of any anticipated absence or delay in reporting to work may result in loss of compensation during the absence and may be grounds for disciplinary action.

    B. An employee must be at his workstation at the prescribed time after breaks. Employees who for any reason will be delayed more than a few minutes in reporting for work are required to call their supervisor promptly to explain their circumstances. If the supervisor is unavailable, employees should contact the Church Administrator or Human Resources Department.

    C. Employees who are delayed in reporting for work more than (   ) minutes and who have not notified their supervisors of their expected tardiness may lose their right to work the balance of the work day. Habitual tardiness shall result in discipline, up to and including termination.

    D. Employees whose duties do not require them to leave the building in which they work must obtain permission from their supervisor in order to leave the (Church) during working hours, except for scheduled rest/lunch breaks.

    E. Employees who are absent from work for (   ) consecutive days without notice and good cause shall be considered as having resigned.

PERSONNEL RECORDS

1.   POLICY:

It is the policy of the (Church) to maintain certain records on each employee, which are related to the employee's job with the (Church). A confidential employment and personnel file is maintained for each employee. It is important that up-to-date records be maintained for employment and benefits purposes. Therefore, an employee is required to notify the Human Resources Department immediately if there is a change in employment status or in personal information, such as marital status, number of dependents, address, telephone number, beneficiary or legal name. All information in the personnel file is (Church) property.

The (Church) will not provide information, except name, job title, job site, and employment date, regarding its current or former employees, unless required by federal or state law or court order. All employee information requests must be referred to the Human Resources Department. The supervisors or other employees are not permitted to respond to a reference request. Telephone inquiries will not be answered. Only written inquiries from the person seeking the information on that person's letterhead with name and title will be considered.

2.   GUIDELINES OF THE POLICY:

A.   Each employee's personnel file will contain necessary job-related and personal information needed by the (Church) in conducting its activities or as is required by federal, state, or local law. This information normally will include:

(1)   Basic identifying information (i.e., employee's name, address and job title)

(2)   Completed employment applications or other hiring-related documents

(3)   Payroll information

(4)   Benefit coverage information

(5)   Performance Appraisals

The (Church) reserves the right to supply information without notifying the individual involved in cooperation with law enforcement, public safety or medical officials who demonstrate a legitimate need to know the specific information.

G.   The (Church) will ordinarily honor subpoenas demanding production of information with respect to any employee, but will seek to advise such employee with respect thereto unless otherwise prohibited by law. The (Church) has no obligation to contest the validity of any such subpoena.

H.   The filing of a claim by, or on behalf of an employee, pursuant to a company or public benefit program is deemed to be consent by the employee for release of any medical information appropriate in connection with processing of such claim.

I.   In order to keep personnel records up to date, employees are urged to notify the Human Resources Department in writing of any changes in:

   (1)   Name

   (2)   Address

   (3)   Telephone Number

   (4)   Marital status

   (5)   Number of dependents

   (6)   Beneficiary designations for any of the (Church's) benefit plans

   (7)   Persons to be notified in case of emergency

   (8)   Education

J.   When a change in the number of dependents or marital status occurs, the employee should report to the Human Resources Department to complete a status change, and appropriate forms for federal and state tax withholding.

K.   The interpretation of this Policy is the sole responsibility of the Human Resources Department with the advice of the Office of General Counsel.

TRAVEL AND BUSINESS EXPENSE

1. POLICY:

    It is the policy of the (Church) to reimburse employees for authorized business expenses incurred in the normal course of conducting the (Church's) business.

2. GUIDELINES OF THE POLICY:

    A. Specified business expenses procedures and reimbursement rates are issued by the Finance and Church Administration. All the (Church's) employees who anticipate business expenses should be aware of the current reimbursement rates and necessary procedures before incurring such expenses.

    B. Activities that justify the reimbursement of expenses include approved (Church's) business, and the attendance at business meetings, conventions, seminars or other selected educational functions related to the employee's job. Prior approval of travel, however, must always be obtained from the appropriate division director or Administrator.

    C. All employees shall travel coach or economy class and shall stay and eat in moderately priced establishments while traveling on the (Church's) business. Any deviation from this policy must demonstrate a bona fide business necessity and be approved by the Administrator before such travel.

    D. Under normal circumstances, all travel arrangements for transportation, lodging and car rentals must be made through the authorized travel agent.

    E. Family members accompanying the employee on a trip will do so at the employee's personal expense. Airfare and other expenses for relatives are not reimbursable nor can they be charged to the (Church). Exceptions to this policy may be made for good cause upon prior approval of the Administrator.

    F. All employees traveling overseas should be accompanied by another staff member. If one person absolutely has to go and no one else is able to accompany him, it may be appropriate to delay the trip.

    G. Employees will not be reimbursed for the expense of entertainment while on a business trip unless the entertainment has a bona fide business purpose. Expenses for meetings with employees of the (Church) or affiliated organizations are not normally reimbursable. If legitimate business purposes necessitate the meeting of employees of the (Church) during a normally scheduled mealtime, reimbursement of such expenses shall be permitted after obtaining the approval of the Administrator.

    H. Employees who take more expensive flights, unnecessary connecting flights or less convenient flight times to accrue airline mileage points for "promotional traveler programs" shall do so at their own expense.

I.   Independent contractors who have been approved for travel subsidy by the appropriate authority should place their travel orders including airfare, hotel and rental cars through the authorized (Church) travel agency.

J.   Reasonable expenses incurred during pre-employment interviews or other pre-placement activities by non-employees are generally reimbursable.

K.   A cash advance for expenses of approved travel may be obtained through administration or by check through the Accounting Department during regular working hours. Requests must be submitted a minimum of (   ) day(s) prior to the need. After normal business hours, an emergency fund will be available and disbursed only for extreme emergencies through the Accounting Department.

L.   Upon completion of travel, the employee must complete an Expense Report form within (   ) working days and attach the necessary supporting receipts with any unspent funds from the cash advance, if applicable. The amounts claimed less the cash advance, if any, must be approved by the Administrator before submitting the expense report to the Accounting Department for payment.

M.   Unused airline tickets and vouchers must be returned to the authorized travel agency.

N.   The (Church) will not be responsible for "no shows: billings (charges for reservations employees have neglected to cancel because of a change in travel plans) with reference to hotel and motel reservations. If the "no show" is the result of a matter beyond the employee's reasonable control, then the employee will not be charged for the "no show."

AUTOMOBILE USAGE

1.   POLICY:

It is the policy of the (Church) to provide use of the (Church's) owned vehicles or to reimburse employees for use of their personal vehicles while employees are engaged in the (Church's) business in accordance with the guidelines of this policy.

2.   GUIDELINES OF THE POLICY:

A.   THE (CHURCH) VEHICLES:

   (1)   The (Church) may assign vehicles to those departments that have special and continual vehicle needs. Acquisition of departmental vehicles must be approved through the Administrator's request process. Each department is expected to assign to one individual the responsibility of operation and maintenance of vehicles. This individual should coordinate his assignment with the Transportation Department, which establishes detailed guidelines for the operation of departmental vehicles.

   (2)   The (Church) may provide a vehicle to an individual whose job duties require the daily and exclusive use of a vehicle. Individually assigned vehicles must be requested in writing by the employee's supervisor through the Transportation Department

B.   EMPLOYEES' PERSONAL VEHICLES: Employees may use their own vehicles for the (Church's) business only with the prior approval of their supervisors. Employees must demonstrate personal vehicle insurance with adequate coverage for property damage, liability and personal injury.

C.   SHORT-TERM RENT VEHICLE: Arrangements for rental vehicles are made through the Transportation Department and are subject to the policies of that department. Additional insurance coverage sold by rental agencies should be refused. The (Church) will pay rental agencies directly for the rental. Rental agencies generally have their own arrangements for emergency service to their vehicles should the employee require such service during the short-term vehicle rental.

D.   MAINTENANCE AND USE OF VEHICLES:

   (1)   The following apply to all the (Church's) vehicles.

      (a)   Drivers should use local gas stations where the (Church) has arranged to charge gas purchases.

      (b)   Maintenance and repairs must be performed by the (Church's)

Transportation department. If they cannot accomplish the work, other arrangements should be made through the Administrator's office. (Employees should make their own arrangements only under bona fide emergency conditions).

(c)   The (Church's) vehicles should be driven by employees on the (Church's) payroll only.

(2)   The following applies to EMPLOYEES' PERSONAL VEHICLES being used for the (Church's) business:

(a)   Repairs or services performed on any employee's vehicle are not reimbursable.

(b)   Expenses reimbursable are those for a per-mile figure based on the current IRS approved mileage allowance.

(3)   The following apply to ALL VEHICLES being used for the (Church's) business, whether assigned by the (Church), a rental vehicle or the employee's personal vehicle:

(a)   All vehicles must be operated legally and safely by the (Church's) employees with a valid driver's license.

(b)   Vehicles must have a current registration and inspection sticker and be in proper repair.

(c)   Traffic tickets, parking fines or other fines incurred while on (Church) business are not reimbursable expenses.

(d)   Normal reimbursable expenses include parking and tolls.

MEMBERSHIP IN TRADE AND PROFESSIONAL ASSOCIATIONS

1. POLICY:

   It is the policy of the (Church) to promote the communication of new ideas and information between employees and other industry experts through participation in the activities of work-related trade and professional associations.

2. GUIDELINES OF THE POLICY:

   A. Subject to prior approval by the Administrator or the Human Resources Department, the (Church) will reimburse employees for membership fees in trade and professional associations. Each approved membership is subject to annual evaluation by management.

   B. Subject to prior approval by the Administrator, the (Church) will reimburse employees for registration fees and reasonable expenses to attend meetings and conferences of trade and professional associations.

   C. Time spent in such activities normally should be outside of the employee's working hours and will not be considered hours worked for pay purposes. However, time spent participating in trade and professional associations at the (Church's) request or under its direction or control shall be considered hours worked for pay purposes.

   D. Employees who are invited to or seek to serve in any official position in a trade or professional association must obtain the approval of the Administrator before accepting. The (Church) will reimburse these employees for reasonable expenses incurred in attending to their duties. Prior approval of the employee's immediate supervisor will be required for all time away from work.

OUTSIDE EMPLOYMENT

1.   POLICY:

It is the policy of the (Church) to review employees' requests for permission to work at a second job on a case-by-case basis, and if appropriate, to allow its employees to hold second jobs, subject to certain restrictions as outlined below. If outside employment is not prohibited, however, prior approval of management must be obtained before any such outside employment is accepted.

2.   GUIDELINES OF THE POLICY:

A.   Request for permission to accept outside employment shall be submitted in writing to the employee's department manager and the Administrator. The request shall state the name and address of the outside employer, the nature of the job and the hours of employment. The department manager shall forward the request to the Director of Human Resources recommending either approval or disapproval. The decision of the Administrator in concurrence with the Human Resources Department with respect to the request shall be final, subject to Complaint and Appeal.

B.   In considering a request to accept outside employment, the Administrator and Human Resources Department shall be guided by the non-exhaustive following standards:

(1)   Whether the outside employment will in any way lessen the employee's efficiency in working for the (Church) or is inherently in conflict with the teaching and tenets of the (Church).

(2)   Whether the outside employment is with an organization which does business with or is a competitor or the (Church).

(3)   Whether the nature of the outside employment adversely affects the (Church's) image in the community.

C.   It must be realized that employment with the (Church) is the employee's primary responsibility. Outside employment will not be considered an excuse for poor job performance, absenteeism, tardiness or refusal to work overtime. Should the outside employment cause or contribute to any of these situations or otherwise affect the employee's performance to the detriment of the (Church), it must be discontinued or the employee will be terminated.

D.   All employees are expressly prohibited from engaging in any activity that competes with the (Church) or compromises its interests. This prohibition includes performing any service for persons on non-working time that are normally performed by the

(Church) personnel and the unauthorized use or application of any confidential trade information or techniques. In addition, employees are not to conduct any outside business during paid working time.

E.   Employees who have accepted outside employment are not eligible for paid absence, other than accrued sick leave, when the absence is a result of injury on the second job or illness associated with the second job.

PERFORMANCE APPRAISALS (EVALUATIONS)

1. POLICY:

    It is the policy of the (church) that the job performance of each employee be evaluated periodically by the employee's supervisor.

2. GUIDELINES TO THE POLICY:

    A. The (Church's) Performance Appraisal manual sets forth the details and procedures of the performance appraisal process. Generally, the components of your work product to be evaluated are: knowledge, quantity, accuracy, judgment, innovation, appearance, habits, cooperation, initiative, reliability and attendance.

    B. The performance appraisal may consist of:

        (1) A completed Performance Appraisal form setting forth the rating for each task objective and the overall rating.

        (2) The supervisor's written comments on each task objective and comments on the overall performance.

        (3) A review session with the employee at which time the performance ratings are discussed and, if necessary, a plan for improvement is developed and tasks/objectives are established for the next appraisal period.

    C. Performance appraisals will generally be completed upon the following occasions:

        (1) After the first ( ) months of employment (see performance appraisals).

        (2) Every ( ) months following employee's anniversary date of hire.

        (3) When the employee is transferred or promoted to a new job.

        (4) At the time of the employee's termination.

        (5) More often, as appropriate, to maintain performance or improve performance.

    D. Except in the case of probation or termination, if a performance appraisal has been completed on the employee within ( ) months prior to one of the above occasions, a new appraisal need not be completed.

    E. Supervisors may keep documentation substantiating job performance of individuals under their supervision. (Originals should be kept in the HR Dept.)

F.   Each written evaluation by the supervisor shall not be final until reviewed and signed by the Administrator before the review session with the employee.

G.   After the written evaluation has been reviewed and signed by the rating supervisor and the Administrator, the supervisor and employee shall meet and discuss the evaluation, assess the employee's strengths and weaknesses in a constructive manner, and set objectives and goals for the period ahead. The employee shall be given the opportunity to examine the written evaluation and make written comments about any aspect of it. The employee shall then sign and date the evaluation. A copy of the approved form shall be given to the employee.

H.   If the written evaluation contains an unfavorable comment or rating which the employee believes is unfair or unjustified, and the matter has not been resolved to the employee's satisfaction during the discussion with the supervisor, the employee may take further action by using the regular complaint procedure.

I.   Nothing contained in this Policy should be construed to prohibit or discourage supervisors from discussing an employee's job performance with the employee on an informal basis whenever the need arises.

J.   Performance appraisals may be forwarded to the Human Resources Department, along with any necessary status change forms for inclusion in the employee's personnel file.

K.   The Human Resources Department may publish instructions periodically defining how performance appraisals shall be linked to compensation, promotions, transfers and merit increases.

PAY INCREASES

1.   POLICY:

The (Church) attempts to maintain competitive salaries based upon the responsibilities of each employee's job and rates paid in other ministries and church-related organizations. A "salary range" is typically set for each position according to factors such as level of responsibility, knowledge and skill required and overall value of the position to the Church.

2.   GUIDELINES OF THE POLICY:

Supervisors and employees are strongly encouraged to discuss job performance and goals on an informal, day to-day basis. Usually, a formal written performance evaluation will be conducted at the end of an employee's initial period of hire, known as the introductory period. Additional formal performance evaluations are usually conducted to provide both supervisors and employees the opportunity to discuss tasks, identify and correct weaknesses, encourage and recognize strengths and discuss positive, purposeful approaches for meeting goals. You are encouraged to frequently reflect upon and compare your performance to the goals established by the (Church) for your job position.

Performance-based pay adjustments are awarded by the (Church) in an effort to recognize truly superior employee performance. The decision to award such an adjustment is dependent upon numerous factors, including the information documented by the formal performance evaluation process. The decision whether or not to award such an adjustment is entirely within the discretion of the (Church).

PROMOTION

1. POLICY:

    It is the policy of the (Church) to attempt to promote employees from within the organization and, thus, to train and develop the employees for promotion to higher level positions as their abilities warrant.

2. GUIDELINES OF THE POLICY:

    A. Generally, job openings will be posted on the employee bulletin boards and announced in employee publications.

        (1) Employees who desire to apply for a particular job should notify the Administrator and Human Resources Department, in writing, within five business days after the initial posting or announcement of the job opening.

        (2) Department managers may also recommend employees for consideration as candidates for promotion, or to fill a job opening.

        (3) In the absence of, or in addition to candidates applying or being recommended for a job opening, the Administrator or Human Resources Department may use outside sources of candidates.

    B. To insure that the records are current and accurate, the supervisor will review the records of all employees who are candidates for a promotion or a transfer.

    C. The manager of the department in which the job opening occurs will interview qualified candidates.

        (1) Employees are allowed time off with pay for job interviews related to promotion.

        (2) It is the responsibility of the department manager to select the most qualified applicant for the position, subject to the approval of the Administrator and the Human Resources Department.

    D. The Administrator and the Human Resources Department may use all or any combination of the following methods to evaluate employees for promotion.

        (1) Attendance and work records.

        (2) Performance appraisals.

        (3) Job-related selection tests.

(4)   A job-related medical examination arranged by the Human Resource Department.

(5)   Personal Interviews.

E.   Employees selected for promotion will be placed on "introductory status" for a period not to exceed (   ) months.

F.   At the end of the introductory period, the supervisor will prepare a written evaluation of the promoted employee's job performance with his recommendations to keep the employee in the new position. Copies of the evaluation will be forwarded to the Administrator and the Human Resources Department.

G.   If the promoted employee is unable to perform the job, he may be reinstated to the former job and assigned his prior rate of pay. If the employee's former position is not available or if other circumstances so warrant, the employee will be placed on layoff status subject to recall into the prior job, or will be released from employment.

H.   Normally, an employee will not be permitted to apply for promotion to a new position until he has been in the present job for a minimum of (   ) months.

TRANSFER

1.   POLICY:

It is the policy of the (Church) to permit transfers of employees from one job to another, either at their own request (assuming suitable openings are available in another department, and the new supervisor agrees to the transfer) or as a result of a decision of the Administrator or the Human Resources Department.

2.   GUIDELINES TO THE POLICY:

A.   Reasons for transfers may include, but shall not necessarily be limited to, fluctuations in department workloads or production flow, the more efficient utilization of personnel, increased career opportunities, personality conflicts, reasons of health and personal situations.

B.   Temporary changes in work assignments may be made with both the transferring and the new supervisor's approvals for periods of up to ( ) months. Such temporary assignments may be extended for an additional ( ) months when the reasons for the original change in assignment continue to be applicable.

C.   An employee's eligibility for transfer is determined by the requirements of the new job and the employee's suitability for that job. Generally, an employee must have been performing in a satisfactory manner in his current job for a period of ( ) months and performed in the current job for less than ( ) months in appropriate circumstances. The Administrator's discretion prevails in approving transfers in concurrence with the Human Resources Department.

D.   While the needs of the department are primary, employees are often considered as candidates for transfer in the following order of eligibility.

  (1)   Eligible employees in the same department as the job opening.

  (2)   Eligible employees in other departments who have submitted requests in accordance with this Policy to transfer to or to be considered for job openings in the particular department.

  (3)   Eligible employees who are being considered for layoff due to the elimination of their jobs.

E.   Employees are free to inquire about possible job transfers at any time. When an employee desires a transfer to another job, the following procedure will be followed:

  (1)   The employee will submit a written Transfer Request form to his department manager. The request must include the reason for the transfer. If the employ-

ee desires a transfer to a specific job, this also must be included in the request. The department manager will forward the request within ( ) days to the Administrator and the Human Resources Department recommending approval or disapproval and the reasons.

(2) The Administrator and the Human Resources Department will determine whether the desired job or suitable job opening exists. If a suitable job is available, the Human Resources Department will arrange an interview between the employee and the manager of the department in which the job opening exists.

(3) Employees will be allowed time off with pay for interviews related to transfers, with prior approval of their supervisor.

(4) The decision whether to effect the transfer will be made by the manager of the department and the Administrator in which the job opening exists, with the concurrence of the Human Resources Department.

(5) Generally, the interval between the approval of the transfer and the implementation of the transfer shall not exceed ( ) calendar days.

F. When an employee desires a transfer to another location, the above procedure will apply. Travel expenses incurred in going to the desired location for job interviews will be handled according to the policy. The time off with pay will be limited to one day unless the manager of the department or the person considering the request needs additional interviewing time.

G. Transferred employees will be given up to ( ) months of introduction/probation. During this period they may be assisted in adjusting to their new jobs. In the event that the employee's performance is unsatisfactory, at the discretion of the manager in charge acting in conjunction with the Human Resources Department, the employee may revert back to his original position, or a comparable position.

H. Requesting a transfer does not jeopardize the employee's job.

I. An employee who is transferred will be paid at the rate of pay authorized for the new job, effective as of the date the person begins the new job.

J. In cases of a temporary assignment to a higher paying job, the employee may be compensated at the rate of the new position. If temporarily transferred to a lower-paying job, the employee will continue to receive the employee's regular rate of pay.

K. Job openings will be posted on a regular basis on the employee bulletin boards and announced in employee publications.

L. Successful job applicants shall usually be limited to one transfer every ( ) months.

M.   If a manager wants to solicit the transfer of a person working in another department, the manager must first coordinate directly with the Administrator and the present department manager as well as the Human Resources Department.

LAYOFF

1.   POLICY:

It is the policy of the (Church) to stabilize employment conditions to the extent possible. In the event that a reduction in the work force becomes necessary, employees will be selected for layoff at the discretion of the Administrator and the Director of Human Resources.

2.   GUIDELINES OF THE POLICY:

A.   Although circumstances may require a different process, usually employees will be selected for layoff in the following order:

(1)   Employees who have not completed the introductory period.

(2)   Temporary, on-call and part-time employees.

(3)   Regular full-time employees.

B.   In the case of regular, full-time employees, seniority, performance and training will be taken into consideration. The staffing needs of the (Church) will be of paramount concern in determining the order of layoff.

C.   Supervisors will, if possible, give notice to affected employees at least two weeks before the layoff is scheduled to occur. In addition to the notice, supervisors shall inform employees of the reason for the layoff, the estimated length of the layoff, and the employee's chances for recall, if known. This information is provided for guidance only and is not binding on the (Church).

D.   In cases where layoff is for an indefinite period and chances for recall are considered remote, the Human Resources Division shall attempt to provide assistance to affected employees, including:

(1)   Outplacement counseling.

(2)   Referral to employment agencies.

(3)   Information concerning unemployment benefits and food stamps.

E.   All layoffs will be treated as termination of employment for the purpose of employee benefits.

RELOCATION

1. POLICY:

It is the policy of the (Church) to provide assistance to regular, full-time employees who are asked to relocate to other (Church) facilities and to certain regular, full-time new hires who are relocating to join the Ministry provided the former residence is at least ( ) miles from the new place of employment. All moving arrangements must be coordinated and approved by the Administrator and the Human Resources Department. The affected employee has the duty of submitting any such request for assistance to the appropriate Ministry department for consideration.

2. GUIDELINES OF THE POLICY:

   A. Department heads should avoid geographical relocation of current or newly hired personnel for employment or position changes whenever possible.

   B. If the move is at the employee's request and convenience, such move shall be at the employee's expense.

   C. Each application of the Relocation Policy will be on an individual basis, subject to approval of the Administrator and the Human Resources Department. An information package will be made available to all employees relocating to the area.

   D. Any requests for exceptions to this Policy must be submitted to the Administrator in writing or the Director of Human Resources for approval, prior to relocation of the employee.

   E. It shall be the responsibility of the department manager to audit and forward all relocation expenses as submitted by the relocated employee to the Administrator and the Human Resources Department on the appropriate form for approval. No alternate authorization signatures will be accepted on any relocation expense forms.

      (1) Receipts, invoices, used and unused travel tickets, and so forth, should be attached to the expense form. (Only receipted amounts for food expense will be reimbursed). All expenses should be reported within ( ) working days after the final move is made. Only expenses specifically outlined in the Policy will be reimbursed.

      (2) The Human Resources Department or Administrator will arrange for the move of authorized household items. Disallowed expenses will be deducted from the invoices by the Accounting or Human Resources Department. The moving company will bill the employee directly for all disallowed items the employee has authorized the mover to ship.

F. This Policy will comply with existing Internal Revenue code, income tax regulations and local taxing authority regulations regarding withholding. The employee should seek competent tax advice regarding reporting requirements as to relocation compensation paid to an employee.

G. Self-moves using rental trucks are encouraged. The (Church) may share the savings of a self-move compared to the expense of a vendor move. A portion of the savings goes to the new employee in a lump sum payment, the amount of which will be determined by the Administrator and the Human Resources Department and paid on a cash available basis. The (Church) will pay the moving costs and arrangements will be made through the Human Resources Department.

H. All reimbursable moving expenses must be submitted within ( ) year from date of hire or they will not be reimbursed.

I. The purpose of this Policy is to provide the employee with necessary relocation assistance while keeping costs to the (Church) at a minimum. Therefore, relocation benefits are not negotiable or interchangeable.

J. The (Church) will not be responsible for relocating discharged employees.

3. GENERAL PROVISIONS (EXEMPT EMPLOYEES ONLY):

A. INTERVIEW EXPENSE: If a pre-employment interview is requested by the (Church), travel, food and accommodation expenses for a potential employee may be paid by the (Church). These expenses must be approved in advance by the Administrator and the Human Resources Department.

B. HOME FINDING IN THE NEW LOCATION: The (Church) may provide one home-finding trip to the new location to include the employee and spouse, not to exceed ( ) nights, with the following reimbursable expenses:

(1) MEALS: Receipted amounts not to exceed present approved corporate reimbursable rate for employee and spouse.

(2) LODGING: All reservations need to be made through the Human Resources Department or Administrator's office and costs will be directly billed or prepaid. The (Church's) housing will be utilized when possible. Motels and alternate lodgings will be used only when the (Church's) housing is not available and arrangements will be made by the Human Resources Department.

(3) CAR RENTAL: If necessary and with prior approval by Administrator.

(4) AIRFARE: Coach only. Arrangements will be made through the Administrator and the Human Resources Department.

(5)   MILEAGE: Mileage from the old location to the new location is reimbursable at the current approved corporate reimbursable rate when a personal automobile is used.

(6)   All expenses, unless stated otherwise, are to be out-of-pocket. Attach all receipts for reimbursable expenses to the appropriate form and give them to the department manager for his/her audit and forwarding to the Human Resources Department or Administrator prior to departure.

C.   TEMPORARY LIVING EXPENSES – EMPLOYEE ONLY: If a move is delayed because of the sale of a house or similar reasons, the (Church) may pay, with the approval of the Administrator and the Human Resources Department, interim living expenses of the employee, until receipt of his first full paycheck or up to (   ) days, whichever occurs first. Managers will be responsible for facilitating all paperwork on time. The Human Resources Department and the Administrator may approve interim living expenses beyond (   ) days in an appropriate case. This will include lodging that will be arranged by the Human Resources Department and the receipted amounts of breakfast and dinner not to exceed the approved corporate reimbursable rate. The expenses of travel, laundry and cleaning, telephone, parking, tolls, etc. will be the employee's responsibility. The manager and the employee are expected to make every effort to minimize temporary living expenses.

D.   RETURN TRIPS HOME: The (Church) may approve reimbursement for the employee's trips home during the actual interim living. A maximum of (   ) trips will be paid by the (Church). One of these trips may be used by the employee to assist the family with the moving of the household goods. If transportation arrangements are required, they must be coordinated through the Human Resources Department or Administrator.

E.   TRAVEL ALLOWANCE: Individual travel advances may be given to relocating employees to cover out-of-pocket expenses of the family move when relocating. This must be approved by the Administrator. (Managers should initiate the request for an advance with sufficient time for processing). Receipts must be retained and turned in on the appropriate form for reimbursement within (   ) days of completion of the trip to the division manager for audit and forwarding to the Administrators office.

F.   MOVING HOUSEHOLD GOODS: Upon receipt of an Employment Relocation form from the Human Resources Department the HR department will arrange with the mover selected to handle shipment of the household goods. Subject to Section 3, Item H of the Relocation Policy, the (Church) may pay for packing and van transportation for up to (   ) pounds of household goods only, and replacement coverage insurance of the household goods at the current contract agreement with the vendor. Packing and shipping of household items must be coordinated to occur during the normal working hours of the moving company. The (Church) may pay for moving household goods for the former principal, personal residence to the new location.

▲

The (Church) WILL NOT PAY STORAGE OR STORAGE RELATED CHARGES.

G. MOVING THE FAMILY:

(1) TRAVEL TO NEW LOCATION:

(a) AUTOMOBILE: The employee is expected to drive his automobile to the new location. Reimbursement for mileage for ( ) automobile, at the current corporate approved rate, is limited to travel by the most direct route from the old location to the new location. Mileage distance will be determined by mileage charts. Mileage will be paid only when the employee's personal car is used. Shipment of automobiles will be at employee's expense.

(b) AIR TRANSPORTATION: Reservations will be coordinated between the Administrator, Human Resources Department, employee and hiring manager and paid directly by the (Church). Air transportation must be coach class.

(c) RAIL OR BUS TRANSPORTATION: Ticket cost will be reimbursed when receipt is presented on the appropriate expense form.

(d) DUPLICATE COSTS: The (Church) will not pay mileage in addition to other transportation expenses.

(e) LODGING IN OLD LOCATION: One night of lodging in the city of residence if necessary, after the furniture is loaded will be reimbursed for receipted amounts only. The most economical lodging should be used.

(f) FOOD ALLOWANCE: Food may be reimbursed for receipted amounts only, not to exceed the current corporate approved rate.

(2) TEMPORARY LIVING EXPENSES: Following the relocation of the employee (and family) temporary living expenses will be paid through the morning after the arrival of the employee's furniture at the new location. Lodging at the new location will be arranged by the Human Resources Department. In the event the family arrives at the new location before the shipment of household goods, the family will not be eligible for food allowance or accommodations and all expenses will be the responsibility of the employee. Scheduling advance housing for a family in this instance may be on a space-available basis and requires prior approval. A maximum of ( ) days will be allowed in any case.

H.   NON-REIMBURSABLE EXPENSES (the cost of which will be totally paid by the employee):

(1)   Household goods in excess of (   ) pounds.

(2)   Moving of unusually large or bulky items requiring special handling such as trailers, boats, heavy equipment or machines, motorcycles, automobiles and/or grand pianos. Items replaceable for less than the moving cost should not be moved.

(3)   Disassembling or assembling pool tables and play equipment, draining and disassembling water beds and/or portable swimming pools or related items.

(4)   Adjusting television sets, removing or installing outside antennas.

(5)   Special electrical or plumbing services in excess of regular services required to connect or disconnect electrical appliances.

(6)   Storage fees.

(7)   Deposits on public utilities (electric, water, telephone, etc.).

(8)   Replacement or appliances that cannot be used at the new location.

(9)   Firewood, patio bricks, greenhouses and contents.

(10)   Relocating pets.

(11)   Upgraded insurance costs on moving household goods.

(12)   All costs associated with selling or leasing prior residence.

(13)   Security deposits.

(14)   Miscellaneous household set-up expenses.

NOTE: Stamp collections, jewelry, firearms, coin collections, antiques, works of art, and other articles of sentimental or extreme monetary value should be carried with the employee during move or insured separately at the employee's cost.

I.   REIMBURSEMENT IN EVENT EMPLOYEE TERMINATES:

(1)   RESIGNATION OF NEWLY HIRED AND TRANSFERRED EMPLOYEES: Employees previously relocated at the (Church) who voluntarily resign will be required to reimburse the (Church) for moving expenses (including house-hunting trip, transport of household belongings, food and mileage and allowances and temporary housing) as follows:

(a)   Resignation during the first (   ) months of employment – reimburse all relocation cost.

(b)   Resignation during second six months of employment reimburse (%) of the relocation cost.

(c)   Resignation after (   ) year of employment – no reimbursement required.

(2)   LAYOFF: No reimbursement required.

(3)   DISCHARGE (Involuntary Termination): No reimbursement required.

J.   GENERAL PROVISIONS (NON-EXEMPT EMPLOYEES ONLY):

(1)   NO INTERVIEW EXPENSES WILL BE REIMBURSED.

(2)   HOUSEHOLD GOODS MOVE: The (Church) may pay reasonable charges for a truck or trailer rental required to move employee's possessions.

(3)   AUTOMOBILE MOVE: Employee may be reimbursed at the approved corporate mileage rate for driving one car to the new job location.

(4)   TRAVEL EXPENSE TO NEW LOCATION: Employee (only) may be reimbursed at the approved corporate rate for food, lodging and transportation while en-route to the new location.

(5)   TEMPORARY LIVING: The (Church) may, if approved by the Administrator and the Human Resources Department, reimburse employee for temporary expenses for food and provide lodging for up to (   ) weeks while employee

works at new job prior to finding a suitable residence. Food reimbursement will be limited to the receipted amounts for breakfast and dinner, not to exceed the approved corporate rate.

TERMINATION OF EMPLOYMENT

1.   POLICY

It is the policy of the (Church) to terminate employment because of an employee's resignation, discharge at management's sole discretion (with or without cause), retirement or as a
result of a permanent or temporary reduction in the workforce. Discharge can result from
an employee's misconduct or unsatisfactory job performance or for other reasons. In the
absence of a specific written agreement signed by the Administrator and the Director of the
Human Resources Department, employees are employed on an at-will basis, and free to
resign at any time. The (Church) reserves the right to terminate employment for any reason,
or for no reason.

2.   GUIDELINES TO THE POLICY:

    A.   RESIGNATION: All employees shall give written notice of their intent to resign.

        (1)   Supervisory employees are expected to give ( ) weeks' notice.

        (2)   Clerical and administrative employees are expected to give ( ) weeks' notice.

        (3)   All other employees are expected to give ( ) weeks' notice.

        (4)   Failure to give a required notice will result in forfeiture of the (Church's) ben-
efits, liability for damages, and ineligibility for re-employment.

        (5)   Resigning employees receive no separation pay.

    B.   LAYOFF: Employees terminated because of a reduction in the workforce may, if pos-
sible, be given advance notice of the termination or pay in lieu of the notice. Though
circumstances may necessitate less notice, in most cases the notice period will be at
least ( ) weeks before the layoff is scheduled to occur.

    D.   TERMINATIONS: All terminations must be reviewed, in advance, by the
Administrator and the Human Resources Department. The procedure to be followed
will be decided upon at that time. After all levels of management have approved the
termination, the last person in the chain of command will forward notices of termination to the Administrator and Human Resources Department for final review and
concurrence. Then the employee shall be made aware of the decision to terminate his
employment.

        (1)   Where the termination is for cause, no separation pay will be paid.
           (a)   Accrued vacation pay up to the date of termination will be paid to
employees terminated for cause.

(b)   Any vacation time taken in excess of that accrued will be deducted from the final paycheck.

(2)   Where the termination is other than for cause or disciplinary reasons, the terminated employee will receive the following benefits:

   (a)   The Human Resources Department may make outplacement services available to these terminated employees.

   (b)   At the (Church's) sole discretion, finances permitting, separation pay may be paid. The amount of such pay, if any, shall be determined by the Human Resources Department

   (c)   Accrued vacation pay up to the date of termination will be paid to these terminated employees

   (d)   Any vacation time taken in excess of the accrued amount of time will be deducted from the final paycheck, with the exception of employees who are "laid off" because of a reduction in workforce.

E.   EXIT INTERVIEWS: Generally, the Human Resources Department shall attempt to conduct termination or exit interviews no later than the employee's last working day. The interviewer will:

   (1)   Attempt, if the termination is voluntary, to determine the real reason or reasons why the employee is leaving, so that, where appropriate, action may be taken to correct any issues that come to light.

   (2)   Discuss, if the termination is for cause, the circumstances leading to the termination, so that misunderstandings can be minimized.

   (3)   Explain any conversion or continuation of benefits under the (Church's) group insurance plans and any other vested benefits available to the employee under the (Church's) benefit plans.

   (4)   Determine the employee's availability for future employment, should the supervisor's written evaluation recommend such employment.

   (5)   Obtain the correct address for mailing Internal Revenue Service Form W-2.

   (6)   Remind the employee to take with him or her any personal belongings and obtain any items belonging to the (Church).

F.   TERMINATION INTERVIEW:

    (1)   A written report of the termination interview should be prepared and placed in the employee's personnel file. Pertinent items requiring managerial review and possible change of policy should be brought to the attention of the Director of Human Resources. The supervisors will be responsible for the return by terminated employees of all of the (Church's) possessions, including the (Church's) identification badges and keys. Supervisors must inform employees that they are responsible for items issued to them by the Ministry or in their control, such as the following:

        (1)   Music, including songbooks and compact disks

        (2)   Credit cards

        (3)   Equipment

        (4)   Keys

        (5)   Manuals

        (6)   Pagers

        (7)   Tools

        (8)   Vehicles

    (2)   All church property must be returned by employees on or before their last day of work. Where permitted by applicable laws, the Ministry may withhold from the employee's check or final paycheck the cost of any items that are not returned when required. The church may also take all action deemed appropriate to recover or protect its property.

    (3)   If any of the (Church's) property in the employee's possession has been lost or damaged, the cost of replacing such property shall be deducted from the employee's final paycheck where permissible.

G.   Refer to the Policy Manual for details regarding entitlement to severance allowance and benefits in event of termination.

H.   FINAL PAYMENT
The Human Resources Department shall distribute the final paycheck.

SEVERANCE ALLOWANCE

1. POLICY:

    It is the policy of the (Church), at the discretion of the Administrator and upon written approval of the Human Resources Department, to grant a severance allowance to terminated employees under certain circumstances in order to provide them with a temporary income to assist in their transition to other employment. Please note that the church is under no obligation to provide terminated employees with a severance allowance and when it does so, it is an act of benevolence.

2. GUIDELINES OF THE POLICY:

    A. An employee will be eligible for severance allowance if employee is permanently terminated after one year of regular, full-time or part-time (30 or more hours per week) service because of:

        (1) A reduction in the (Church's) work force

        (2) Elimination of the job or position

        (3) An insufficient aptitude for continued employment with the (Church) not attributable to any willful cause or act of misconduct.

    B. An employee will not be eligible for severance allowance if the employee:

        (1) Leaves the (Church) voluntarily

        (2) Is terminated for misconduct or other cause.

        (3) Retires from the (Church).

    C. Loss of a particular job shall not be considered a termination on account of reduction in the workforce or elimination of the job if the employee refuses to accept other employment which is offered by the (Church) unless the offered employment requires the employee to relocate or take a reduction in salary.

    D. When the church elects, and finances permit the church to provide a terminated employee with severance, the amount of severance allowance shall be (   ). Severance allowances will be paid on regular paydays during the period the terminated employee is eligible to receive severance allowance. The severance allowance is subject to all applicable taxes and withholdings.

E. Generally, when practical, the (Church) will attempt to give the employee ( ) week's paid notice of termination in addition to the above stated severance allowance, where the termination is due to reduction in force, elimination of the job or position, or insufficient aptitude on the part of the employee. Employee may or may not be required to work during this period of time, at the Administrator's and the Human Resources Department's discretion. However, no notice of termination shall be required prior to termination. No notice need be given where termination is for misconduct

F. In unusual situations or cases involving key management personnel, a severance allowance in excess of that stated in Item "C" may be approved by the Administrator with the concurrence of the Human Resources Department.

G. The purpose of severance allowance is to provide income for the specified period of time while the terminated employee seeks other employment. The severance allowance may, therefore, be terminated should the employee find other employment prior to the end of the severance pay period.

H. Severance allowance will be granted to eligible employees in addition to pay for any unused vacation, but not unused sick leave, that has accrued during the year in which termination occurs for which the employee may be eligible.

I. A Letter of Separation and General Release may be required to be signed by an employee or former employee at the (Church) as a condition precedent to the employee receiving severance allowance described in this policy.

J. This policy is only a guide. Management reserves the right to vary this policy or to eliminate severance pay. Management determines the circumstances that warrant disclosure of benefits.

PARTICIPATION IN PUBLIC SERVICE ACTIVITIES

1. POLICY:

It is the policy of the (Church) to fulfill its responsibility to the community it serves by encouraging all employees to participate in civic affairs and to practice good citizenship. However, employee participation in public service activities must not adversely affect the employee's job performance or be detrimental to the (Church).

2. GUIDELINES OF THE POLICY:

   A. Employees are encouraged to take an active interest in community activities of a charitable, religious, fraternal or civic nature and to apply for membership in service organizations. Time spent in such activities normally should be outside of the employee's working hours and will normally not be considered hours worked for pay purposes, although management may attempt to accommodate the employee by rescheduling work hours, at management's discretion. However, civic activities should not interfere with job performance or reflect adversely on the (Church).

   B. If the employee has participated in public service activities on the (Church's) time and receives compensation for his participation in public service activities, the gross compensation received will be deducted for the employee's church wages.

   C. Time spent working for charitable, public or similar purposes at the (Church's) request, or under its direction or control shall be considered hours worked for pay purposes. Under these circumstances, approved expenses incurred shall be reimbursed by the (Church).

   D. Voluntary employee participation in public service activities that may involve an extended period of time away from the job shall be handled in accordance with the policies contained in LEAVES OF ABSENCE.

   E. The reimbursement for membership fees and expenses in public service organizations, where such membership is not required by the church, shall be subject to the provisions of MEMBERSHIPS IN TRADE AND PROFESSIONAL ASSOCIATIONS. Each approved membership is subject to periodic evaluation by the Administrator. The employee may be asked to submit an individual activity report to his department manager to justify continued participation in the organization.

   F. Employees are not encouraged to accept invitations to speak before civic groups. However, if any such communication might be construed as representing the (Church's) position on any subject, prior approval must be obtained from the Administrator. Such approval will not be granted if the topics deal with the (Church's) internal affairs or organization.

SECURITY: VISITORS, PROPERTY, PHONES, COMPUTERS, MAIL

1. POLICY:

It is the policy of the (Church) to protect and maintain integrity of its proprietary information, security for its property, its employees and persons visiting its premises. Security is the responsibility of all the (Church's) employees. The (Church) cannot guarantee the safety or security of any person or property.

2. GUIDELINES OF THE POLICY:

A. The Security Director and his staff are responsible for all the (Church's) security programs.

B. Identification badges are issued to all personnel at the time they are hired. These badges will be required for employee access to the (Church's) premises and must be worn at all times while at work. Employees are permitted only in those areas where their work requires them to be or in designated employee rest areas.

  (1) If an employee loses his identification badge, the Administrator and security should be informed. Arrangements will be made with security to have a new identification badge made at a charge to the employee.

  (2) In the event that an employee is terminated or resigns, the immediate supervisor is responsible for obtaining the employee's identification badge and returning it to the Human Resources Department.

C. Employees taking property off the premises with them are required to obtain a "Material/Equipment Pass" from their supervisor. The material/equipment to be removed must be described on the pass signed by the employee's supervisor or department manager. A pass must be obtained for any personal belongings which could be mistaken for the (Church's) property including radios, tape recorders, tools, etc. All packages being taken from the premises are subject to search by the security officers.

D. All employees may be subject to search, surveillance, interview or other investigative techniques when warranted. These activities will be conducted when deemed necessary by management.

E. All keys for use on secured gates, doors and vehicles shall be stamped "do not duplicate", and will be issued to those employees whose duties require them to have keys. The issuance and security of these keys, as well as the maintenance of key records are the responsibility of the Security Director. Employees will be required to return issued keys when the nature of their job changes or when their employment is terminated. The unauthorized duplication of keys will be considered a breach of the (Church) security and will subject the employee to disciplinary action.

F. Visitors, telephones and electronic communications (e-mail) jeopardize the security of the (Church) and distract from productivity. You must not send or receive junk electronic mail. Likewise, computers and the information stored therein belong to the (Church). All employees must strive to protect the integrity of the Ministry's many data systems using them only for their intended business purposes. The (Church) discourages personal visitors to employees during normal working hours. All such visitors are subject to approval. The security desk will advise the "host" by telephone of the presence of the visitor(s). The "host" is required to escort the visitor physically to his destination. No one is permitted beyond the immediate access doors without an escort. This is necessary as a matter of common courtesy to our guest but particularly necessary for security/safety reasons. If a visitor wishes to visit with others while in the building, the original "host" will escort him to the next "host", who in turn will escort the visitor back to the reception area upon completion of the visit. The visitor must have an escort at all times while in the (Church) building.

G. Personal calls should be kept to a minimum. The (Church) does not wish to prevent employees from taking care of necessary personal business that cannot be completed outside office hours. However, these calls should be made during the lunch hour whenever possible. Employees are required to reimburse the (Church) for any charges resulting from their personal use of the telephone. Employees are required to reimburse the (Church) for any postage used for personal correspondence.

H. Employees are responsible for maintaining control over all lockable files and/or cabinets. They should be secured at the close of business or when the employee is called away from his work area for a prolonged period.

I. All vendors wishing to conduct business with the (Church) or to visit executives or staff, will be required to sign a log. They will be issued an identification tag which is to be displayed on the upper left shoulder of the visitor's garment and is to be worn during the visitor's stay.

J. The (Church) may be entered outside of normal working hours only by employees who have been authorized to do so by their supervisor. The Security Director maintains a list of authorized personnel for use by the security guards.

K. Employees must exercise reasonable care for their own protection and that of their personal property. In addition, employees are expected to respect the property of others. Articles of personal property found on the premises should be returned to the owner, if known, or turned into security. Inquiries regarding lost property should be directed to Security.

L.   The (Church) will assume no responsibility for employee losses resulting from robbery or theft.

SOLICITATION

1.   POLICY:

It is the policy of the (Church) to prohibit solicitation of employees on its premises, whether made by employees or by individuals or groups not associated with the (Church) except in circumstances as outlined below:

2.   GUIDELINES OF THE POLICY:

A.   Unrestricted solicitation on the (Church's) premises interferes with normal operations, is detrimental to discipline and efficiency and impacts church security.

B.   All solicitations of funds, signatures, membership drives, distributions of literature or gifts and offers for sale of merchandise or tickets by individuals or groups not associated with the (Church) are prohibited unless prior approval of the Administrator is obtained. Employees may solicit only in the cafeteria and only during non-working hours such as lunch breaks, subject to the approval of the Administrator.

C.   Solicitations for gifts or expressions of sympathy to fellow employees or their families may be permitted on certain occasions, provided the prior approval of management is obtained.

D.   Distributions and solicitations by an employee during the employee's working time are prohibited anywhere on the (Church's) premises. However, this prohibition does not apply to times such as lunch and rest breaks.

E.   Distribution of literature in work areas by an employee is prohibited, whether during the employee's working time or during his own time.

F.   Distribution of literature in such a manner to cause litter on the (Church's) property will not be permitted.

G.   Distribution of literature is prohibited in the Sanctuary or anywhere the public is present.

H.   The Security Director shall ensure that solicitations and distributions authorized under the solicitation policy are conducted so as not to interfere with the security of the (Church).

POLITICAL ACTIVITIES

1   POLICY:

The (Church) policy encourages employees to become active individuals in public affairs and to support the party and candidates of their choice.

2.   GUIDELINES TO THE POLICY:

A.   If an employee engages in any political activity, he must do so as a private citizen. The employee should not identify himself as a representative of the (Church) in any political activity, nor in any communication to any news source. Campaigning, fund raising and other partisan political activities must be conducted on the employee's own time.

B.   Employees must obtain the prior approval of the Administrator before seeking public office or accepting an appointment to public office. If such activity involves an extended period of time away from the job, a leave of absence may be given, depending upon the nature of the office and any restrictions which may be imposed by state or federal laws.

C.   The (Church's) equipment and facilities may not be used for any political activity. The (Church's) letterhead should not be used in connection with political activity.

D.   The (Church) does not make contributions or expenditures in connection with any election or any political office, or in connection with any primary election or political convention or caucus held to select candidates for any political office. Under no circumstances shall expenses incurred by an employee relating to political activity be reimbursed from (Church's) funds.

E.   All solicitations of signatures, distribution of literature, posting of signs and posters, or petitions of a political nature are prohibited.

SUGGESTION PROGRAM

1.   POLICY:

It is the policy of the (Church) to encourage employees to submit constructive suggestions that could benefit and enhance the operation and environment of the (Church). This program has been established to encourage all employees to become more aware of their job functions and responsibilities, and to make maximum use of available resources.

2.   GUIDELINES OF THE POLICY:

A.   A suggestion is defined as a constructive idea that might help the (Church) solve a problem, improve procedures, streamline operations, reduce costs or in any other way make the (Church) more effective in the accomplishment of its mission. Examples of constructive suggestions might include:

(1)   A more efficient way to do a job.

(2)   A better method to handle materials.

(3)   A method for improving working conditions.

(4)   Suggestions on raising employee morale.

B.   The Human Resources Department is responsible for development, implementation and management of the Suggestion Program. Rules and operational procedures for the Suggestion Program may be obtained from the Human Resources Department.

C.   Suggestions should be submitted in writing on the Employee Suggestion form to both the employee's supervisor and the Human Resources Department.

D.   If the suggestions can be adopted immediately or if the idea has merit but cannot be adopted at present, the employee will receive recognition for the suggestion in a manner to be determined by the Human Resources Department.

E.   If the suggestion does not seem practical, the employee will be advised of this in writing.

HORORARIUMS AND MINISTRY OUTSIDE THE (CHURCH)

1.   POLICY:

It is the policy of the (Church) to give directives to employees who may be invited to minister or speak outside the (Church) on the handling of honorariums and the reimbursement of travel expenses.

2.   GUIDELINES OF THE POLICY:

A.   If an employee is invited to speak or minister as an individual and not as a representative of the (Church) nor on the (Church's) time, he is entitled to keep any honorarium.

B.   If any employee is invited to speak or minister because he is associated with the (Church) and is serving as a representative of the (Church), any honorarium less approved travel and/or out-of-pocket expenses incurred by the employee, will be turned over to the (Church's) Accounting Department.

C.   If the organization that has invited the employee to speak or minister specifically desires, and on their own initiative, give a gift to the (church), all of the gift shall be turned over to the (Church's) Accounting Department.

D.   Travel and other expenses should normally be paid for by the inviting organization. It is best to have an understanding of this at the time the invitation is accepted. If these expenses are to be a part of the honorarium that will be turned over to the (Church), travel arrangements can be made with the understanding that reimbursement will be forthcoming.

E.   Travel or other expenses for the (Church) sponsored or initiated promotional engagements will be paid by the (Church).

F.   If engagements are multi-purpose, partially the (Church's) and partially unrelated, the ministry will determine the fair apportionment of expenses in coordination with the employee.

COMPLAINT AND APPEAL

1.   POLICY:

While nothing in this Policy should be construed in any way as limiting the at-will nature of employment at the (Church), it is the policy of the Ministry to encourage employees to bring to the attention of management their valid complaints related to work. Employees will be provided with an opportunity to present their complaints and appeal decisions by management through a Complaint and Appeal procedure. All complaints will be resolved promptly whenever possible.

2.   GUIDELINES OF THE POLICY:

A.   A complaint is defined as an employee's expressed feeling of dissatisfaction concerning conditions of employment or treatment by management, supervisors or other employees. Examples situations which may warrant use of the Complaint and Appeals procedure are:

   (1)   Application of the (Church's) policies, practices, rules, regulations and procedures believed to be to the detriment of an employee.

   (2)   Treatment considered unfair by an employee such as coercion, reprisal, harassment or intimidation.

   (3)   Alleged discrimination.

   (4)   Improper or unfair administration of employee benefits or conditions of employment such as vacations, fringe benefits, promotions, retirement, holidays, performance reviews or salary.

B.   Employees shall use the Complaint and Appeal procedure as set forth below. Supervisors are responsible for insuring that the complaint is investigated to the employee's satisfaction with the decision, or until the appeal procedure is exhausted.

C.   "Reasonable time" for reaching a decision concerning a Complaint and Appeal issue at any organizational level will be (   ) working days.

D.   Information concerning an employee's use of the Complaint and Appeal process will usually be received in confidence, although the (Church) may find it necessary to discuss the complaint or the facts underlying the complaint with relevant persons. The Administrator will discuss a Complaint and Appeal issue only with those individuals who are involved in or have information relevant to the situation.

E.   Reasonable time spent by grieved employees in Complaint and Appeal discussions with management during their normal working hours will be considered hours worked for pay purposes.

F.   Whenever two or more employees have a common or similar complaint, the employees may select one or more of them to represent the group. The final decision on the complaint will be binding on all members of the group.

G.   The Administrator's decisions on Complaint and Appeals will not necessarily be precedent setting nor binding on future Complaint and Appeals.

DISCLOSURE OF BENEFITS

1. POLICY:

One of the greatest assets of the (Church) is its employees, their efforts, skills and cooperation. In recognition of this, together with the (Church's) interest in the welfare of each employee, certain benefit programs have been established. Information and summary communications intended to explain these benefit plans are furnished to all plan participants and beneficiaries on a timely and continuing basis. Benefits, carriers, and plan particulars are all subject to change without prior notice.

2. GUIDELINES OF THE POLICY:

A.   All benefits provided by the (Church) are described in official documents which are kept on file in the Human Resources Department and are available for examination by any plan participant or beneficiary. These documents are the only official and binding documents concerning the (Church's) benefits and all summaries and communications, both written and verbal, must refer to these documents as the only binding documents. The (Church) reserves the right to modify, amend or terminate any or all of its benefits.

B.   The Director of Human Resources, or such person or persons as he may designate, shall serve as Administrator of the (Church's) benefits. The Director of Human Resources is responsible for all communications and disclosures concerning benefits and for compliance with all applicable laws and regulations. In addition, the Administrator, or such person or persons as he may designate, shall be available to answer employee questions concerning benefits and shall provide counsel to new employees, employees as they achieve eligibility, retiring employees and employees' beneficiaries as to specific benefit coverage and required forms and designations. The Administrator is specifically authorized to use outside professional assistance as needed.

C.   ELIGIBILITY:

(1)   Regular employees working (   ) hours or more per week are eligible for full employee benefits.

(2)   Regular employees and introductory employees working less than ( ) hours per week, but (   ) hours or more do not qualify for employee benefits with the exception of vacation, holidays and sick leave.

(3)   Regular employees as stated above in Items 1 and 2 on "introductory employ-ees" are eligible for employee benefits ninety (90) days after their date of hire, without counting vacation time.

(4)   Regular employees working less than (   ) hours per week, as well as temporary and on-call employees are not eligible for any employee benefits.

HOLIDAYS

1. POLICY:

It is the policy of the (church) to observe holidays each year as may be determined by management. Eligible employees will be given time off with pay for each holiday observed.

2. GUIDELINES OF THE POLICY:

A. The schedule of holidays to be observed during each calendar year is as follows:

    (1)   New Year's Eve

    (2)   New Year's Day

    (3)   Christmas Eve

    (4)   Christmas Day

    (5)   Memorial Day

    (6)   Thanksgiving Day

    (7)   * ( ) Personal Preference Days

B. Regular, full-time employees will receive their regular rate of pay for each holiday. Regular, part-time employees those working ( ) or more hours per week will receive pro-rated hours pay based only upon their average number of part-time hours worked per week.

    Example: A regular, part-time employee who is working an average of ( ) hours per week would receive ( ) hours of pay for each holiday.

C. Temporary employees, on-call employees and employees on unpaid leaves of absence are not eligible to receive holiday pay.

D. To receive holiday pay, an eligible employee must be at work, or on an authorized paid absence, on the work day immediately preceding and immediately following the day on which the holiday is observed. If an employee is absent on one or both of these days because of illness or injury, the (Church) reserves the right to deny holiday pay.

E.   A holiday that occurs on a Saturday or Sunday may be observed on either the preceding Friday or following Monday at management's discretion.

F.   If a holiday occurs during an employee's vacation period, the employee will receive holiday pay instead of vacation pay for the holiday only.

G.   An observed holiday will be considered a day of work for the purpose of calculating weekly overtime.

H.   The (Church) reserves the right to schedule work on an observed holiday:

    (1)   An eligible hourly or non-exempt employee who works on a holiday shall receive regular pay and holiday pay for all hours worked on the holiday

    (2)   When an exempt salaried employee is required to work on a holiday, his department manager may authorize time off with pay at a later date, equal to the amount of time worked on the holiday. Such time off shall be at the mutual convenience of the (Church) and the employee

I.   PERSONAL DAYS: In the event that Personal Days are given, the following will apply:

    (1)   Personal days are scheduled at the employee's request, subject to the department manager's approval.

    (2)   To be eligible for two (2) personal days, new employees must have been hired and on the payroll prior to the ( ) of the current calendar year.

    (3)   To be eligible for ( ) personal day, new employees must have been hired and on the payroll after ( ) and prior to ( ) of the current calendar year.

    (4)   Employees beginning work after ( ) of the current calendar year will not be eligible for any personal days in the current calendar year.

    (5)   Personal days may not be carried into another year and, if not taken by the end of the current year, must be forfeited.

    (6)   An employee may not receive additional pay in lieu of a personal day.

SICK LEAVE

1. **POLICY:**

    It is the policy of the (Church) to authorize a certain number of sick days per year for its employees, depending on the employee's classification and length of employment.

2. **GUIDELINES OF THE POLICY:**

    A. All regular, full-time employees earn days of sick leave during the calendar year. New regular, full-time employees that are hired during the year only earn ( ) sick day per completed month during the remaining part of the calendar year following the introductory period.

    B. In order to earn a sick day during the employee's first and last months of employment, the employee must work a minimum of ( ) days during that calendar month.

    C. Regular, part-time employees working ( ) or more hours per week, are eligible for sick leave which is pro-rated based upon the number of hours worked per week.

    D. Temporary and on-call employees are not eligible for sick leave.

    E. Employees may choose to utilize their sick leave in the event of illness of dependent children, where it is necessary for the employee to care for the child.

    F. Sick leave may be used for doctor and dental appointments. If the employee does not want to use a full day's sick leave for a brief appointment, employees may take just the number of hours required, or casual "time off."

    G. Generally, time off from work because of illness in excess of earned sick leave cannot be compensated by the (Church).

    H. If deemed appropriate, the (Church) reserves the right to require a doctor's certification of illness whenever sick leave is taken.

    I. In the event of termination of employment for any reason, the employee will not be paid for any accrued, unused sick leave up to the date of termination.

FAMILY AND MEDICAL LEAVE OF ABSENCE

1.   POLICY:

So long as the Family Medical Leave Act (FMLA) applies to the (Church), the (Church) will grant qualifying employees up to twelve (12) weeks of unpaid leave under the federal Family and Medical Leave Act. The FMLA applies to individuals who have worked at least 1,250 hours in the last twelve (12) months (29 U.S.C.§ 2611). For example, an employee who worked an average of twenty-five (25) or more hours per week over the course of a year usually would be eligible for family and medical leave. Some state family and medical leave laws provide additional protections for part-time employees. The Family and Medical leave Act of 1993 (FMLA) provides that the Ministry must provide eligible employees leaves of absence for the employee's, or his immediate family member's serious health condition, the birth of a child, parent's care of child after birth and/or the placement of a child with an employee for adoption or foster care.

2.   GUIDELINES OF THE POLICY:

A.   If you believe you are entitled to leave under this section, please notify your supervisor of your intent to take FMLA leave as far in advance as possible.

B.   The church is dedicated to promptly and fairly examining your request for FMLA leave and responding in a timely manner. The Ministry will comply with the FMLA in all regards including the maintenance of pre-existing health coverage during the leave period and will generally reinstate the employee to the same or equivalent job. However, the Ministry reserves all rights and protections to employers under the Act, statutory, regulatory, common law and otherwise.

LEAVE OF ABSENCE

1. **POLICY:**

   It is the policy of the (church) to grant employees leaves of absence from the (Church) under certain circumstances.

2. **GUIDELINES OF THE POLICY:**

   A. The Administrator's consideration of any request for a leave of absence shall be affected by the following factors:

      (1) The employee's record of performance, particularly attendance.

      (2) The urgency of the employee's situation creating the need for a leave.

      (3) The workload of the (Church) and the department at the time during which the leave is requested.

      (4) Applicable state and federal law.

   B. Whether the employee receives compensation during a leave of absence shall be at the discretion of the Administrator in concurrence with the Human Resources Department.

   C. Normally, all vacation time and accumulated compensatory time off, if permissible, is to be used before a leave of absence will be granted.

   D. The employee is to make the initial request for a leave of absence of his supervisor with as much advance notice as possible. The supervisor will process the request and forward it to the Administrator and Human Resources Department for concurrence and inclusion in the employee's records. The Human Resources Department shall notify the immediate supervisor whether or not the leave is approved.

   E. During a leave of absence, an employee may continue participation in certain benefit programs by paying the total cost of those programs. The Human Resources Department will inform the employee of the details of this coverage should the employee desire.

   F. Vacation days and sick leave days will not accrue while the employee is on a leave of absence.

   G. The normal salary review dates of employees on leave of absence are to be postponed (by the amount of leave time).

H. An employee who returns to work at the conclusion of a leave of absence may be restored to his former position or to a comparable position at the same rate of pay unless circumstances have changed so as to make it impractical to reinstate the employee. The employee may retain credit for prior service, accrued retirement benefits and accumulated seniority. He may also retain sick leave days accrued prior to requesting leave of absence only if the leave of absence is other than medical.

I. An employee failing to report to work on the first working day following the expiration of the leave may be considered to have voluntarily resigned. If an employee does not return to work following a leave of absence, the termination date may be the last day worked.

3. APPLICATIONS OF THE POLICY:

A. SHORT-TERM ABSENCES: Department managers may approve leaves of absence from ( ) to ( ) days. Leaves of absence over ( ) days require the approval of the Administrator and the Human Resources Department.

B. LONG-TERM ABSENCES: The following leaves of absence may be granted to employees who have completed at least ( ) year(s) of service. The duration of each leave of absence shall be at the discretion of the Administrator in concurrence with the Human Resources Department.

(1) A Personal Leave of Absence may be granted to an employee in cases where an extended period of time away from the job will be in the best interest of the employee and the (Church).

(2) An Educational Leave of Absence may be granted to an employee who desires to continue his education in order to prepare himself for added responsibilities in his employment.

(3) A Missionary Leave of Absence may be granted to an employee who desires to work with an organization devoted to community betterment.

C. VOLUNTARY AND INVOLUNTARY MEDICAL LEAVES OF ABSENCES.

(1) A Medical Leave of Absence may be granted to an employee whose non-occupational illness or injury continues beyond the coverage afforded in the SICK LEAVE policy. During a Medical Leave of Absence, the employee may be compensated by the (Church's) disability plan if the disability insurance provider approves the claim. Before granting a Medical Leave of Absence and during the course of the absence, the (Church) reserves the right to have the employee examined by a physician selected by the (Church).

(2)   The (Church) reserves the right to initiate a Leave of Absence if the employee's attendance, quality or quantity of work is adversely affected by the condition. A Medical Leave of Absence may continue until such time as the employee's physician certifies that the employee is able to return to work. However, management's decision in concurrence with the Administrator and Human Resources Department as to the duration of or necessity for a Leave of Absence shall be final. An employee on Medical Leave of Absence is required to contact the Human Resources Department and report the return-to-work plans or medical status at ( ) intervals.

D.   MATERNITY LEAVE OF ABSENCE: Disabilities caused by or contributed to pregnancy, childbirth or related medical conditions are treated as temporary disabilities for the purpose of this policy and any health or temporary disability insurance or sick leave plan maintained by the (Church). Employees who are granted Maternity Leave of Absence will be eligible for the same sick leave benefits received by the employees suffering from illness or other temporary disabilities.

E.   EMERGENCY CLOSING OF THE (CHURCH) PREMISES: Employees are expected to make a good faith effort to get to work during inclement weather conditions if the (Church) is operating and does not declare an emergency closing and such conditions do not make travel to work unreasonably dangerous. You will be notified by the Administrator's office if weather conditions force the church to close.

F.   MISSIONARY LEAVE OF ABSENCE: Employees who have been employed by the (church) for ( ) consecutive years are eligible for ( ) week(s) paid Leave of Absence during their ( ) year of employment, as well as every ( ) year thereafter, for missionary service. This Leave of Absence provision is primarily for international missionary service, however, domestic missionary endeavors may also be considered. Missionary service Leaves of Absence must be approved by the Administrator and Pastor.

BEREAVEMENT LEAVE

1. POLICY:

    It is the policy of the (church) to grant time off from work without loss of pay for employees bereaved by the death of an immediate family member or relative.

2. GUIDELINES OF THE POLICY:

    A. ELIGIBILITY: All regular full-time and part-time employees working ( ) hours per week are eligible for Bereavement Leave beginning with their first full day of active employment. This benefit does not apply if death of the relative occurs while the employee is on Leave of Absence, layoff or absent for any other reason.

    B. AMOUNT OF LEAVE TIME:

        (1) Spouse, children, parents, guardians, mother-in-law, father-in-law, brothers/sisters: ( ) consecutive working days.

        (2) Grandchildren, grandparents, brothers-in-law, sisters-in-law: ( ) working days.

        (3) Aunts, uncles, nieces, nephews: ( ) working days.

    C. Bereavement Leave must be approved by the Administrator.

    D. Compensation allowance will not exceed ( ) hours per day at the regular hourly rate based on the employee's salary. Time off granted in accordance with this policy shall not be credited as time worked for the purpose of computing overtime.

    E. Regular, part-time employees will be compensated per day according to the average hours worked per day the previous ( ) workdays.

    F. The (Church) may request verification of the absence (i.e., death certificates, newspaper article) prior to granting bereavement leave.

JURY DUTY (COURT APPEARANCES)

1.   POLICY:

It is the policy of the (Church) to recognize and support the civic responsibility of an employee to serve as a juror when called upon to do so. If an employee is called on to make an appearance in court to serve or as a witness he is normally eligible for remuneration under the guidelines of this policy. Timespent in court for personal business is not reimbursable.

2.   GUIDELINES OF THE POLICY:

A.   The employee shall notify his Administrator and supervisor immediately upon receipt of the summons, subpoena or other document that gives instructions to report for jury duty.

B.   There may be cases where an employee's extended absence would have a serious effect on the operating efficiency of the (Church). In such instances, the department manager in coordination with the employee, the Administrator and the Human Resources Department will request that the employee be excused from jury duty or that his assignment be postponed by the proper authority.

C.   The employee's pay during the performance of jury duty will be an amount which is the difference between his regular pay and the jury duty pay. The (Church) shall continue to issue the employee's regular pay and the employee shall endorse the jury duty check to the (Church).

EDUCATIONAL ASSISTANCE

1. POLICY:

    It is the policy of the (Church) to develop a better-educated and more highly skilled work force by providing educational assistance to its employees with the guidelines established below.

2. GUIDELINES OF THE POLICY:

    A. Educational assistance in the form of partial reimbursement will be provided only for courses of study which are directly related to the employee's present job or which will enhance the employee's potential for advancement to a position within the (Church) which the individual has a reasonable expectation of achieving. In addition, the courses or programs must be offered by accredited institutions of learning.

    B. Education programs or courses of instruction which meet the above criteria may be announced by the Human Resources Department. Certain educational courses may be offered to the employee by the (Church) at no cost to the employee.

    C. Other requirements for educational assistance include the following:

        (1) Only regular, full-time employees and part-time employees working (   ) or more hours per week are eligible.

        (2) The employee who is eligible to receive financial aid from other sources, such as the Veterans Administration or educational institutions, must utilize such benefits. The (Church) will not duplicate educational assistance that is available from other sources.

    D. In order to be eligible for reimbursement of educational costs, requests for educational assistance must be approved by the Administrator prior to enrollment or no reimbursement shall be available. A completed Educational Assistance Application shall be submitted to the Administrator and Human Resources Department by way of the employee's supervisor. The supervisor and administrator shall recommend either approval or disapproval of the request. It is the employee's sole responsibility to process the application for educational assistance and to complete all steps required for reimbursement.

    E. In determining whether to approve a request for educational assistance, the supervisors, Administrator and the Human Resources Department are directed to consider the following factors:

        (1) Nature and purpose of the course of study.

(2)   Benefits to be derived by the employee and the (Church).

(3)   Level of responsibility and length of service of the employee.

(4)   Estimated cost.

F.   The amount of assistance paid by the (Church) shall be based upon the following criteria:

(1)   A maximum of (   )percent of tuition fees for approved courses are reimbursable.

(2)   A maximum of (   ) percent of costs for approved home-study type schools is reimbursable.

(3)   To be eligible for reimbursement, it is required that an employee receive a passing grade of (   ) or better for undergraduate courses.

(4)   To be eligible for reimbursement, it is required that an employee receive a passing grade of (   ) or better for graduate courses.

(5)   For passing a "pass-fail" course, the amount of assistance shall be (   ) percent of reimbursable costs.

(6)   Reimbursement will be limited to tuition fees only. There shall be no reimbursement for textbooks, tools, instruments, laboratory fees or supplies, registration fees or other such costs.

(7)   Reimbursement is limited to not more than (   ) courses for the school quarter or semester and a maximum of $(   ) per school year (month - month).

(8)   Educational assistance paid to the employee is subject to all applicable taxes.

G.   To obtain reimbursement upon completion of the course, the employee shall submit to the Administrator and Human Resources Department a certified transcript of grades received and receipts for expenses incurred. The (Church) may them reimburse the employee the applicable percentage of the cost of tuition. Employees who take courses at the specific request or direction and with prior written approval of management may at the Administrator's discretion be reimbursed in advance.

H.   Class attendance and completion of study assignments shall be accomplished outside of the employee's regular working hours. Class schedule or activities shall not interfere with the employee's work.

I.   An employee who is terminated during enrollment in an education program or course of instruction because of reduction in the work force or elimination of the job, or who is unable to complete the course because of transfers within the (Church), shall be reimbursed for the amount of the costs incurred up to the date of termination or transfer. An employee who voluntarily leaves the (Church) or is terminated for cause prior to completing a course shall not be reimbursed for the expenses associated with the course.

J.   If the employee leaves the (Church) voluntarily within six months of completion of the course, the employee must repay the full amount reimbursed by the (Church) for educational assistance. If the employee leaves the (Church) voluntarily between ( ) months and ( ) year(s) after completing the course, (%) of the amount will be repayable. After ( ) year(s), no reimbursement is required.

K.   Records will be maintained by the Human Resources Department of all education programs completed by each employee.

EMPLOYEE COUNSELING AND PERSONAL MINISTRY

1. POLICY:

    It is the policy of the (Church) to provide pastoral counseling, ministry and referral services to aid employees in areas of professional, vocational and personal needs.

2. GUIDELINES OF THE POLICY:

    A. Employees are encouraged to seek assistance with personal, family, financial, emotional, interpersonal and spiritual problems impacting their ability to work effectively within the (Church).

    B. Employees shall be permitted to seek such assistance in an environment of mutual trust. In the event of life threatening situations or in areas that compromise the welfare, safety, security or integrity of the (Church) or any individual, the counselor may choose to involve other appropriate people in the process. In such cases, there shall be no obligation to maintain confidentiality.

    C. Supervisors shall be alert to detect the existence of personal problems that adversely impact performance and the work environment. Indications of such problems include excessive absenteeism, changes in employee behavior, attitude and substandard performance.

    D. Should the supervisor become aware of such problems, generally, an informal interview should be conducted to determine the nature of the problem and assist with its resolution. Should counseling be required, the supervisor shall contact the Pastor of Counseling to schedule an appointment for evaluation and possible referral. If an employee is referred to a service outside of the (Church) for further counseling, expenses incurred from this referral may be the responsibility of the employee.

    E. Career counseling services are available in the Human Resources Department to those employees desiring assistance in their education and/or career planning. Outplacement counseling services are also available to employees terminated other than for cause as well as to those planning for retirement.

SERVICE AWARDS

1.   POLICY:

It is the policy of the (Church) to recognize long and faithful service to the organization by presenting service awards to eligible employees in accordance with the guidelines set forth below.

2.   GUIDELINES OF THE POLICY:

A.   All regular full-time and part-time employees working ( ) or more hours per week may receive a service award upon completion of ( ) years of continuous service and at the end of every ( ) years of continuous service thereafter.

B.   The Pastor or his designee shall present Service awards.

C.   The Human Resources Department along with the Administrator and supervisors are responsible for identifying those employees to be honored and for administration of the service awards program.

FLOWERS FOR DECEASED RELATIVES

1.   POLICY:

It is the policy of the (Church) to send flowers or to make a donation to an appropriate charity in the event of the death of an employee's spouse, child (including miscarried babies), parents or spouse's parent.

2.   GUIDELINES OF THE POLICY:

A.   The employee's department manager will be responsible for ordering the flowers through the Administrator's office, or making a donation to the appropriate charity.

B.   The flowers may be sent to either the funeral home or the home of the deceased whichever is more appropriate.

C.   This policy is applicable for all the (Church) employees.

D.   Flowers or donations paid for by the (Church) should be sent on behalf of the (Church) rather than the department placing the order.

E.   Departments or groups of individual employees may send flowers or make donations on their own initiative, and at their own expense. The (Church) will not reimburse such expenses.

This publication is designed to provide information in regard to the subject matter covered. It is sold with the understanding that neither author nor publisher is engaged in rendering legal, accounting or other professional services. If legal advice or other professional assistance is required, the services of a qualified professional should be sought.

EMPLOYEE SAFETY AND HEALTH

1. POLICY:

    It is the policy of the (Church) to provide a safe and healthy work environment for all employees. Employees are expected to comply with all safety and health requirements whether established by management or by federal, state, or local law. You are responsible for immediately reporting any accident to the Director of Security involving an employee or church member. If you witness or discover any accident or you or another employee are involved in one, you must report the situation to the Administrator.

    The (Church) provides a comprehensive worker's compensation insurance program at no cost to employees. This program covers any injury or illness sustained in the course of employment that requires medical, surgical, or hospital treatment.

    Employees who sustain work-related injuries or illnesses should inform their supervisor immediately. The injury or illness must also be reported immediately to the Administrator and Human Resources Department. No matter how minor an on-the-job injury may appear, it is important that it be reported immediately. This may enable an eligible employee to qualify for coverage as quickly as possible. You may be asked to complete a Worker's Compensation form. Notify your supervisor before seeing a doctor for work related accidents.

    When an employee is absent with a covered injury or illness, the employee's vacation and sick leave benefits may continue to accrue. Also, the Ministry may continue to provide the employee and his or her dependents with the same group insurance coverage.

    Neither the church nor the insurance carrier will be liable for the payment of workers' compensation benefits for injuries that occur during en employee's voluntary participation in any off-duty, recreational, social or athletic activity sponsored by the Church.

2. GUIDELINES OF THE POLICY:

    A. The Administrator's Office shall make its best efforts to protect the safety and health of our employees.

    B. The Human Resources Department's responsibilities include:

        (1) Monitoring compliance with the (Church's) safety rules, regulations and the applicable safety and health standards established pursuant to the Occupational Safety and Health Act of 1970.

        (2) Investigating, correcting and working to reduce unsafe and unhealthy working conditions or potential hazards.

(3)   Conducting periodic informal safety and health inspections of work areas, machinery, equipment, elevators, lift trucks, warehouses, grounds and any other potentially hazardous (Church) facilities.

(4)   Coordinating investigations conducted by the Occupational Safety and Health Administration (OSHA), state and health, and insurance carrier personnel.

(5)   Organizing the training of employees as required by OSHA.

(6)   Managing compliance with the various requirements established by OSHA, the state and the insurance carrier regarding record keeping and the retention of records.

(7)   Posting notices ad records as may be required.

(8)   Investigating serious accidents and injuries involving the (Church) employees or accidents that occur on the (Church) premises.

C.   All observed safety and health violations and any accidents resulting in injuries to employees shall be reported to their immediate supervisor who shall immediately advise the Security office and the Director of Human Resources.

D.   If safety clothing or equipment is required by OSHA regulations, the (Church) will either provide the clothing and equipment without cost to employees or will reimburse employees for the expense of such items upon presentation of a sales receipt. The Church will likewise replace damaged or broken safety clothing and equipment at its cost, providing the damage was not caused by the lack of care by the employee.

E.   No employee may be discharged or discriminated against in any manner because the employee has instituted a proceeding with OSHA, has testified in such a proceeding or has otherwise exercised any right afforded by OSHA.

CONTROLLED SUBSTANCES AND BEHAVIOR POLICIES

1. POLICY:

The Church recognizes that its future is dependent upon the spiritual, physical and psychological health of its employees. The use of drugs and alcohol pose serious threats to the church its employees and members. It is the responsibility of both the (Church) and its employees to maintain a safe, healthy and efficient-working environment. Employee's behavior at work, including their decision to never use illegal drugs or alcohol, determines the safety and efficiency of the (Church) more than any other factor. In recognition of the nationwide problem of drug and alcohol abuse, the (Church) seeks to develop and maintain, with the cooperation and assistance of its employees, a drug and alcohol-free work environment. In order to achieve this goal, the (Church) has adopted the following policies with regard to the use, possession, transfer and sale of drugs or alcohol by its employees.

A. Pre-Employment Screening: The (Church) may conduct pre-employment screening practices designed to prevent hiring individuals who use illegal drugs or individuals whose use of legal drugs or alcohol indicates a potential for impaired or unsafe job performance.

B. Use, Possession, Transfer or Sale of Drugs or Alcohol:

(1) Illegal Drugs: The use, possession, transfer, manufacture, dispensing, purchase or sale of an illegal drug by an employee of the (Church) is prohibited. Being under the influence of or in the presence of any detectable levels of an illegal drug is also prohibited. The term "illegal drug" includes, but not limited to, the use of marijuana, cocaine, narcotics, opiates, opium derivatives, hallucinogenic substances, inhalants and any other substances that have either a stimulant or depressant effect on the central nervous system such as amphetamines or barbiturates. The use of prescription or "legal" drugs is permitted on the job only if it does not impair an employee's ability to perform the essential job functions in a safe manner. Any employee who violates this policy is subject to immediate discharge.

(2) Alcohol: Employees of the (Church) are required to totally abstain from the use of all alcoholic beverages. Consumption or possession of alcohol on (Church) premises is prohibited. Being under the influence of alcohol while engaged in the performance of (Church) business is prohibited. Any employee who violates this policy is subject to immediate discharge.

C. Drug and Alcohol Screening: The (Church) may require a blood test, urinalysis, or other drug/alcohol screening of those persons suspected of using or being under the influence of a drug or alcohol, or where circumstances or workplace conditions otherwise justify it. An employee's consent to submit to such testing is required as a condition of employment. An employee's refusal to consent to drug and alcohol testing is grounds for immediate discharge. Questions regarding the (Church's) drug testing policy should be directed to the Administrator.

D. Injury: An employee who is injured in the course and scope of their employment and subsequently tests positive on a drug or alcohol test, may forfeit their eligibility for Worker's Compensation medical and indemnity benefits.

2. GUIDELINES OF THE POLICY:

A. All employees are expected to conduct themselves and behave in a manner consistent with the ethical and religious purpose of the (Church). Such conduct includes:

(1) Reporting to work punctually as scheduled and being at their workstation, ready for work, at the assigned starting time.

(2) Notifying the supervisor when the employee will be absent from work, or is unable to report for work on time.

(3) Complying with all the (Church's) safety and health regulations.

(4) Wearing clothing appropriate for the work being performed.

(5) Performing assigned tasks efficiently.

(6) Eating meals only during meal periods and only in designated areas.

(7) Maintaining their work place and work area with cleanliness and orderliness.

(8) Treating all visitors and church members as guests of the (Church).

(9) Refraining from behavior or conduct in violation of Biblical principles, the STATEMENT OF FAITH of the (Church), or otherwise offensive or undesirable behavior.

B. The following conduct is prohibited and will subject the individual involved to disciplinary action up to and including termination. This list is not comprehensive and other conduct of employees on or off the job may result in disciplinary action, up to and including termination. The ministry retains the right to use its own discretion in discipline and in termination of the employment relationship.

(1) The use of alcoholic beverages other than for medicinal or religious purposes at any time, either on or off the job.

(2) Possession, sale or use of illicit drugs or other controlled substances.

(3)   The use of profanity or abusive language.

(4)   The possession of firearms or other weapons on the (Church's) property.

(5)   Insubordination – the refusal by an employee to follow management's instructions concerning job-related matter.

(6)   Assault on a fellow employee, customer or visitor.

(7)   Theft or misuse of the (Church's) property or of another employee's property.

(8)   Gambling on the (Church's) property.

(9)   Falsifying any of the (Church's) records or reports, such as an application for employment, production record, time record or shipping/receiving record.

(10)   Unauthorized distribution or use of copyrighted material, or any other material or work in process produced by or for the (Church).

C.   The possession , sale or use of a controlled substance other than a drug prescribed by a physician is detrimental to the health of employees, to their job performance and to the reputation of the (Church):

(1)   Any employee found to be selling or distributing unauthorized drugs will be subject to immediate termination.

(2)   In other cases of drug abuse, management will consider the employee's work record and his willingness to undergo treatment before deciding whether termination is required.

D.   Supervisors should be alert to signs or symptoms which may suggest drug use:

(1)   An employee who is suspected of drug abuse should be reported at once to the Administrator, Security and Pastor of counseling.

(2)   Supervisors should not attempt to provide counseling services to suspected drug users, since diagnosis and rehabilitation are the functions of qualified experts.

PERSONAL APPEARANCE OF EMPLOYEES

1. POLICY:

It is the policy of the (Church) that an employee's dress and grooming be appropriate to their work situation. Radical departures from conventional dress or personal grooming are not permitted. The (Church) retains the sole right to determine whether an employee's dress or grooming is appropriate in the (Church's) workplace.

2. GUIDELINES OF THE POLICY:

A. Every office employee has some contact with the public and, therefore, represents the (Church) in his/her appearance, as well as by their actions. The properly attired man or woman helps create a favorable image for the (Church). Accordingly, the personal appearance of office workers shall be governed by the following standards:

(1) Employees are expected to dress in a manner that is normally acceptable in business establishments. The wearing of dungarees, jeans, shorts, sandal, T-shirts and similar items of casual attire is not permitted, as they do not present businesslike appearance. Exceptions to this paragraph shall be considered by the Administrator, based on the dictates of a particular job.

B. If an employee reports for work improperly dressed or groomed, the supervisor shall instruct the employee to return home to change clothes or to take other appropriate corrective action. The employee will not be compensated during such time away from work and repeated violations of this policy will be cause for disciplinary action.

PERSONAL FINANCES OF EMPLOYEES

1. Policy:

    It is the policy of the (Church) that all employees are expected to discharge their financial obligations promptly. Failure by an employee to comply with this policy reflects poorly upon our Christian purpose and witness and subjects the (Church) to unnecessary expenditures in assisting creditors in collection of amounts owed them.

2. GUIDELINES OF THE POLICY:

    A. Whenever the (Church) is served a writ of garnishment or attachment, a notice of levy by the Internal Revenue Service or other taxing authority or any other similar order requiring payment of a portion of an employee's compensation to someone other than the employee, management must immediately refer the matter to the Administrator for appropriate action. Failure to act promptly may render the (Church) legally liable.

    B. In the event that garnishment or similar proceedings are instituted against an employee, the (Church) will deduct the required amount from the employee's paycheck. The amount deducted from an employee's disposable earnings will not exceed that permitted by law.

    C. Compliance with writs of garnishment and similar orders imposes an administrative and financial burden on the (Church). In addition, the failure of an employee to meet his financial obligations does not reflect favorably on the (Church) and frequently has an adverse effect on the employee's job performance.

    D. Whenever a supervisor has reason to believe that an employee is experiencing severe financial difficulties, the supervisor shall investigate the situation and, if circumstances require, proceed in accordance with the *Employee Counseling And Personal Ministry policy.*

    E. No employee will be terminated because his earnings have been subjected to garnishment for his or her indebtedness. Repeated garnishments for more than one indebtedness may result in appropriate discipline, depending upon the circumstances of the case, the employee's record of performance and the recommendation of his supervisor.

    F. The (Church) may not deny employment to or terminate employment solely because the employee has filed a petition for bankruptcy.

CONFLICTS OF INTEREST

1. **POLICY:**

    It is the policy of the (Church) to prohibit its employees from engaging in any activity, practice or act which conflicts with the interests of the (Church) or working with businesses or other organizations in competition with the (Church). Several examples of conflicts of interest which should be avoided are set forth below. Similar situations which create an actual conflict of loyalty or interest, or even the appearance of such a conflict, must be scrupulously avoided unless approved in advance by the Pastor or Administrator.

    An actual or potential conflict of interest occurs when an employee is in a position to influence a decision that may result in personal gain for the employee or relative as a result of the (Church's) business dealings. For the purposes of this policy, a relative is any person who is related by blood or marriage or whose relationship with the employee is similar to that of persons who are related by blood or marriage.

    The (Church) allows the employment of relatives but requires that relatives take active steps to inform the (Church) when any one of the following situations exists:

    A. Relatives that works directly for or with another relative.

    B. ( ) or more relatives report to the same supervisor.

    C. A relative's supervisor could be influenced by that relative.

    D. The marriage of two employees.

    The (Church) reserves the right to take any action deemed appropriate to remedy a perceived conflict of interest.

    No "presumption of guilt" is created by the mere existence of a relationship with outside firms. However, if employees have any influence on transactions involving purchases, contracts or leases, it is imperative that as soon as possible, they disclose to the Administrator the existence of any actual or potential conflicts of interest, so that safeguards can be established to protect all parties.

    Personal gain may result not only in cases where an employee or relative has significant ownership in a firm with which the (Church) does business, but also, when an employee or relative receives a kickback, bribe, substantial gift, or special consideration as a result of a transaction or business dealing involving the (Church).

2. **GUIDELINES OF THE POLICY:**

    A. Any employee who owns a financial interest in or accepts full-time or part-time work with a firm which is a competitor of the (Church) must make that fact known to the Administrator immediately for appropriate action. The term "employment" shall mean that "paid service" of an employee, one who is hired by another or by a business or firm to work for wages or salary and shall include independent contractors. The term "financial interest" shall not include a non-controlling interest in a publicly traded stock.

Certain employees may be requested to become directors of other religious organizations or serve in similar capacity. Such associations, with prior written approval of the Pastor or Administrator, are acceptable under this policy, as are remuneration for travel expenses and honorariums.

B.   Employees at or above the level of department manager are prohibited from all outside employment. Such prohibition does not prevent individuals at this employment level from engaging in personal business activities that provide income but are not normally considered in the category of employment.

C.   Employees below department manager level can engage in outside business activities and/or take employment subject to Item A, provided such employment does not negatively affect the employee's job performance. In the case of outside employment, prior approval by the Administrator of the respective division is also required.

D.   If a family member or an employee has a financial interest in a firm which does business with the (Church), an employee must report the interest to the (Church) and must not represent the (Church) in such transactions.

E.   No employee or member of the employee's immediate family shall accept gifts from any person or firm doing or seeking to do business with the (Church). Such gifts should be returned or turned over to the Administrator. However, employees are not prohibited from accepting advertising novelties such as pens, pencils, calendars or other gifts of nominal value when circumstances clearly show that the gifts are offered for reasons of personal esteem and affection. The Pastor or Administrator may grant a waiver from the limitations in this paragraph. Employees shall disclose all gifts to their immediate supervisor.

F.   The (Church) will not contribute to political parties or candidates for office, nor will any member of management directly or indirectly suggest that employees contribute to any particular party or candidate.

G.   Acts of hospitality toward public officials should be of such a scale and nature in order to avoid compromising the integrity or impugning the reputation of the (Church). No employee shall directly or indirectly engage in conduct which is disloyal, disruptive, competitive or damaging to the (Church).

BUSINESS GIFTS AND ENTERTAINMENT

1.   POLICY:

The Internal Revenue Service limits business gifts to any business associate to $ (   ) per year and the (Church) must use caution in the purchase of such gifts. Since the Ministry is a nonprofit organization, the excess spent above $(   ) for a gift could be classified by the Internal Revenue Service as an expenditure not for an exempt purpose. This could jeopardize the (Church's) exempt status.

2.   GUIDELINES FOR THE POLICY:

A.   Business gifts must be substantiated. A receipt is required stating the cost of the gift and the date of purchase. Also, the name of the person receiving the gift, the business reason for the gift and the business relationship of the recipient must be noted. Gifts to employees are taxable compensation to the employee and must be added to the employee's wages. See tax attorney concerning amount.

B.   Entertainment – The cost of meals or entertainment must be directly related to, or associated with the active conduct of business. These expenses must be fully documented and supported by receipts. Also, a written explanation of each of the following is required:

(1)   The name(s) of the person(s) involved.

(2)   The type of activity.

(3)   The reason for the meal or entertainment.

(4)   The date, time and location of the meal or entertainment, including the place of the business meeting the expense is associated with.

CONFIDENTIAL NATURE OF THE (CHURCH'S) AFFAIRS

1. POLICY:

It is the policy of the (Church) that the business affairs should not be discussed with parties outside the organization, except to the extent required by the normal course of business. Due to the need for confidentiality on behalf of the (Church), confidentiality of information is mandatory. All records, of whatever nature, whether financial, or not, are to be kept in the strictest confidence with transfer of information being restricted to authorized personnel. All information received in the ordinary course of employment is confidential and is not to be discussed with any party in the normal course of performance of the employee's duties, except for authorized exceptions.

Your personal salary has been established and based on the nature and content of your responsibilities, your previous experience and other assets that complement your abilities. It is the policy that you maintain your rate of pay as confidential information, as well as respect the rights of others by not asking them their rate of pay. This applies to all other means of compensation, such as bonuses and life insurance policies.

When you move, change your telephone number or have other changes in your personal information, please notify the Church Administration and Human Resources Department of such changes so the (Church) can keep personnel records accurate and up-to-date. Remember to notify the Administrator and the Human Resources Department of any changes involving your marital status or the birth of a child, which may affect your insurance coverage. It is your responsibility to see that the (Church) has your current address and other information, so that we can communicate with you as needed.

2. GUIDELINES OF THE POLICY:

A. Inquiries into the business affairs of the (Church) are to be directed to the Church Administrator and Public Relations department or your supervisor. No information is to be given to newspapers, magazines, TV or radio reporters or photographers on the telephone or in person, by employees other than those authorized to do so.

B. Access to certain (Church) information and operating procedures will be limited to those authorized employees who "need to know."

C. All information obtained by virtue of employment at the ((Church)) should be held in strictest confidence to protect the (Church) and its constituency. Employees are prohibited from disclosing such information to anyone outside the organization.

D. Requests for personnel information by persons outside the ((Church)) shall be referred to the Human Resources Department. Supervisors are not authorized to divulge such information without the prior approval of the Administrator and Human Resources Department.

E. Nothing contained in this policy is intended to prohibit the disclosure to outsiders of information about the (Church) that is routinely made available to the public.

F. Violations of this Policy may subject an employee to disciplinary action.

DISCIPLINARY PROCEDURE

1. POLICY:

While nothing herein should be construed to limit the "At-Will" nature of employment at the (Church), it is the policy of the (Church) to discipline employees who violate the (Church's) policies, rules, regulations and standards of employee conduct. Employee discipline may or may not be progressive in its application and administration, depending on the circumstances. The (Church) disclaims adherence to a progressive discipline system in every situation.

2. GUIDELINES OF THE POLICY:

In the event the (Church) elects to use progressive discipline, these guidelines will usually be followed:

   A. FIRST VIOLATION: On the occasion of the first violation, the employee's supervisor will usually take the following action:

   (1) Meet with the employee to discuss the violation, formally reminding the employee of the (Church's) expectations.

   (2) Inform the employee of the specific nature of the problem and the action needed to correct it.

   (3) Prepare a memorandum to the employee detailing the discussion, specifying the problem and the agreed upon steps for correction. The supervisor shall keep a copy of the memorandum for future reference.

   B. SECOND VIOLATION: Should a second violation occur of either the same or different nature, the supervisor shall usually meet with the employee to:

   (1) Review the written record of the initial meeting.

   (2) Re-clarify the expectations for improved performance.

   (3) Warn the employee that a third violation could result in a more severe disciplinary action, including suspension or dismissal.

   (4) Prepare a written summary of the meeting for the employee's signature. Copies of the written reprimand with employee's signature are to be sent to the Administrator and to the Human Resources Department for inclusion in the employee's personnel file.

C.   THIRD VIOLATION: Should additional violations occur, the supervisor shall usually:

(1)   Consult with the Administrator and the Human Resources Department for assistance and guidance in the next step of discipline.

(2)   Request a meeting with the Administrator and the employee to discuss the matter.

(3)   The supervisor, after consultation with the Administrator and the Human Resources Department may take one of the following steps:

(a)   Place the employee on a one ( ) day disciplinary suspension "with pay" during which the employee is to make a final decision whether he/she can (a) solve the immediate problem, and (b) is willing to make a total performance commitment to the (Church).   (c)The employee shall return to work on the day after suspension and inform his/her supervisor of his/her decision.

(b)   Place the employee on probation for an appropriate period of time with the understanding that further violations could lead to suspension and/or dismissal.

(c)   Suspend the employee "without pay" for a specified period of time.

(d)   Discharge the employee following procedures and recommendations from the Human Resources Department.

D.   In cases where serious misconduct has occurred such as dishonesty, compromise of church security or threats to personnel or facilities, the supervisory staff in consultation with the Administrator and the Human Resources Department may move directly to suspension or dismissal of the employee.   At the discretion of management, there may be immediate discharge when the circumstances warrant such action.

E.   No employee compensation or benefits shall be accrued or paid to an employee suspended "without pay" or terminated for disciplinary reasons.

The following are terms and their definitions as used in the Handbook:

(1)   The words "shall" or "will" are to be construed as mandatory and the word "may" as permissive.

(2)   The masculine gender shall be construed to include the feminine gender.

(3)   "Supervisor" means an individual with the authority to assign, direct and review the work of two or more employees.

(4)   "Immediate family" means the employee's spouse, children, parents, guardians, brothers, sisters, father-in-law, mother-in-law, brothers-in-law and sisters-in-law.

This publication is designed to provide information in regard to the subject matter covered. It is sold with the understanding that neither author nor publisher is engaged in rendering legal, accounting or other professional services. If legal advice or other professional assistance is required, the services of a qualified professional should be sought.

SAMPLE LETTER TO SUPERVISORS

Over the past several years, we have been privileged as supervisors here at the (Church) to witness the astounding growth of the ministry under the blessing of God. I know you rejoice as I do to see this thrilling growth, together with the tremendous increase in (Church) employees and in the benefits we are able to offer them.

Naturally, this phenomenal growth has made a more formal approach to the (Church) and employee relationship necessary. For this reason the (Church's) PERSONNEL POLICY MANUAL has been designed to help you maintain a harmonious and productive work environment for all your employees. Every good organization lets the employees know what is expected of them and what they can expect from the organization. This manual, written by the Human Resources Department and approved by the Organization's board, together with new policies that are developed, and the interpretation of those policies will help you in doing just that.

I urge you to read these materials carefully. As you know, good policies remain good only as they are well implemented. You as a supervisor bear the responsibility for translating the ideas and principles contained here into action – and I have every confidence that you will do so effectively.

A caution: Nothing in this manual should be interpreted as creating a contractual relationship. You will need to exercise wisdom in applying many of the more broadly stated policies to specific situations. If you have questions or comments, please feel free to contact the Administrator or the Human Resource Department at any time. The Human Resources Department is committed to evaluating the effectiveness of all personnel policies and implementing changes as the need arises, with the approval of the Pastor.

As a Christian organization, the (Church) has had both the unique opportunity and the even greater responsibility of seeking God's wisdom so as to reflect His principles in the formulating of our personnel policies.

INTRODUCTION AND DISCLAIMERS

WELCOMING STATEMENT

Although welcoming statements normally do not involve many legal issues, the (Church) should be careful not to use language or make any statements that create new or additional legal rights for employees beyond those guaranteed by federal, state, or local law. The major legal concern for (Church) is avoiding the use of language or phrases that might turn an at-will employment relationship into an implied or expressed contractual relationship. For example, the welcoming statement *should not include assurances of long-term or permanent employment or commit the organization to a just cause discipline or discharge policy.* In fact, most handbooks include, either as part of or an appendix to the welcoming statement or introductory section, a prominently displayed notice outlining the at-will nature of the employment relationship. Examples of other types of legal disclaimers that often appear in or adjacent to a welcoming statement include:

- A statement stressing the non-contractual, non-binding nature of the handbook's policy provisions and terms, usually accompanied by a reservation of management's right to change any of the policies, procedures, benefits, or language at any time without further notice.

- A notice that any and all employment agreements or understandings granting rights or benefits beyond those specified in the handbook must be in writing and signed by the chief executive officer or other specifically designated top management official.

To reinforce these legal disclaimers, (Church) requires workers to sign an acknowledgment form indicating that they have received the handbook or policy manual and agree to abide by its terms and provisions. These receipts or acknowledgment forms can be general in scope, although many specifically address the at-will nature of the relationship and other legal issues. Some churches include these acknowledgment forms as a tear-out section or page in a handbook's introductory section.

POLICY HELPS

Policy Issuer

Ordinarily, the Pastor of the organization prepares and sign a handbook's welcome statement. In a few organizations, this responsibility is exercised by another top-level manager – for example, the Administrator or the organization's Board of Directors.

PRACTICAL CONSIDERATIONS

Scope and Purpose

The (Church) usually inserts contract disclaimer language at or near the beginning of an employee handbook or policy manual. Typically, contract disclaimers appear either as part of the welcoming message that introduces a handbook or separate, but prominent appendix to a welcoming statement or other introductory materials. To ensure that employees see and read these notices, you would frequently print disclaimers in a larger, more noticeable typeface or frame them in an eye-catching, boxed-in display on a single page of the manual.

An at-will disclaimer focuses on and asserts the right of both the (Church) and individual workers to terminate the employment relationship at any time for any legally permissible reason. An at-will disclaimer puts employees on notice that they are not working under any guarantee of employment, and that either they or the (Church) can end the relationship at any point. In recent years, courts have recognized a number or exceptions to the at-will termination rights. For example, courts in many states have upheld wrongful discharge claims filed by workers who claimed that their dismissals violated public policy or an implied employment agreement.

General contract disclaimers usually are broader than an at-will disclaimer in that they aim to negate any potential interpretation of a handbook policy, procedure, program, or provision as a binding agreement between the (Church) and its workers. Typically, a general disclaimer emphasizes that the handbook's policies and provisions are guidelines only and are not intended to create any agreement or contract between the (Church) and its workers. Similar to an at-will disclaimer, general contract disclaimers almost always appear near the front or in the introductory section of a handbook. You would frequently place such disclaimer language near or even in the welcoming statement. To ensure that employees notice the general disclaimer used in front of a handbook, many ministries print these provisions in separate, larger-type or boldface section.

Most courts agree that disclaimer language in an employee handbook or policy manual protects from liability against an employee's claim that certain handbook provisions created a binding employment agreement. A statement stressing the non-contractual, non-binding nature of the handbook's policy provisions and terms, accompanied by a reservation of management's right to change any of the handbook's policies, procedures, benefits, or language at any time without further notice, usually provides the organization with an adequate defense against an employee's contract claim. However, courts generally insist that for a disclaimer to be effective, it must be:

- Clear and unambiguous.

- Prominently displayed or communicated.

A clear and unambiguous disclaimer is one that cannot be misunderstood and is consistent with the rest of the handbook's provisions. For example, a common handbook inconsistency occurs when a disciplinary policy indicates that the (Church) follows certain disciplinary procedures, while the disclaimer says the (Church) does not necessarily follow disciplinary procedures in certain termination situations. To avoid such conflicts, the (Church) should include such language in its handbook stating that the steps in a disciplinary procedure are discretionary and that management reserves the right to deviate from disciplinary procedure as circumstances warrant (with the rest of the handbook's provisions.)

To communicate a disclaimer effectively, the (Church) must make sure that the language is so prominently displayed that employees cannot claim that they failed to notice it.

To reinforce the defense provided by disclaimer language, many ministries require workers to sign an acknowledgment form indicating they have received the handbook or policy manual and agree to abide by its terms and provisions. These receipts or acknowledgment forms specifically address the at-will nature of the employment relationship and other legal issues covered by disclaimer language.

POLICY POINTERS

The organization should make sure that its handbook policy manual includes a clear statement that each worker's employment is at-will, not governed by any oral or written contract, and terminable by either the (Church) or employee at any time, with or without cause or notice. This at-will disclaimer should be printed in a prominent typeface at the beginning or the handbook and possible in other relevant sections of the manual. Many organizations also include at-will disclaimer language in their employment application forms, as well as the acknowledgment forms that employees sign on receiving the handbook or policy manual.

Employee handbooks should include provisions that explicitly recognize the (Church's) right to change, add, eliminate, or otherwise deviate from any of the handbook's policies or procedures at any time. Some churches include a statement that they reserve the right to issue new policies or a new handbook and specify that any new policies or procedures supersede any previously issued verbal or written policies.

The (Church's) obligation under many federal and state employment and tax laws can vary depending on whether workers are classified as employees or independent contractors within the meaning of the particular law. Some of the legal obligations the (Church) has with respect to employees, but not independent contractors, include:

- Withholding federal income taxes.

- Withholding employee's FICA taxes and paying the (Church's) portion of FICA.

- Paying federal and state unemployment taxes.

- Guaranteeing overtime and minimum wages required under the FLSA.

- Paying premiums required under state worker's compensation laws.

- Guaranteeing protection under the Employee Retirement Income Security Act (ERISA), the Labor Management Relations Act, Title VII of the Civil Rights Act of 1964, and the Americans with Disabilities Act.

EMPLOYEE ORIENTATION PLANNING GUIDELINES

Planning for a new employee's arrival is essential. The following are tips that can help supervisors prepare for a new hire's arrival and ensure that the employee's socialization is successful:

- Inform staff that a new employee is joining the department and provide some background information, such as the new hire's name, work experience and scheduled start date. Communicate this information verbally or by memorandum.

- Assign a buddy or sponsor to provide day-to-day support for the new hire and review that individual's responsibilities before the new hire's first day.

- Make sure that the new employee's workstation is ready, all necessary equipment and supplies have been obtained, and the area is neat and clean. If office nameplates are used, make sure the nameplate of the new hire is in place before the employee arrives.

- Prepare a tentative schedule of first-day and first-week activities that includes daily and weekly check in times during which the new employee can ask questions and obtain feedback.

- Anticipate the kinds of questions the new employee might ask and be prepared to answer them.

- Have work ready and waiting for the employee. A new hire should not be expected to mark time reading instruction or policy manuals. While the first assignment should not be complicated, it also should not be mindless or menial.

- Be present to greet the new employee and introduce his or her co-workers and buddy.

- Help the new employee locate essential departments and facilities, such as workstation, restroom, cafeteria, parking lot, photocopy or fax room. Provide the employee with a diagram showing the layout of offices and their occupants' names.

- Go over the day's planned orientation activities and provide the employee with a list of scheduled events.

- Note or review any forms that the employee has to complete.

- Discuss general expectations for performance and behavior. The worker should be given a written job description that should be reviewed orally.

- Immediate job duties should be briefly and simply discussed. Starting and quitting times, lunch breaks, procedures for obtaining work supplies, and the use of time sheets or a time clock should be explained. Workplace rules should be outlined clearly to prevent misunderstandings, reduce errors, and help establish positive work habits.

EMPLOYEE ORIENTATION CHECKLIST FOR SUPERVISORS

Employee Name: _____

Department: _____

Job Title: _____

Schedule/Shift: AM _____ PM_____ SHIFT ☐ 1ST ☐ 2ND ☐ 3RD

INITIAL WELCOME

- Introduce yourself
- Determine name employee wishes to be called
- Give brief history of the (Church)
- Introduce employee to lead person and co-workers
- Assign a co-worker or other responsible employee as lunch buddy to join new employee for lunch during the first few days

HOURS OF WORK/PAY POLICIES

- Work hours – starting and stopping times
- Overtime requirements
- Lunch and break periods
- Time card/time clock procedures
- Starting rate of pay
- Paycheck distribution – when, where, how
- Pay discrepancies
- Performance review/appraisal procedures
- Merit/pay increases
- Vacations/holidays
- Sick/personal leave procedures

THE JOB

- Tour of department/work site
- Department structure
- Employee's job duties and job scope
- Employee's job as it relates to total product
- Performance expectations
- Quality requirements
- Systems/tools/procedures
- Suggestion system/procedures

GENERAL PROCEDURES AND REGULATIONS

- Location of restroom, cafeteria, vending machines, lockers, storage areas, pay phones
- Tardiness policy
- Absenteeism policy
- Tardiness/absenteeism call-in procedure
- Personal use of telephones and other company equipment or facilities
- Care of equipment
- Name badges
- Parking location and sticker
- Where to get information and help

SAFETY

- Fire extinguishers and emergency exits
- Copy of general safety rules
- Job or equipment hazards
- Reporting accidents and illnesses
- Proper clothing and footwear
- Proper lifting techniques
- Eye protection and other protective equipment requirements
- Storage and disposal of solvents and hazardous chemicals
- Location of first aid/CPR assistance/medical care

JOB POSTING PROCEDURES - STANDARD POLICY

Introduction. To promote the efficient filling of job vacancies and provide opportunities for career growth, the (Church) follows a promotion-from-within procedure where qualified candidates exist for open positions. As part of that procedure, all vacant non-management positions are posted at the work-site where they occur, and bids or applications are accepted from interested employees in accordance with the general procedures set forth below.

Job requisition. Supervisors or managers who have a job vacancy in a non-management position that they do not intend to fill with someone on the present staff should complete a Job Requisition Form (available for the Human Resources Department). A current job description for the position must be attached to the completed Job Requisition Form. If the vacancy involves a pre-existing position, the immediate manager of the hiring supervisor or manager also must sign the Job Requisition Form. If the vacancy is a new position, both the immediate manager and the department head must sign the Job Requisition Form.

Job posting locations. All non-management vacancies are posted at the work-site where the job is located. Vacant positions are posted on the specially designated "Job Openings Bulletin Board" that is found in the Human Resource Department and in the Employee Lounge.

Posting and bidding time limits. The job vacancy remains posted ( )working days. During that time, bids from all eligible employees are accepted. After the job has been posted for ( ) working days, management can begin considering outside applicants, if the hiring supervisor has not selected an internal candidate to fill the position. However, employees who have applied for a posted job during the first ( ) days of the posting period are given preferential consideration. Qualified employees who express an interest in a posted position after the first ( )days are considered for the position along with any outside applicants.

Eligible employees. Employees who work at the location of the vacant position can apply for a posted job on the following conditions: (1) They meet the minimum qualifications included in the job description and vacancy announcement, (2) they have been in their present position at least ( ) months, (3) they have bid on no more than ( ) other job vacancies in the past ( ) months, and their present job grade is equal to or lower than the job they are bidding on.

Responses to job postings. Interested employees should complete a Job Bid Form (available from the Human Resource Department), which includes a description of how candidates meet the minimum qualifications listed in the job posting. A note or memo from an employee also can be accepted as a showing of interest, but employees are still required to complete a Job Bid Form. Telephone calls are not considered an acceptable or sufficient response to a job posting. The completed form or appropriate substitute should be submitted to the Administrator and the Human Resources Department.

Notification to bidders. Bidders who were not selected are notified in writing by the Human Resource Department. This notification includes an explanation of the reasons the employee was not selected. Employees are encouraged to discuss these reasons with the hiring supervisor, Administrator or the designated staff member from the Human Resources Department.

Job posting and bidding deadline. A Job Vacancy Announcement describing the job duties and minimum qualifications is posted in the Human Resource Department on the electronic Human Resource Bulletin Board that employees have access to on the (church) computer network. Each announcement remains posted for ( ) weeks. During that time, only employee applicants eligible to bid are considered. All interested employees must submit during this ( ) period.

Late bids. Bids on posted jobs that are submitted after the two-week deadline are considered only if the employee is qualified and was on approved leave or away from the worksite on business for the entire ( ) period.

Eligible employees. All regular-status employees who meet the minimum qualifications for the vacant job and have completed the probationary period in their current position are eligible to bid. Employees working a regular part-time schedule also are eligible to bid on posted positions, but bids from temporary workers are not accepted or considered until all other internal candidates have been eliminated from consideration. Bidders who work at a different location than the hiring supervisor are interviewed initially by the Administrator or the Human Resource Department.

SAMPLE JOB VACANCY ANNOUNCEMENT FORM

JOB VACANCY ANNOUNCEMENT

The following position is available. Interested employees who are eligible to bid should submit a completed Job Bid Form to the Human Resources Department or the Administrator.

Job Title:

_____

Grade:

_____

Department:

_____

Shift:

_____

Essential Functions of the Job:

_____

_____

_____

_____

MINIMUM QUALIFICATIONS REQUIRED

Skills:

_____

Knowledge:

_____

Education:

_____

Experience:

_____

Licenses of Certifications:

_____

_____

GENERAL RELEASE FORM

I _____,

 authorize the (Church) to contact any organization or individual that I have listed on my employment application or resume or mentioned in job interviews and obtain from them any relevant information about my job qualifications, including my experience, skills, and abilities. I understand that I am consenting to the release of any reference-related information about me held or known by my former supervisors, and co-workers. In addition, I consent to the release of any information about my education, experience, abilities, or work-related characteristics or traits held or known by other business associates, and friends and acquaintances that the (Church) might contact in the course of conducting a reference check or background investigation of my suitability for employment.

I understand and acknowledge that this release of information can involve my qualifications, performance, credentials, or other characteristics or factors affecting my suitability for employment with the (Church).

Specifically, I am authorizing the release of any information about my performance, experience, capability, attitude, or other work-related characteristics that currently are in the possession of the following organizations or their managers or representatives:

_____

_____

_____

_____

_____

(Note: use a separate form for release to check criminal background)

NOTICE OF REQUEST FOR CONSUMER REPORTING AGENCY INVESTIGATION

Dear _____:

This is to inform you that as part of our employment application process, we have requested a consumer report agency to prepare an investigative report on your qualifications for employment. As the basis for this report, the agency conducts a background investigation to obtain information through personal interview with third parties, such as family members, business associates, financial sources, friends, neighbors, or others to whom you are acquainted. This inquiry is designed to produce information on your character, general reputation, personal characteristics and mode of living, whichever might be applicable.

Please be advised that this type of investigation and report is a normal part of our employment.

<u>REJECTION NOTICE BASED ON INVESTIGATIVE REPORT</u>

Dear _____:

We regret to inform you that your application for employment has been denied. This action was influenced by information in a consumer report, which was prepared at our request by (name and address of service, credit bureau, or consumer report agency), a nationally known, reputable source of information for business decisions. Please contact the agency if you have questions about the specific information in this report.

Thank you for your interest in the (Church)

Sincerely,

(Signature)_____

CHURCHSTRATEGIES™
for the 21st century

For more information about

CHURCHSTRATEGIES™

seminar locations, materials and training videos

and other related services write:

CHURCHSTRATEGIES™

P.O. Box 210488 Dallas, Texas 75211

or call 214-215-0050